Following Characters into Meaning

BUILDING THEORIES, GATHERING EVIDENCE

LUCY CALKINS ◆ KATHLEEN TOLAN

*first*hand

HEINEMANN

DEDICATED TO TEACHERS

Dedicated to Melanie Brown, with thanks for unending support and generosity.

DEDICATED TO TEACHERS

firsthand
An imprint of Heinemann
361 Hanover Street, Portsmouth, NH 03801
www.heinemann.com

Offices and agents throughout the world

"Dedicated to Teachers" is a trademark of Greenwood Publishing Group, Inc.

© 2010 by Lucy Calkins and Kathleen Tolan

The asterisked tradebook titles in this text have been officially leveled by Irene Fountas, Gay Su Pinnell, and their trained levelers. Other systems that use level designations are not equivalent to theirs.

Post-its ® is a registered trademark of the 3M company.

The authors and publisher wish to thank those who have generously given permission to reprint borrowed material:

Excerpts from THE TIGER RISING. Copyright ©2001 by Kate DiCamillo. Reproduced by permission of the publisher, Candlewick Press, Somerville, MA.

Photographers: Peter Cunningham and Melanie Brown
Cover and Interior Design: Jenny Jensen Greenleaf
Composition: Publishers' Design and Production Services, Inc.

Library of Congress Cataloging-in-Publication Data
CIP data on file with the Library of Congress

ISBN 10: 0-325-03066-9
ISBN 13: 978-0-325-03066-1

Printed in the United States of America on acid-free paper
14   13   12   11   10   ML   1   2   3   4   5

Following Characters into Meaning

VOLUME
2

BUILDING THEORIES, GATHERING EVIDENCE

Units of Study for Teaching Reading, Grades 3–5

Contents

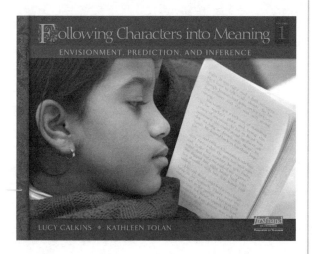

FOLLOWING CHARACTERS INTO MEANING

VOLUME 1: Envisionment, Prediction, and Inference

PART ONE   WALKING IN A CHARACTER'S SHOES

SESSION I   **Making Movies in Our Minds As We Read**   **2**

"If we read well, we become the character in a book. We read the words and then poof! We are one of the characters in the mental movie we're making. Poof! I'm Willy, bundled up on that sled, snow flying into my eyes, my heart racing, urging Searchlight on."

ASSESSMENT   DEVELOPING CONCRETE, OBTAINABLE READING GOALS   19

SESSION II   **Living in the World of a Story**   **28**

"When we read, you and I need to be the ones to notice if we are just gazing out at the text, thinking, 'It's as pretty as a postcard.' We need to notice times when we are reading on emotional autopilot—maybe understanding the text, but not taking it in. And we need to say, 'Stop the car. Pause the reading.' When we read, we need to see not just words, but also the world of the story through the eyes of the character. There is a rap on the door, and we hear it. Even before the character calls, 'Come in,' we practically call out a greeting ourselves."

SESSION III   **Stirring Our Empathy Through Personal Response**   **44**

"When we read ourselves awake, really envisioning what's happening in the story so that we are almost in the character's shoes, we often find ourselves remembering times in our lives when we lived through something similar, and we then bring feelings and insights from those experiences to bear on our understanding of whatever we are reading."

SESSION IV   **Letting the Text Revise Our Image of the Characters**   **56**

"A reader not only sees, hears, and imagines as if in the story, making a movie in the mind. A reader also revises that mental movie. Often when we read on, the story provides details that nudge us to say, 'Oops, I'll have to change what I'm thinking.'"

SESSION V   **Spinning All We Know into Predictions**   **70**

"One way readers read actively and wisely, then, is we empathize with the main character, we feel with the main character, in a way that leads us to anticipate what the character will do next."

SESSION VI   **Detailing Predictions to Bring Out Personalities**   **88**

"To predict well, it helps to make a movie in your mind of what has yet to happen. Those movies need to show not only what will happen next, but also how it will happen. We can anticipate how things will happen by remembering what we already know of our characters."

SESSION VII   **Mining Details About Characters**   **104**

"When you read in such a way that you are connected with a character, when you open your heart to him or her and care the same way you would about a friend, then envisioning, predicting, and thinking about a character happen all at once, in a whoosh."

**ASSESSMENT   ANALYZING TEXT DIFFICULTY TO INFORM   120
                 (AND TRANSFORM) INSTRUCTION**

FOLLOWING CHARACTERS INTO MEANING
VOLUME 2: Building Theories, Gathering Evidence

PART TWO   BUILDING THEORIES ABOUT CHARACTERS

SESSION VIII   Talking to Grow Theories About Characters   2

"We pull in to read, yes, but we also pull back from reading to think. We read like we are a character in the book, but we also read like we are a professor, growing intellectual ideas about the book. We read like we're under the covers, reading by flashlight, but we also turn the imaginary lights on in the room and scrutinize the text to grow ideas. The most fervent ideas center on the people in our books."

ASSESSMENT   DEVISE A SYSTEM OF RECORD KEEPING THAT   16
SCAFFOLDS ASSESSMENT-BASED TEACHING

SESSION IX   Developing Nuanced Theories About Characters   24

"Researchers have found that some people, like my husband, are good at reading people, and those who can read people in real life can also read people in stories. To read people—in life and in stories—it is important to remember that actions can be windows to the person. In life and as we read, we can pause after a character has done something and say, 'Let me use what just happened as a window to help me understand this person.'"

SESSION X   Expecting Complications in Characters   40

"It is important to keep in mind that characters are complicated; they are not just one way. And here's a key point: To grow nuanced and complex ideas about characters it helps to think deeply about times when a person seems to act out of character."

SESSION XI   Attending to Objects that Reveal Characters   58

"Paying attention to the objects that a character keeps near and dear is one way to grow ideas about what kind of person that character is. Those objects are often windows into the mind and heart of our characters. The possessions that a character keeps close almost always reveal something important about the person."

SESSION XII   Seeing Characters Through the Eyes of Others   70

"When readers want to think deeply about a character, we examine the ways that people around the character treat the character, looking especially for patterns of behavior. We not only notice how other people, other characters, treat and view the main character; we also notice what others call the character and the voice and body language people assume when talking to the character."

SESSION XIII   Reaching for Exactly True Words   82

"Readers sharpen our ideas about characters by using precise language to describe them and their actions. {Author: please expand)

Contents

PART THREE FROM INFERENCE TOWARD INTERPRETATION

SESSION XIV   Synthesizing Insights into Ideas About Books   100

"When readers get about halfway through our books (or when our books are bursting with ideas), it is wise to take some time to organize our thoughts. One way to do this is to sort our Post-it notes into piles of ideas that seem to go together."

SESSION XV   Seeing Texts Through the Prism of Theories   120

"As Jasmine showed us yesterday, once readers have grown a theory, a big idea, we reread and read on with that theory in hand. And I want you to know that we hold a theory loosely, knowing it will have a life of its own as we travel on. It will take up places we didn't expect to go."

SESSION XVI   Bringing a Narrative Frame to Theories About Characters   138

"Expert readers believe that when thinking about stories, it can especially pay off to pay attention to characters in general and to their motivations and struggles in particular."

SESSION XVII Authoring Ideas About Texts   154

"A simple, obvious idea about a character or a book is a great place to start, even if your goal is a complex idea. To take that simple idea as a starting place and to climb to higher levels of thinking, it helps to use a few phrases as thought prompts, grasping those phrases like we grasp rungs on a ladder, using them to help us climb higher and higher."

SESSION XVIII Tracing Ideas Through Texts   168

"The stuff that keeps recurring, that resurfaces often, that is threaded in and out of the fabric of a narrative, is the biggest stuff. That's true in life, and true in books. In books, the things that the author mentions again and again are the ones that she really wants you to notice, the ones that are critical to understanding the essence of the character and the story."

SESSION XIX Intensifying Interpretations by Finding Motifs   182

"I want to teach you a way that readers can intensify our reading, a way readers can catch some of the spirit of the book, to hold onto for themselves even when they are finished reading."

SESSION XX   Spying on Ourselves as Readers   190

"We can look back on the jotted notes we make as we read, and research our thinking, asking, 'What sort of thinking do I tend to do as I read?' After we spy on our own thinking, we can put together all the clues that we see, and together, these can help us construct a sense of ourselves as readers. We can come away from this saying, 'I'm the sort of reader who does a lot of this kind of thinking..., and who doesn't do a lot of that kind of thinking.' We can then give ourselves goals so we deliberately outgrow our current habits as readers and thinkers."

SESSION XXI Celebration: Creating a Self Portrait in Books   202

ASSESSMENT TAKING STOCK OF ALL WE'VE LEARNED   211

Building Theories About Characters

Talking to Grow Theories About Characters

ecause this session launches the next bend in the road of this unit, it needs to shine a spotlight on the upcoming trail, helping readers anticipate the new reading work they'll be doing over the next period of time. Of course, the session also needs to draw a line in the sand, suggesting that was then, this is now.

You'll convey to your readers that "previously in" the reading workshop, they learned that readers author reading lives, developing systems for finding books that matter, establishing the habit of reading long and strong, becoming accustomed to looking back over the texts we've already read to recall (and sometimes share) highlights of those texts, and you'll convey that they've also learned that readers read with imagination, becoming lost in stories, reading as if we are characters in the stories. As part of this, readers worry about and hope for and predict what will come next.

After synthesizing all that readers have already learned, you'll convey that during the upcoming bend in the road, children will learn that readers read not only with a flashlight, following the story line as it lures us deeper and deeper into the plot, but also with a spotlight, backing up to grow ideas about the whole text. This sort of reading is less about imagination and vicarious experience, and more about scrutiny and critical reflection. The effect on the brain, though, is no less electrifying. This upcoming bend in the unit of study will help children read with their minds on fire, growing ideas as they read and as they talk about their reading. In teacher language, children will learn that readers

GETTING READY

- By the time you teach today's minilesson, you should have completed Chapter 12 of *The Tiger Rising*.

- Bring your class read-aloud to today's lesson. If you are using *The Tiger Rising*, you will reread a portion of Chapter 12 during today's active involvement.

- Remind students to bring their "My Reading Life" folders and reading notebooks to the meeting area.

- Refer to the chart, "Strategies Readers Use to Grow Ideas About Characters" during the link section of the minilesson.

- During the next five minilessons, you will be revisiting parts of *The Tiger Rising* that you and your children have already read. Therefore, be sure to pace your read-alouds so that you continue to move forward in the book. In Session XIII, we reread a portion of Chapter 14. In Session XVI, we reread a portion of Chapter 21 in the mid-workshop teaching point, and in Session XVII we read part of Chapter 25 in the minilesson. You may wish to use these as guideposts as you plan your read-aloud time.

grow theories as we read and reflect on reading. You'll help them learn that reading involves the thrill of coming to a realization, of asking questions, of following a dawning idea, of fashioning a theory, of watching that idea grow in significance, and of exploring the ramifications of it. That is, reading is an intense kind of thinking. During this upcoming bend in the road, you'll focus on teaching higher-level com-

> *As we read, the*
> *conversations that we had*
> *in the air become*
> *conversations in the mind.*

prehension, and as part of that, you'll help children begin to do more writing about reading.

Teaching and assessing comprehension isn't easy, however, because comprehension is invisible and fluid, layered and responsive; it is the work of the mind. When I think about teaching and assessing comprehension, I'm reminded of the lines from *Sound of Music* about trying to catch a moonbeam in your hand. Often, in an effort to teach comprehension, we turn reading into something it is not. Take

the common expectation that readers write our responses to each chapter as we read. I do not know of anyone who hunkers down to read a novel on a Saturday morning, pausing at the end of each chapter to write a page about that chapter. I wonder if I'd read as much if that was what reading entailed. The challenge, then, is to teach and assess comprehension without turning reading into something that it is not.

In this bend in the road, you'll teach children that reading involves a sort of double consciousness. Readers not only participate in a text, envisioning what's happening and worrying about what will happen next; we also think about the story, the story world, and especially the people in the story. While on the one hand, we allow ourselves to get lost in the book, we meanwhile also read with our minds on fire, bursting with ideas about the book and the people in it. One of the great joys of reading is that sometimes we have reading friends with whom we can share our ideas about a text, and when we have a chance to share those ideas, they become deeper and more significant.

This session will emphasize the fact that readers grow ideas as we read, and then we share those ideas, engaging in heady conversations about our reading. The session, and the bend in the road that it launches, will also channel readers to realize that when we return to the page after a book talk, we read a little differently for the fact that we have been in those conversations. More specifically, as we read, the conversations that we had in the air become conversations in the mind.

In other words, this upcoming bend in the road aims to support deeper comprehension by helping children grow ideas as they read and as they talk.

MINILESSON

Talking to Grow Theories About Characters

CONNECTION

COACHING TIPS

Tell children you've noticed them talking up a storm *outside* reading time and talking far less *during* reading time. Their extracurricular talk is usually about people—which after all, is what readers talk about, too.

"Readers," I began. "You know, I watch you! I listen with my ears and my eyes. I pay attention to what is going on. A few days ago, I started to notice that before school starts, and in the lunchroom, and when the day is over, you all explode into talk!

"And then, I got to thinking that even though you seem to explode into talk before and after school and during lunch, sometimes when I ask you to talk to me or each other about the book you are reading, you seem to have little to say, and you talk robotically.

"So I confess, I decided to listen in when you talk zealously (that means passionately or eagerly). Yesterday morning and this morning, when I saw a couple of you engrossed in really heated talk, I sidled over toward you and (I cupped my ear and tilted my head) I listened to what you were saying. I know, I know, it sounds nosy. But this wasn't really *eavesdropping* so much as *research*. I was doing an investigation that I hoped would help me teach you to talk (and think) about your books.

"What I learned is this. When you talk with each other as you enter the class in the morning, or when you are in the lunchroom, you are usually talking about people. You talk about your friends, your family—sometimes even your teachers! You seem to love conversations that go like this."

In countless connections, I start by telling a little bit of my personal life. This connection begins instead with me telling a little bit of the kids' personal lives. The minilesson may sound lightweight, but the truth is that there are enormously important concepts underlying what I am saying. We know that the best way to make school come to life for kids is to tap into their social energy by creating a culture of learning. When John Goodlad asked children, "What's the best part about school?" almost all children answered, "The kids." We can disparage kids, complaining that they have the wrong priorities, but when Goodlad asked teachers, "What's the best thing about school?" the vast majority of teachers answered, "My colleagues." The truth is, we are social beings to our core. As long as reading is an isolating activity, children will turn their backs on it. So it is crucial for all of us, as educators, to consider ways in which we can make reading into a rich interpersonal activity.

I spoke in an intense, gossipy tone of voice, using sentence starters that could, just as easily, be used in book discussions as in gossip.

"I can't believe he (she) did that! Why did he? What's going on? I bet it's because. . . . Or maybe it's because. . . . But he should. . . . I know I'd. . . . But then, he's nothing like me. He probably acts like that because. . . ."

"And you know something? If you could be a fly on the wall in the faculty room, you'd find that the other teachers and I *also* love having conversations that go just that way. It seems that people are made in such a way that we love to talk about other people."

"So far in this unit of study, you have learned that readers read, feeling as if we are almost one of the characters in a book, losing ourselves in the story. Today marks an important shift in our reading lives. Today I want to teach you that we *also* read in a very different way."

Name your teaching point. Specifically, tell children that readers not only read, identifying with the characters and feeling lost in the story line, but we also pull back to think and talk about the book and especially about the characters.

"Today I want to teach you that we pull in to read, yes, but we also pull back from reading to think. We read like we are a character in the book, but we also read like we are a professor, growing intellectual ideas about the book. We read like we're under the covers, by flashlight, but we also turn the imaginary lights on in the room and scrutinize the text to grow ideas. The most fervent ideas center on the people in our books."

I hope children come away from this realizing that they, too, can turn around and research themselves, asking questions such as, "Why do I find myself bursting to talk when I'm not in a reading partnership and unable to say anything when I am expected to do so in class?" Ideally, children will become active observers of their actions, their interactions, their patterns, and their words, authoring not only their reading lives but also their learning lives.

Notice that today's minilesson doesn't channel kids toward particular kinds of ideas. We're inviting readers to approximate the whole activity of reading with their minds on fire, jotting ideas, bringing those to partner talks, and then growing their ideas by talking about them. For today, we simply want children to learn that they can read, thinking about grand ideas that they're dying to share, and that they then can have book talks with a partner that resemble the talks they have during read-aloud with the whole class.

Teaching

Reiterate the teaching point, accentuating the fact that instead of seeing the drama of the story from a participatory stance, readers will be more paradigmatic, expository, and objective.

"Today we're going to shift toward a new kind of thinking about books. We're still going to get lost in the text, but then we're also going to stop, turn on an imaginary light in the room, and we're going to think and say smart things about what we've just read. We're going to become professors, developing theories about the characters in our books.

"I know you all will be amazed at growing smart ideas about characters, because every morning, you're practicing doing just this. Every morning, you say things like, 'I can't believe he . . . Why'd he do that? I bet it's because . . . Or maybe. . . .' You may not realize that the sorts of ideas you are sharing about each other are exactly the sorts of ideas that professional readers develop and share about the people we come to know in books. As we read, we watch a whole social scene unfold, and our minds are full of the same kinds of thoughts that I hear you sharing with such energy when you arrive in the room in the morning."

I know, I know, it is overstating things a bit to say that the kids are going to read like professors, or, as I say a few lines later, like professional readers. But then again, the kids are accustomed to being told in the writing workshop that they're adopting the strategies of professional writers, writing like authors. And in any case, I want kids to understand that I'm asking them to assume a new stance, to read with new eyes. I want them to understand that readers, like writers, make the shift John Ciardi talks about when he says we shift between being passion hot and critic cold. I want them to understand that this bend in the road is calling for them to pull back from the text, to cast a discerning eye over characters' comings and goings, and to speculate, analyze, and theorize. I link this to the sort of thinking the kids do about each other to help them feel that this stance that I've made out to be so very intellectual is within reach for them, and also because, of course, the analogy is very true.

We accentuate the fact that this bend in the road marks a change of course because when we piloted these units of study, despite all the emphasis we placed on growing ideas about characters during Part 2, many readers continued to respond to texts by envisioning and predicting. While we rejoiced that children had held onto the teaching of Part 1, we realized that for them to undertake a new sort of thinking about books, we needed to make the demarcation between the first two bends crystal clear.

Tell children the story of one time when you were bursting to talk about your thoughts but had to bottle them up. Liken this to what readers do during reading time, when we read stories to ourselves and save up our responses to share later.

"In a way, reading reminds me of a time when I was little. Once, when I was about nine years old, I heard my parents downstairs in the kitchen yelling at each other. I gestured to all my siblings—I have eight of them—that something was going on downstairs in the kitchen, and so the nine of us sat on the back stairway, quiet as church mice, listening. Mum said something like, 'I can't take it any longer. I just can't take it' and started crying, and Dad said, 'Virginia, stop it.' Our minds were full of all the things we were dying to say to each other but couldn't—not then (or they'd hear us). Finally, after things subsided, my brothers and sisters and I crept back to one of our bedrooms, and we started this huge talk about what that interaction between our mum and dad meant.

"There are ways in which reading is a little bit like sitting on the back stairs, quiet as mice, dying to react, saving up stuff to talk about later. We read, and it is like we are peeking in on the scene in our character's kitchen, and we're full of all these thoughts.

"Whether we are reading a book aloud together, during read-aloud time, or alone during independent reading, reading is definitely like that scene, because we can't talk as we read. We need to sit quietly, saving up the things we want to say about the book, holding onto our ideas for a little while. Then, after reading for a bit, we find a way to talk to someone about it. In school, those conversations come during 'turn and talk' times or grand conversations during read-aloud and during partnership times at the end of each day's independent reading.

"When we read on our own, sometimes we don't figure out ways to talk about books. If we have no book partner, sometimes we don't even save up our thoughts. That's a huge loss! If there's no chance for us to have a gigantic conversation about our reading, sometimes when we read on our own, we end up not even *having* all those thoughts in the first place. Remember how I mentioned before that the famous reading researcher, Alan Purves, once said, 'It takes two to read a book.' He's reminding us that we need to set up book partners in life. And we need to read, planning for the conversations that we'll soon have about a book."

I am hoping this story will ring true for kids—that they'll recall similar times in their own lives. What child hasn't, at one time or another, overheard something important and needed to refrain from saying anything at that moment, leading the child to practically burst at the seams from holding back his or her reaction? I'm hoping to catapult children into their own memories of times they've been dying to talk, and to then say, "Reading is just like the time you are recalling."

Notice that in a session about growing ideas, I'm spotlighting what readers eventually do with those ideas. That is, I'm spotlighting not the construction of ideas but the sharing of them.

The upcoming minilessons all convey particular ways for kids to grow ideas about characters, but I think it is all too easy for us as teachers to get caught up in the specifics of that. The truth is you can think about the character's name and grow ideas from that; you can think about the objects the character carries and grow ideas about that. The risk is that we begin to think it matters that readers think about this or that particular thing. It doesn't. Lots of very skilled grown-up readers read a book without ever giving thought to the character's name, for example, or to the object the character carries. But skilled readers do read with our minds on fire; we do find little things to be significant; we do become accustomed to seeing significance in what others might pass by. And skilled readers go through life talking about books. This minilesson aims to recruit kids to the big work, the main task, of growing ideas as one reads, and that is very important indeed.

Of course, this is repetitive. Take the passages and parts that resonate for you, and share those with your kids. Leave the rest. I've essentially reiterated the same idea three or four times!

Active Involvement

Set children up to listen as you read a revealing passage aloud. Sit them in groups of four and then prepare those clusters to have grand conversations. As children talk, coach in.

"Readers, you're going to be talking in small groups for this active involvement, so right now I want you and your partner to pull together with the partnership nearest you and to sit so you can all talk together. Each group should be made up of two partnerships.

"I want you to try something a little different today. You're going to listen with your eyes closed. Some people say that when you lose one sense, your other senses are sharpened. For example, people who lose their sight have crystal clear hearing. In a minute, I'm going to reread a passage from *The Tiger Rising*, and as I do so, I want you to have that razor-sharp listening ability. Do the kind of listening that my brothers and sisters and I did on those steps years ago. Listen with your minds turned on.

"Listen so closely to this passage that you're bursting with things to say. After I'm finished reading, you'll have a chance to have a grand conversation with your group about your thoughts. Remember to focus especially on what you learn about the characters in this passage. And remember that you all are great at talking about people. You can talk about characters just like you talk about people in your life: 'I can't believe he. . . .' 'Why'd he do that? I bet it's because. . . .' 'Or maybe. . . .'"

> Then she [Sistine] saw his carvings, the little wooden village of odd things that he [Rob] had made. He had them all on a TV dinner tray beside his bed.
>
> "Oh," she said—her voice sounded different, lighter—"where did you get those?"
>
> She went and bent over the tray and studied the carvings, the blue jay and the pine tree and the Kentucky Star sign and the one that he was particularly proud of, his father's right foot, life-sized and accurate right down to the little toe.
>
> She picked them up one by one and then placed them back down carefully.
>
> "Where did you get them?" she asked again.
> "I made 'em," said Rob. She did not doubt him, as some people would.

Notice that in this active involvement, I ask children to engage in conversations involving two partnerships. You may decide to invite these larger conversations often.

You might wonder why I ask children to close their eyes to listen. The truth is that there is no special reason. We vary things to keep kids alert. This is one way to do that. If I catch a few kids peeking, that won't be important to me.

This is not the easiest passage in the world to grow ideas about. If you think your students will grope around for words after you read this aloud, choose a different, more provocative section.

Instead, she said, "Michelangelo—the man who painted the Sistine ceiling—he sculpted, too. You're a sculptor," she said. "You're an artist."

After I'd finished reading, I said, "Okay, readers, open your eyes and begin your conversation. Take turns sharing with your group the things you were dying to say as I read. Begin!"

I crouched low and listened in to one group talking. Josh started the conversation. "Sistine seems really different in this passage. Nicer."

"I agree," replied Aly. "When I heard Sistine's lines, her voice sounded soft and I could picture her smiling at Rob. She really likes his carvings. I bet she feels like she and Rob are the same."

Fallon nodded her head emphatically. "Yeah, Sistine really cares about art and now she's seeing this other side of Rob. She's seeing that he's creative. It's like—Rob's softer side brings out Sistine's softer side. They're like, soul mates!"

Sam, who'd been thoughtfully listening as the others spoke, said, "To add on, I think that before, Sistine kind of doubted Rob. Maybe she grouped him with the other kids. And now she's seeing that he's different, like her. She seems impressed by all those carvings. It's like there's this new understanding between them. I wonder if she'll open up to him now. Maybe they'll even become friends."

"I think maybe they already are," Aly said softly, her face pensive.

Listening to this foursome speak, I rejoiced silently at their seamless ability to listen and add on to each other's thoughts and to push themselves to see these characters so deeply.

I tore myself away from that group and hurried to another cluster. I listened for a minute to their talk.

Brianna said, "I think Sistine wants some of Rob's carvings."

Lily said, "I think so, too. She's giving him a compliment. Maybe she wants them. I know I'd love one of those carvings, and maybe I could make a house for it out of cardboard."

Sometimes when a teacher approaches a small group, the conversation stops as children in the group turn to the teacher, summarizing what they've been talking about and conversing with the teacher. You will need to be crystal clear with kids that whenever you approach a partnership or a small group discussion, you expect children ignore you for a time and carry on as if you were not there. Otherwise, how can you ever observe their conversations if these cease the moment you arrive on the scene? To train kids to continue their discussion in your presence, you may want to resist interrupting a group right away even if in that particular instance, you'd like to do just that.

Not all children, of course, will land so quickly on this kind of deep character analysis. You may need to coach children on what to notice about characters. What does a character value? Fear? What makes a character open up or shut down? What does a character take notice of? How does a character speak? Is there a shift in how this character is acting?

LINK

Remind children to read with their minds on fire, scrawling their ideas onto notes so as not to lose them.

"Eyes up here, readers," I said and waited for the talk to subside. "Today, I want to suggest that when you read your independent reading book, you do so with your mind on fire. Try to have thoughts about your book as you read. These will probably be thoughts about the people in the book. Let's add 'Read with our minds on fire' to our chart on growing ideas about characters. And just so those thoughts don't float away, scrawl the big ones onto Post-it notes. We'll be doing a whole lot with those Post-it notes, so even if you are the sort of reader who hates to pause as you read, please force yourself to jot some of your thinking—at least for now. Remember that you already know how to buzz with ideas about people in your life. Use that proclivity, that ability, to buzz with ideas about the characters in your independent reading book. And later, we will engineer things so that you *do* have grand conversations."

Strategies Readers Use to Grow Ideas About Characters

- We make a movie in our mind, drawing on the text to envision (or become) the character.

- We use our own experiences to help us walk in the character's shoes, inferring what the character is thinking, feeling, experiencing.

- We revise our mental movies as we read on, getting new details from the text.

- We notice when we feel connected to a character and use that feeling to deepen our understanding of the character.

- We read with our minds on fire and capture thoughts that lead us into grand conversations.

You will notice that I'm not reminding readers to envision and predict as well as to grow ideas about their characters. This is because the last time we taught this unit, children clung too vigorously to the sorts of thinking they'd learned earlier in this unit and didn't really push themselves to do a new sort of thinking. Notice, too, that I am a bit apologetic when I assign every reader to record a few Post-its during any one day's reading time. I'm always holding myself to the ideal of asking readers to do the sorts of work I do as I read, and if someone told me the kinds of thinking I was to do while reading a particular book, I'd balk a bit. I'm careful, therefore, to emphasize that no, readers do not go through life with someone else as our job captain, telling us the sorts of ideas we are meant to have at any one moment as we read. When I do channel children to do some mental work that I'm hoping they become accustomed to doing, I always point out that this is temporary and meant as a means for me to help them.

CONFERRING AND SMALL-GROUP WORK

Help Readers Grow Theories About Characters

Today marks the start of the second bend in this unit of study. Sometimes the bends in the road of a minilesson are bigger in the mind of the teacher than in the minds of readers, themselves. Today needs to be an exception. You will want to help children understand that a line has been drawn in the sand. Starting today, you will be asking them to tackle some new sorts of thinking as they read.

This may puzzle you. "Hmm," you might think. "How is it so different? Before. readers were thinking about characters, and now they're thinking about characters." It is true that then and now, characters will be important to your readers. But there are big differences in the ways you are hoping readers relate to characters.

Before now, you essentially wanted children to read as if they *were* the character. You wanted your kids to *be* Brian, trying to exist in an Alaskan wilderness with the help only of a hatchet. You wanted your readers to eye the raspberry bush hungrily, to hear the plunk, plunk, plunk as the ripe raspberries fell into the bottom of their hat. You wanted your readers to hope and dream, to worry and scheme, as if they were in the skin of the characters. The reading skills

you were supporting all combined, really, into one big thing. You wanted readers to know that lost-in-a-story feeling when the line between reading and living is thin indeed.

In this second portion of the unit, you are asking readers to engage with texts in an entirely different way. Yes, you are still asking them to be attentive to characters. But now, instead of *being* the character, you are asking your readers to stand back from the story, to assume the stance of an objective scholar studying patterns in the character's behavior, constructing and testing and refining theories about those characters.

Be prepared, then, to let readers know that a line has been drawn in the sand, and that starting today, you're going to help them to think in wise ways about characters. And then don't expect that children will be particularly proficient at this work.

Rely on a Whole Range of Conferring Methods to Help Readers Grow Ideas About Characters

The easiest way to help children understand and care about the work you'll be asking them to do is to help them see that just as we can watch people in real life and grow theories

---

> ### MID-WORKSHOP TEACHING POINT
>
> #### Readers Let Book Conversations Reverberate, Becoming Conversations in the Mind
>
> "In a minute, I'm going to suggest you have a grand conversation with your partner. But first, let me help you rehearse for that conversation. You know how in school, when we put on a play, we rehearse for it? People can also rehearse for grand conversations, and doing so makes those conversations more likely to go well.
>
> "One of the ways to do this is to look through your thoughts, your jottings, even before you meet with your partner and think, 'Will this idea spark a lively conversation?' If you find a thought that feels talk-worthy, you'll probably want to reread the section of your book that prompted the thought.
>
> "Usually, when I do this, I find the jottings that can spark a good conversation are ones that get *me* talking back to the idea even before I share it with anyone. That is, if I read my jotting and think, 'Another place I saw this in the book is . . . ,' or think 'This Post-it note goes with this other one I wrote,' or think "And to add on . . . ,' then I've probably got an idea that will provoke my partner and me into a great conversation.
>
> "As you look through your jottings, you may discover (as some of you have already confessed to me) that sometimes when you thought you had written *an idea* onto your Post-it, you actually got yourself started by just writing a fact that comes directly out of the book. If you find that
>
> *continued on next page*

about those people, so, too, readers can do this as we read. You'll want to approach your conferences ready to share a story or two of how you have been coming to know someone. I find my teaching is vastly more intimate when I share stories about my sons, so I'm apt to draw on the fact that my boys are away from home and to suggest that now I listen to their stories, seeking little indicators that tell me what life is like for them, seeing everything as suggestive and revealing. Then I'll point out that readers, too, can live with a similar sort of receptivity, ready to see signs that suggest what a character is like, and ready, too, to deduce all sorts of theories from whatever we see.

You can rehearse for your conferences by thinking of the personal insights you'll share about times in your life when you are especially tuned in to telltale signs that help you understand a person.

If two children are talking back and forth about a character, you might decide to coach from the sidelines, whispering prompts to one child or another such as, "Ask her why she thinks that" or "Aren't you dying to hear more about that idea? Tell her so!" Don't worry that you'll be putting words into kids' mouths. That is the whole point!

You may also decide to convene a cluster of children to talk about the main character in the whole-class read-aloud text before (or instead of) talking about a character in their independent reading books. Because the class as a whole will have studied the read-aloud text, children will have lots of ideas—some original and many borrowed. After children have a chance to develop smart insights about the protagonist from the read-

---

MID-WORKSHOP TEACHING POINT

continued from previous page

you've jotted lots of facts, not ideas, onto your Post-its, you may want to push yourself right now to have a thought about whatever you recorded. Write, 'The thought I have about this is . . .' or 'This is important because . . . ,' and then really stretch your mind to find a provocative, compelling idea. Even if you have, in fact, recorded ideas, not facts, you can extend those ideas by writing the thought prompt, 'This is important because . . .' or 'This makes me realize that . . .' and then writing some more."

After children had talked for a bit, I intervened. "Can I stop all your conversations so I can talk with you? Last night, after the talk we had about *The Tiger Rising*, I couldn't stop thinking about all the ideas you suggested. That's how good book talks go. They reverberate, like church bells reverberate. The bells ring—bong, bong, bong—and then, after the last bong ends and it seems like they are done ringing, they keep ringing, just more quietly, for a long time. That's how good conversations go. They continue even after they're over.

"I can see that conversations you have reverberate. You come into the classroom in the morning, talking about something—someone's birthday, or plans for the weekend—and then an hour later, when we're doing something completely different, I'll hear one of you whisper to another, 'What time?' For a minute I think you are asking what time it is, but then I realize you are still on that morning conversation, the one about the birthday, or the weekend plans. Long after that conversation is over, you're still thinking about it. You are still involved in it.

"So it is time for you to go back and read, but try letting the conversation you just had reverberate. Try to read differently because you are continuing the conversation in your mind—and on your Post-it notes—as you read on."

---

aloud book, you can ask members of the group to continue the conversation, this time shifting to talk about the main characters in their independent reading books, perhaps comparing them to those in the read-aloud.

No Matter How You Teach, You'll Be Helping Readers Extend Their Thinking About Their Characters

I sat beside Lily as she jotted on a Post-it. "Ooh, Lily, I see you've recently begun reading *Because of Winn-Dixie*! I love that book. What are you writing on your Post-it?"

"I wrote 'Opal made a friend with the library lady,' Lily said. "I just read it."

"I remember that part when Opal and the librarian became friends. What was her name? I can't remember," I said, prompting Lily to be more specific. Lily glanced at the book for a moment, recalled the name of the librarian, Miss Franny, and scribbled it on her Post-it. As she scrawled the name, I murmured, "Smart to include specifics like names."

I asked Lily what she was thinking about Opal now that she'd read a few chapters of the book. When she replied simply, "Well, she made friends in her new town." I noted that at least in that one response, Lily seemed to be thinking mostly about the actions, the events, involving Opal rather than considering what those actions and events revealed about Opal. That is, I do not wait for long in a conference before developing a hypothesis about the reader, though I fully expect that the initial hypothesis may be altered as I continue to listen. Pushing a bit, I said, "So what are you thinking specifically about Opal as a character?" and again I heard about what Opal had been doing with the librarian.

I decided to teach Lily to extend her thinking so that when she noticed *events* in a text, she would think about whether there were patterned ways in which the characters acted across those events. I knew *Because of Winn-Dixie* was a good book for teaching how to see interactions with people not just as isolated incidents but rather as linked, one to the next.

First, I complimented Lily for getting right to the heart of the story—noting that Opal is making friends. Her response may seem simple, but in fact it captures the main thrust of the first few chapters in *Because of Winn-Dixie*. I already knew that Lily is the kind of reader who takes in books with a wide-open heart, ready to feel strongly with her characters, and it was clear that Opal had made friends not only with people in her new town but also with at least this one young reader. When I pointed this out, Lily agreed that she'd taken Opal into her heart.

Then I said, "Lily, I think you're ready to push your thinking even further. You're ready for the next step. Here it is: One of the things that thoughtful readers do when we notice something going on with our character is we think, 'Hmm, how does this connect to other events, and what does this pattern make me think about my character?'"

I made an analogy to putting together a puzzle, explaining that Lily needs, as she reads, to think about how new pieces of information—like Opal's relationship with the librarian—fit with other pieces of information that Lily had gleaned earlier in the book. Then I asked her to try it.

"You just noticed that Opal made another friend, Miss Franny. Let's put this information alongside what you've already learned about Opal to see how it fits together. Think back on things you've learned about Opal and ask yourself, 'How does this fit in with what I already know, and what does it make me think?'"

Lily looked at me, willing me to start the process. "Okay, so what do I know about Opal? Let's see," I said, thinking alongside Lily.

Lily wrinkled her forehead and adjusted her black-rimmed glasses while she looked through her Post-it notes. She read two of them aloud. "Opal has a friend, Winn-Dixie," and "Opal's dad is hard to talk to."

"Okay, hmm, let's put that information alongside the new information you just found that Opal has another friend, Miss Franny the librarian.

How do these pieces go together to tell us something about our character, Opal?"

"Opal makes friends?" Lily said, essentially repeating the idea she'd voiced earlier, this time with a questioning intonation.

"Say more. Stretch your thinking by reaching back to the story." I swung my hand over my head to refer to the work we did back in unit one. "Try to give specific information about each character."

"Well, Opal makes friends with Winn-Dixie, who is a dog, and with Miss Franny, who is a librarian, and that's not that usual."

"And that makes me think . . . ," I said, prompting Lily to go further. I gestured with my hands to suggest that Lily repeat the language of my prompt, and then continue talking.

"And that makes me think," Lily said with a bit of reluctance in her voice, "that Opal makes friends with a dog and a lady so far."

I gestured for Lily to say more, and most importantly, I was silent.

"Well, I think it's different that she doesn't have kid friends yet, and it makes me think maybe she's shy or maybe she's scared the kids won't like her or something."

I looked at Lily and nodded, using nonverbal cues to encourage her to say more.

"Maybe Opal really wants friends because her dad doesn't talk to her, and she's looking for friends she can talk to easily. And those are the best kinds of friends—the easy to talk to ones. Even a dog."

"Wow, Lily. Let's step back for a moment and look at the thinking work you've just done. First, you noticed something that happened—Opal made friends with the librarian. Then you thought about how this connects with other stuff that happened. It's like you put the events side by side, saw a pattern across them, and came up with some new thinking about Opal. She seems to make friends with unexpected people, oh, and animals, but not kids. Then, you did a really big thing. You thought, 'What does this make me think about Opal?' That gave you an idea about her, something you can keep in mind as you read on. As you move forward in the story, remember to always ask yourself, 'What does this make me think about Opal?' You might find things occur in the upcoming story that match your theory about her friendships, or you might find things that make you revise your ideas. That's the fun of reading!"

TEACHING SHARE

Readers Aim for—and Rehearse for—Grand Book Conversations

Rally children to the task of having book conversations that will last.

"Right now, think about a time in your life when a book mattered to you because you were in a grand conversation about that book. It might be *The Tiger Rising*, or *Stone Fox*, or it might be a book someone read aloud to you last year, or a book you shared at your church or temple. Think about a book that meant a lot because it was shared."

After a moment's pause, I said, "Now think about the book you are reading right now. Look at it.

"Starting today, I'd like you to set a goal for yourself. Aim to have grand conversations about this book, letting those conversations reverberate so that you have book talks in your mind as you continue to read, and do this in a way that turns this book that you are reading right now into one that really matters to you. That's what great book talks can do. They can turn what would otherwise be an okay book into a deeply meaningful one."

Offer children some pointers on ways to have powerful book talks. Ask them to talk with a partner and later, at home.

"If you are going to have a really powerful conversation about your book, one that you can carry with you as you read on, you can't just hope *your partner* brings a ton of brilliance to the conversation. *You* need to bring a whole head of mental steam. The best way to do that is to rehearse for your conversation. Reread your Post-its and see if a couple of them go together, and suggest a line of thought that feels interesting to you. Consider which ideas might be interesting to your partner as well. One way to do that is to think between the book you are reading and books you and your partner have shared (think perhaps of ideas that link your independent reading book and *The Tiger Rising* or *Stone Fox*).

"As I said earlier, when deciding whether it will be easy to think and talk long about a Post-it, let your Post-it spark more ideas in *your* mind. That way it will be apt to spark ideas in your partner's mind as well. I'm going to give you some time to put a couple Post-it notes that go together onto one double-spread page of your reader's notebook. Then jot

Note that because this session is the start of Part 2, I'm devoting as much time and energy to preaching as to teaching. I cannot teach people strategies for doing something unless they first have the intention to do that thing. Motivation comes first. In this minilesson, I am doing my best to rally kids to engage in the big picture of this work. The specific how-to tips can come later. This means I need the work to seem both doable and worth doing.

We've actually seen that children ramp up their mind work to very high levels when they have a limited amount of time and a big job to do. So it is no accident that we're telling them they have only five minutes to rehearse for the grand conversations we hope they'll have with each other.

ideas and questions and connections about or between those Post-its, making arrows or marginal notes or stars that capture your thinking. In five minutes exactly (I set a timer), you'll have a chance to have a grand conversation with your partner."

After five minutes, I said, "Partners, check in with each other, decide which of you has ideas that could prompt a great conversation, and talk about that person's ideas. If you can't choose between the two of you, go with Partner 2. Get started."

After allotting time for the conversations, I brought the class to a close by saying, "Give me a thumbs up if you are willing to try to read tonight with your mind on fire, finding stuff you are dying to talk about (or almost dying to talk about, or that you can pretend to be dying to talk about). One bit of advice. Remember that interesting stuff is not in the book alone. It comes from the intersection of your mind and the book."

Since you're asking children to try your advice at home tonight, and in nights to come, you will want to follow up with them about this work, making them accountable to the work that you set up in your classroom. Checking in with children can be as simple as asking them about their "mind-on-fire" reading while they walk into the classroom tomorrow morning, or it can be as intimate as asking them about their reading lives during a one-on-one conference.

Devise a System of Record Keeping That Scaffolds Assessment-Based Teaching

You may come upon these pages with a heavy heart. I can imagine you asking, *"Another* assessment section? *Already?"* I suspect you are thinking, "I haven't begun to put the previous section into action, and now there is yet *more* for me to wrap my arms around!"

You can breathe again because this section is geared not toward loading you up with yet more assessment work so much as helping you develop a portable, efficient system for carrying your assessment information with you, on the run, as you move among your readers. And I need to say from the start that the advice in this section draws on work my colleagues and I are piloting now, so there will be details that aren't pinned down; regard this as an invitation to co-construct alongside us.

Let's start by considering the task. When we teach reading to a classroom full of children, the task, by definition, means that we will be pulled in competing directions. On the one hand, we need to lead the entire class in ways that create a culture of excellence, inviting kids into a rich community of text discourse and rallying all kids to work collaboratively on skills that pertain to all readers—skills such as monitoring for sense, reading with fluency, predicting, envisioning, inferring, growing theories about characters, determining importance, word solving, reading for the main idea, interpreting, and reading critically. On the other hand, we need to assess each reader individually, constructing a sense for that particular reader's learning pathway, and we need to ensure that each reader has goals that are within his or her zone of proximal development, a clear sense of ways to work toward those goals, and a constant stream of feedback that enables that reader to refine, extend, adjust, or accelerate his or her efforts.

To carry on with both tasks, teachers absolutely need some of this work to be streamlined and organized. The *Units of Study for Teaching Reading* books as a whole are meant to help with this, and you will presumably construct your own abbreviations of these sessions—outlines or notes you extract from the sessions and from other resources that

you draw upon—so that when you actually go into the classroom, you feel as if you have "cheat sheets" or scaffolds to help you remember all that you want to teach and do.

I expect that in a similar fashion, you'll want to construct cheat sheets or scaffolds of some sort that can help you recall the assessment information you'll need to draw on as you confer and work with small groups of readers. Those cheat sheets that you've created from your own data will need to be continually under construction as you teach because the specific work you did with a reader or the insight you gleaned into her thinking will be information you need to draw upon another day as you make teaching decisions.

This assessment section aims to help you create a record-keeping system that can contain data about individual readers' progress while also functioning as that cheat sheet or set of cue cards to remind you of what you need to know from that assessment for teaching each particular reader.

Clarify the Work This Record-Keeping System Needs to Accomplish

If you think for a moment of the different roles that record keeping needs to play when you are teaching reading as opposed to teaching writing, it will quickly be apparent to you that the demands on your record keeping are far greater in the reading than in the writing workshop.

When Children Are Writing, Some Information Is Available, Quickly and Obviously, to Feed Teaching.

After all, when you pull alongside a writer and ask, "How's it going?" that writer need not be very articulate for you to quickly ascertain how, in fact, it *is* going for the writer.

The writing process tends to be a sequential one, with a writer needing very different support based on whether the writer is brainstorming for a topic, planning how the piece might go, drafting leads, writing an early draft, rereading to revise, and so forth, and in a glance you can see where in this sequence a given writer is working. That knowledge alone will give you lots of ideas about the sorts of help that might be relevant.

Then, too, when conferring with a writer, you can scan just a few pages of text and see what exactly the writer has been doing, the extent to which the writer is utilizing prior instruction and coaching, ways the writer's work illustrates patterns of strength or need, and so forth.

You can also see, in the writer's work, the results of the preceding conferences and small-group work.

This all means that if you simply record in your notes the teaching compliment and the teaching point you convey to the writer, those records will be mostly adequate. They exist alongside the writer's work, and the work itself tells 99% of the story.

When Children Are Reading, Very Little *Information Is Available, Quickly and Obviously, to Feed Teaching.*

Think how different the situation is when you pull alongside a *reader* and ask, "How's it going?" If the reader, like the writer, is not especially articulate about what she has been doing, then you can cast an eye over the book the child is reading. She may be on page 70 of a 130-page book that (let's imagine) you have not read. There could be a scattering of Post-its, left along the reader's trail through the book. A log records the reader's time on task and progress through this book. And that's it. What a sharp contrast this is to the wealth of information available to you when you draw alongside a writer!

After all, reading is not all that different based on whether one is at the beginning, the middle, or the end of a book. Then again, you could say the reader's work varies—from asking questions to predicting to monitoring for sense and so forth—but those different operations all occur at lightning speed, out of sight, and the nudge to do one of these or another is not dependent upon cues that a teacher, pulling alongside the reader, can spot. The Post-its or notebook entries that dot the book don't consti-

tute reading. They are, instead, tiny remnants of a process that is largely invisible. And any teacher who wants to understand how a reader's reading has changed or what a reader has done with earlier instruction will have a hard time gleaning that from any of the available evidence.

This makes it entirely understandable why so many teachers feel as if they're at sea when trying to confer with individual readers once those readers can read fairly proficiently. Teachers will tell me, "I ask, 'How's it going?' The reader tells me fine. I struggle to ask some follow up questions. 'Can you picture it?' I ask. 'Any hard words? Any problems?' I dutifully record what the child says, even though I know I'll never do anything with what I record. Maybe I ask her to read a few sentences aloud, in which case I record any word that gives her a hard time. By that time, I know I am supposed to do something helpful, but I feel like I am grasping at straws, like I'm pulling stuff out of thin air. I don't know the book. I am not all that sure I know what the kid needs, really. So I say something totally inadequate like, 'I'll let you get back to your reading. Don't forget to picture it as you read. Off you go.'"

Some teachers have given up on responsive teaching that aims to help readers progress along learning pathways. Instead, they found stability in leading formulaic small-group work, using one format for essentially every interaction they have with readers. Others bring groups of readers to a text they know and then ground their teaching in that text—introducing it and watching readers work through the predictably hard parts. Neither solution is adequate for a teacher who aims to be responsive.

So the question I believe we need to ask is this: How can we devise a form of reading records that functions, for young readers, rather as medical records function for patients in a hospital. This, of course, is not a new question, and there are many reading researchers who've developed systems (see Myra Barrs' *Learning Records*, for one impressive example). My sense is that the record-keeping systems that have been the most common and well used are tailored especially to K–2 readers, where a good deal of the record keeping revolves around ascertaining the reader's stage of development (preemergent, emergent, beginning, early transitional, late transitional, etc.) and around helping readers draw on the cueing systems (including graphophonics, syntax, and meaning) to read fluently.

Once readers are in or beyond the intermediate stage of reading development, there are fewer agreed-upon developmental pathways along which teachers can track a reader's progress, and most instruction supports intellectual work that can be subsumed under the catch-all term *comprehension*. Think about it: If a teacher is really going to watch over a proficient fourth-grade reader's reading growth, is it enough for the teacher to look for broad, general indications that the reader "is comprehending?" Is it enough for our records to say, "Yep, she's comprehending this book. Yep, she's comprehending that book." We simply can't settle for this level of record keeping for our intermediate-and-beyond readers.

The Big Picture of a Proposed Record-Keeping System

Imagine yourself carrying a simple pocket folder, one for each of your readers. What would that folder contain, and how would we use it to inform and fuel our teaching?

The Left-Hand Pocket of the Folder: Reading Data-in-Short and Goals

You might carry a sequence of sheets on the left-hand side. One of these sheets could contain some quick reference facts to feed your teaching of this child:

- Data from the reader's semiformal assessments such as running records—perhaps the running records themselves and perhaps just the analyses of strengths and needs

- Date for when the child needs to be reassessed with hopes of progressing to another level of text difficulty

- Reading rate data and analysis of what this means

- Spelling inventory data

- High-frequency word data, if relevant

For Marisol, a fifth grader, the information on this one sheet might look like this, in April:

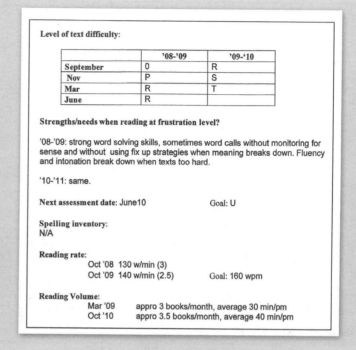

In the pocket on this same side of the folder, you could keep more sheets. These would be dated records of conference and small-group work with your notes pertaining to this reader, probably one page set aside for each unit of study, even if the page isn't completely full of notes. You might record some of those notes at home, while studying the reader's writing about reading or while thinking over the day.

You may or may not want to record your teaching compliment, your teaching point, and the agreed-upon work the reader will be doing. If you want this portion of your records to be heavily formatted, with a place for the date, the compliment, the teaching point, and the plan, make some sheets that you can print in this format that you invent to suit your needs.

The Right-Hand Pocket of the Folder: Text-Difficulty-Related Prompts and Cues for Teaching Reading Skills

In the pocket on the right side of these reading records, you'll have a different kind of sheet entirely.

A Sheet Divided into Quadrants for Note-Taking Related to Reading Skills

For this side of the folder, you could print sheets that are divided into quadrants. In each quadrant, you'd name a particular reading skill that you are focusing on during the current unit of study or portion of the year. (Or one of the skills you name in a quadrant could represent the work you want to focus on uniquely with this reader, regardless of the current unit of study.)

Since, within the sequence of these units, it is now October, and since you are in the midst of *Following Characters into Meaning*, you are helping your kids become more skilled at envisioning, predicting, and growing theories about characters. For Marisol, you also have been working to support fluency. So, in this example, those are your four quadrants. Those quadrants create a space for you to record Marisol's progress in these reading skills you are especially focusing on with her.

A Sheet Divided into Quadrants for Prompts Related to Skills and Text Levels

Beneath this sheet, you can place a similar sheet—with the same four quadrants, named with the same four skills—but this sheet contains notes that you've already placed there. These notes are cues for you, prompts you might use, to remind you of the teaching Marisol, and readers reading at her level of text difficulty or skill level, might need next in each of the skills you've selected. You would have pulled this particular sheet from a set of sheets you've made—a set containing prompts and cues for these four skills for each band of text difficulty.

Printing out, en masse, the same sheet of prompts and cues for all your children reading texts in the R/S/T band of text difficulty is an act of efficiency that will undoubtedly make you uncomfortable. It should; readers differ, one from the next, not only by the band of text difficulty

they can handle but in many, many other ways as well. You will absolutely have to amend these sheets in some cases, tailoring them to your children. These sheets are meant only as a best guess as to where each reader might be—something for you to start with!

These sheets presume that children develop each of their reading skills at roughly the same rate. In other words, if the reader is highly skilled at predicting, he'll also be highly skilled at envisioning and highly skilled at developing theories, say. Of course, this is not always true. A reader might be skilled at envisioning and quite unskilled at developing theories. So, while your preprinted sheet will have suggestions in each quadrant for coaching readers, the suggestions will all be based on the assumption that the reader is at about the same level of development for each skill. If that is not the case, if the reader is developing in one skill and advanced in another, what will you do to amend your prompt sheets?

These sheets also presuppose that you'll choose the same four skills to focus on for each reader. You might do this, or you might tailor your teaching more precisely to each reader.

One solution to both of these problems with the sheets is to use stickers that are about the size of a quadrant (giant mailing labels work). If the prompts for every stage of the development of every skill you want to focus on are printed out on a ready-made stack of stickers, you can easily adjust a prompt sheet for one child by grabbing the right sticker and using it to cover the quadrant on the premade sheet that is at the wrong level, or names the wrong highlighted skill, for the child with whom you are working.

Yes, of course, you could use only the stickers, placing them on blank sheets of paper and tailoring each to the reader's needs, presupposing no particular stage of development within each skill. That will be your decision to make, according to what works for you, your experience level, and your teaching situation.

How Will We Create the Prompts and Cues for Each Quadrant?

Let's go back to our example. Marisol is reading books at the R/S/T band of text difficulty; we know some of the demands those books place on her. In other words, we can deduce from her text difficulty band some of the work she will need to do to understand texts at this level. For example, you'll recall that in the text difficulty band before R/S/T, many stories contained conflicted, complex characters (such as Amber Brown, who is conflicted over whether she wants to be a teenager or a kid), and the texts at these earlier levels tended to state, outright, the nature of that conflict or complexity. For that level, readers needed to carry and apply this information about the character, but they did not need to infer it. Now, at the R/S/T band, however, readers are often left to infer a character's complicated mix of traits. The reader is given windows through which to watch the character, but it is the reader's job to generate descriptors and figure out the character's nature. Ideally, readers will generate ideas about a character and then think more deeply about the character, refining those ideas. We may need to support Marisol in making that leap in her character work!

In the quadrant of your record-keeping sheet that is reserved for "Developing Theories About Characters," you might, then, include some prompts that can help you coach Marisol to think a bit differently than she has about character. Specifically, here's an example of what one quadrant of your record-keeping sheet could look like:

Developing Theories About Characters
R/S/T Text Difficulty Band

*Talk and Thought Prompts Readers Can Use
to Understand Characters in R/S/T Texts*

- *Even though the book doesn't come right out and say this, I think [character] _____ is [some traits] _____. There are hints that show this. For example: _____. Another example is _____.*

- *At first I thought [character] _____ was [some traits] _____, but as I get to know him/her more, I'm coming to think that deep down, she/he's really [some traits] _____.*

- *Sometimes the main character acts and talks one way but really is feeling a whole other way. For example, one time he/she acted this way _____ and said _____, but actually he/she was feeling _____.*

- *One way the author helps us know a character is the author gives that character objects or ways of acting and talking that are meant to represent something about the character. I think it's perhaps significant that the author gave this character [objects or ways of acting and talking] _____. To me, this might show _____.*

- *The main character has different sides to him/her. When she's/he's _____, she's/he's _____. Then when she/he's _____, she's/he's _____.*

You may be perplexed. "What do I do with those blanks?" You might ask. "Do I fill in what the child says?" The answer is "No." These prompts are written in this way simply to help you say them in such a way that children can use these as they use conversational prompts. (I want to add on . . . , I agree because . . . , I disagree because. . . .) And the concept is not that you'll ever run down this whole list, flooding the child with an excess of good ideas. But if Marisol looks up from *The Tiger Rising* and says, "Rob is sort of a soft person," you might glance at the last item on your list and say, "Can I give you a tip? You are reading books where the characters will have different sides to them. Could you think, 'When Rob is doing such and such, he's soft—yet when Rob is doing (you'd have to think of what else) he's . . . what?'" And you could even leave that reader with a Post-it with this prompt on it, suggesting the reader try thinking this way about more characters than just Rob.

Of course, it may seem to you now that Marisol's comprehension skills are not as strong as you thought they were in September when you conducted running records. You may think, "I don't think she is remotely ready for this work that I think of as suited to readers of R/S/T books." In this case, you may look over the Post-its and entries she's already been keeping, thinking, "Is the work Marisol is doing now more like what I envision readers of K/L/M doing, or is it more like I envision readers of N/O/P/Q doing?"

You should be able to look between the prompts I list below and my earlier descriptions of the work that readers tend to do when working at different bands of text difficulty, and in this way understand the genesis of the prompts I have suggested.

Developing Theories About Characters
K/L/M Text Difficulty Band

*Talk and Thought Prompts Readers Can Use
to Understand Characters in K/L/M Texts*

- [Character] _____ is [some traits] _____ because _____.

- She's/he's doing or saying _____. This shows me she's/he's _____.

- In this book, the main character's feelings change. First, she's/he's _____ because _____. Then later, she's/he's _____ because _____.

- She/he could have done this _____ but instead she/he did this _____. This makes me think that she's/he's _____.

Developing Theories About Characters
Text Difficulty Band N/O/P/Q

*Talk and Thought Prompts Readers Can Use
to Understand Characters in N/O/P/Q Texts*

- Sometimes my character is _____. For example, _____. But other times, she/he _____. For example, _____. This makes me think _____.

- In the beginning, my character was _____, but as the story continues, I think my character could be changing. By the end, she/he _____.

- Sometimes the book comes right out and tells readers about the character's personality/feelings. For example, it says _____. Then there are places in the story where it doesn't say this, but it shows this. For example, _____.

Although during this second portion of the unit, *Following Characters into Meaning*, your primary emphasis will be on helping readers develop theories about characters, you'll also be maintaining the development readers made during the first portion of the unit and reminding them that alert, engaged readers predict and envision. You could, of course, take the characteristics of proficient envisionments (Session I) and proficient predictions (Session VI) and turn those into cue cards to nudge your work with readers. Alternatively, you can think about ways in which different bands of text difficulty will require readers to do different sorts of envisionment and prediction, and again, turn your teaching hopes into a cheat sheet of some sort, filled with prompts that you can pass along to readers. These, then, could go in a different quadrant of your record-keeping sheet:

Predicting
Text Difficulty Band R/S/T

Talk and Thought Prompts Readers Can Use
to Predict in R/S/T Texts

- Before, in books, there was often a main problem and a main solution. Now, the problem has many parts. For example, in this books, its not just that _____ but about _____ and on top of that, _____.

- Often the solution doesn't really solve things, but it does help characters understand or see things. For example, _____.

- When reading a story, many experienced readers have a feeling of, "I've read stories like this one before," and this helps the reader speculate how the story will unfold. What other stories have you read that are a bit like this one, and how do those stories help you predict?

A few months from now, if Marisol seems to you to have nailed the sort of prediction work that you expected she'd do when reading in the R/S/T band of text difficulty, you might want to take the prompts designed for more experienced readers, those reading texts in the U/V/W band, and affix them on top of where you'd earlier kept the prompts listed above.

Predicting
Text Difficulty Level U/V/W

Talk and Thought Prompts Readers Can Use
to Predict in U/V/W Texts

- Often in stories, the reader is given one piece of the whole, then another, another . . . and when the story ends, the pieces come together. What pieces of the story am I holding, and when I think how the story will end, which pieces do I think might fit together? How might they fit?

- When reading, we often have a sense that the author is trying to convey an idea or to teach a lesson. The author has some big meaning that is unfolding across the story. What big meaning do I sense is being conveyed in this story, and how does that sense of meaning help me predict what will happen in the upcoming sections of the book?

Using These Record-Keeping Folders

You'll wonder about the record-keeping portion of this. You may be thinking, "Should I check off what readers can do?" And you may wonder, "Can I turn this into a checklist of some sort?" I encourage you to experiment. The idea for creating and using reading records such as I am describing to you is something quite new for our community of teachers, and we'll be exploring and experimenting alongside you. For now, however, let me say that sometimes I think we busy ourselves recording all sorts of stuff that we never use at all. Instead of creating a checklist, maybe the most important thing we could do would be to collect Post-its from time to time that illustrate each reader's ability to grow theories about a character, to predict or envision or anything else. Perhaps the most important thing about records is that these records allow us to "read" what a child is *already* doing, understanding that work so that we can place that child somewhere on a developmental trajectory, to meet him where he is. Maybe the most important thing is that our records allow us to be agile, responding to whichever curve-ball the reader throws our way. You are predicting? Let me help you do that even better. You are growing ideas about characters? Great, let's work on that. Perhaps the best use of these quadrants in the right-hand pocket of our record-keeping folder is as a sort of portable bulletin board, with us affixing the latest bit of evidence that shows the gist of what a child is currently doing as a predictor, an envisioner, or a theorizer.

My son Miles has taken a job at McKinsey, a strategic management firm that advises companies and nonprofits and government agencies across the world. McKinsey is known for coaching organizations in ways that are not unlike how you and I want to coach individuals. There are books about The McKinsey Way, and you won't be surprised that I've been reading them as I try to imagine my twenty-two-year-old stepping into this new role. One of the hallmarks of The McKinsey Way is the notion that when confronting a complex conundrum, one for which simple solutions don't jump immediately to mind, the temptation is to think, "I need to take a lot of time to figure this out right." You and I could say that about our system for record keeping in the reading workshop. We could think, "This is a complicated problem. My colleagues and I need to think this through with the greatest care imaginable, so we get it right."

The McKinsey Way suggests that when confronting a complex conundrum, the best way to proceed is to do exactly the opposite of this. Come up with a solution—right away, by the end of next week. Generate a plan, and start acting on it.

Why? Because that's draft one, and once one draft proposal is out there on the table, work can begin, improving that draft. So my biggest suggestion is this: Invent a plan for record keeping, one that will help you not feel as if you're pulling your teaching out of thin air. Create it now. It won't be perfect—but it will be a perfectly good start.

Developing Nuanced Theories About Characters

IN THIS SESSION,

You'll teach students that readers can develop complex theories about their characters by paying attention to how they act.

y now, you have no doubt gleaned that just as there is a way that fiction books tend to go, there is also a way that these sessions tend to go. You can approach the prelude to any session, anticipating that you'll learn why the upcoming session matters tremendously, why the suggested teaching is so very important that it deserves the time and attention of you and of your children. The preludes are my way of spotlighting the big work underlying the upcoming session. I write them because I know that when teaching ideas are passed from one person to another, sometimes the inspiration and motivation for the teaching drops away, and all that is left are the concrete how-to tips. The result is that teaching that once felt incredibly important all of a sudden amounts to little more than a trinket.

The truth is that for you to teach a really powerful reading workshop, you need to be able to *write* as well as to *read* the preludes to your minilessons. That is, you'll be best able to teach reading strategies in ways that command attention if your teaching emerges from your own felt sense, your own lived experience, of the content. Ultimately, for any reform to work, that reform needs to tap into a teacher's sense of personal purpose. Michael Fullon, in his book *Change Forces*, writes, "Organizations intent on building shared visions encourage members to develop their personal visions. If people don't have their own visions, all they can do is 'sign up' for someone else's. The result is compliance, never commitment."

If you haven't done so already, it's important for you to begin mining your own experiences and drawing from those

GETTING READY

- Bring your class read-aloud to today's lesson. If you are using *The Tiger Rising*, you will reread portions of Chapter 10 during the teaching and active involvement and portions of Chapter 7 during the mid-workshop teaching point.

- Ask children to bring their "My Reading Life" folders and, specifically, their reading logs with them to the lesson. They will fill it out during the link.

- Prepare the anchor chart "Strategies Readers Use to Grow Ideas About Characters," which you will add to during the link.

- During the teaching section, you will need a chart called "To Grow Ideas About a Character, I . . ."

- During the active involvement in Session X, you will be revisiting a portion of Chapter 12 in *The Tiger Rising*, so you may want to reread this on your own to prepare.

when you teach these units. When teaching a reading workshop, this means that you need to become accustomed to turning around in your tracks, noticing what you do when you read. Above all, notice the ways in which you grow ideas as you read.

So pick up a pen and read, and as you read, note the fleeting thoughts that cross the landscape of your mind. Spy on yourself as you progress down the page. Notice ways *you* grow ideas about characters. Then ask yourself, "How can I describe what I did in a way that applies not just to this particular page of this particular book but also to other pages and other books?"

> *So pick up a pen and read, and as you read, note the fleeting thoughts that cross the landscape of your mind.*

This process, of spying on your own reading and then turning what you do as a reader into teaching points, can lead you to easily imagine a score of little things that readers can do to grow ideas about characters. And all of what you notice can become the substance of minilessons in this portion of your unit. If you notice that *the way* a character talks (not just *what* the character says but the character's *distinct lingo*) reveals a lot about the character—then dandy. That can be a minilesson! If you notice that the times when a character is silent reveal things about the character just as surely as do the times when the character is anything but silent, then again, this means you have content to teach. You may notice that you attend to something as specific as the character's name, wondering about its significance. The list of possibilities is long. The ideas for stuff to teach will come fast and furious if you begin to mine your own experience as a source for your teaching.

A word of caution: You don't want to make reading—an experience that presumably is relatively simple and organic and flowing for you—become overly complex. That is, you'll spy on your own reading process and note specifics that you attend to—specifics like the objects that seem to define a character, a character's name, and so forth. As you note these things, however, remember that you do not want to inadvertently convey to children that reading is like a scavenger hunt, with readers holding fast to a long list of small items that need to be found in a text. In scavenger hunts, it is okay to look for four-leaf clovers and pink pebbles, but you do not want *reading* to be all about checking off the items on someone else's list. Your main hope is simply that readers read, appreciating that there is more to a text than first meets the eye.

In today's minilesson and the minilessons that follow, notice that we tuck little disposable tips about particular ways one can think about characters into the bigger message. One part of the bigger message is that there is a thin line between thinking about characters and caring about them. And I'm convinced that caring about the main character in a story gives many of us a through line that draws us into and along a story. But I also believe that thoughtful readers learn to think deeply about people—about the characters we meet in books, and in life, too—and to grow complex, nuanced, and sensitive ideas about people. That is, through reading, people develop social intelligence, becoming more able and more apt to think deeply about people, to forgive people, and to learn from people. This enriches not only a person's *reading* but also a person's *life*. And this is the theme of this session.

MINILESSON

Developing Nuanced Theories About Characters

CONNECTION

Tell a story about someone who is good at reading people. Then suggest that reading people in real life is not unlike reading people in stories.

"When my son Evan was a little boy, he sometimes seemed to do exactly what I told him not to do. I'd scrub and wax the kitchen floor and then say, 'Evan, keep off the floor 'til it's dry.' Evan would stand outside the kitchen as I spoke, nodding. But not two minutes later, I'd see him, out of the corner of my eye, slyly take one toe and dip it quickly onto the still wet kitchen floor.

"I remember talking to my husband, John, about how naughty I thought Evan was being when he did things like this. But John, who is incredibly astute at reading people in the world, pointed out that Evan wasn't necessarily out to defy me. John suspected that Evan was merely figuring out what he could get away with and how to assert himself. 'He just wants his little victories,' John said.

"It was the same way when he became a teenager. Evan was basically a good kid. Sometimes he would test the waters, but for the most part he did his homework, came home on time, was polite to adults. But *one day* he walked through our door with a *stripe* in his hair—a bleached blonde streak that ran right down the middle! I was aghast! But my husband, ever the astute reader of people, pointed out yet again that Evan was basically a good kid. He wasn't intent on defying me. He was just trying to be himself. 'He needs his little victories'," John reminded me.

"Thank goodness for John's advice. He has always been good at reading Evan and has helped me understand Evan's 'little victories' and through them, my son, too."

Obviously you won't feel comfortable talking about my son Evan as if he was your son, so you have a couple of choices. You could tell children that a friend of yours has this son, and carry on like that, or you can substitute a child you know for Evan, or you can rewrite the minilesson altogether. The best option is to rewrite this! The larger point—that people who read people well can also read texts well—is one that will be easy for you to make.

It should be clear to you by now that whenever a minilesson contains two examples, you can streamline it by selecting just one—or by substituting your own example, making it a bit briefer. But don't delete details, because details are necessary in good writing. If you streamline a minilesson so much that you lose the human side of what would otherwise be abstract ideas, you'll find no one listens to you.

Name your teaching point. Specifically, suggest that we can learn to "read" people in stories the way we "read" them in real life.

> "To read people—in life and in stories—it is important to remember that actions can be windows to the person. In life and as we read, we can pause after a character has done something and say, 'Let me use what just happened as a window to help me understand this person.'"

You should, by now, be accustomed to the fact that teaching points often contain the big goal—good readers are good at reading people—and specific tips for how a person can go about doing this big goal. Notice, too, that the specific tips are written in a slightly step-by-step way. The first step to reading characters is to read, then pause after a character has done something, and then say, "Let me use what happened. . . ."

TEACHING

Read an upcoming section of your read-aloud text, demonstrating how you go about letting a character's actions reveal the person. Struggle so you can demonstrate that there is more to see in the text than first meets the eye.

> "Let's return to a chapter we read a few days ago in *The Tiger Rising*, Chapter 10. This is the chapter that introduces Willie May. We'll be making a movie in our minds as we always do, but this time, let's especially notice this character's actions, letting those actions act as windows to the sort of person she is. Watch as I try to read *her*."

You are demonstrating the thinking work of reading. Your hope is that while you demonstrate, you can at the same time provide children with scaffolded support so they actually do the same thinking alongside you. Take your time growing thoughts about what the character's actions reveal so that you leave time for children to beat you to any inferences about these.

>> Rob was sweeping the laundry room when Willie May, the Kentucky Star's housekeeper, came in and threw herself down in one of the metal chairs that were lined up against the cement-block wall.
>>
>> "You know what?" she said to Rob.
>>
>> "No, ma'am," said Rob.
>>
>> "I tell you what," said Willie May. She reached up and adjusted the butterfly clip in her thick black hair. "I'd rather be sweeping up after some pigs in a barn than cleaning up after the people in this place. Pigs at least give you some respect."

> "Let me stop," I said, lowering the book. Looking up into the sky, I mused, "What do I know about Willie May? Hmm. . . . The book hasn't told me that much. Maybe I should read on." I started to duck my head toward the page. But then I stopped myself. "Wait a minute. It might not SAY that much, but I know that if I pay close attention to how a character is acting, this can give me a window into what kind of person she may be. So let me see."

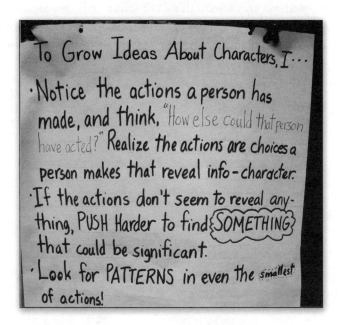

To Grow Ideas About Characters, I...

- Notice the actions a person has made, and think, "How else could that person have acted?" Realize the actions are choices a person makes that reveal info—character.
- If the actions don't seem to reveal anything, PUSH Harder to find SOMETHING that could be significant.
- Look for PATTERNS in even the smallest of actions!

I began quietly rereading, doing so as if I were reviewing the text for myself only, not for an audience. I read aloud a few key sentences from the text.

> She threw herself down in one of the metal chairs. . . .'I'd rather be sweeping up after some pigs in a barn than cleaning up after people in this place. Pigs at least give you some respect.'

Looking up from the book I said, "Isn't Willie May something else? What a spitfire! She really bursts into that room, doesn't she? I can see her collapsing into that chair with a loud plunk and then speaking in a big, frenzied rush. She seems upset to me. I can't believe she'd rather clean up after pigs than people. Pee-ew! (I held my nose, prompting the children to giggle.) Pigs can be really smelly. It could be that she's just had some bad encounters with people. Maybe today is a bad day. *Or* (I paused for effect) it may be that Willie May is the kind of person who stands up for herself. She talks about respect. That's clearly a big deal to her.

"Hmm. . . . The more closely I look at Willie May and her actions, the more I suspect that she is someone who values herself enough to expect fair treatment. Rob, on the other hand, lets people bully him right and left—the Threemonger boys, certainly, and even Sistine. I think Willie May may be a lot tougher than Rob. I mean, she could have just gone about her work quietly, whistling, not letting other people get to her, and certainly not pointing out their discourtesy. But instead, she practically broadcasts her frustration!

Over and over again you will notice that one way to highlight how a person follows a strategy is to demonstrate first neglecting to follow the suggested steps and encountering subsequent difficulty and then to self-correct, give yourself a little pep talk, and this time set out to take the high road.

Notice that I try to embed little tips into a demonstration. In this instance, I point out that it is helpful to think about actions as choices and to consider the other choices a character could have made. No good piano teacher would simply sit beside a child who was eager to learn piano, and say, "Watch me play this sonata," and then proceed to play beautifully, ending with the injunction, 'Now you try.' Similarly, you can't simply say to children, "Watch me grow ideas about characters," and then poof! You proceed to do just that, ending with the words, "So now you go do this work." Instead, you need to convey specific pointers that will help your children. I think of this as a process of tucking little tips into my demonstration.

"Sometimes when I'm trying to think what the actions show, it helps me to think what a character *could* have done but didn't do. I think of a character's actions as choices, keeping in mind that the person could have made different ones. Then I think, 'Why might this person have acted *this* way, not *that* other way?'"

Pause and talk directly to the children, pointing out several strategies you have used to grow ideas about a character.

I put the book aside and leaned in toward the children. "Readers, do you see that when I want to read a person—in this case, Willie May—I take note of the actions the person has made, actions that might not move the plot forward all that much (like when Willie May throws herself into a chair) but that might reveal the person? Notice that first, I named what I noticed and what an action or words might tell me about that character. And then, I thought about how else that character might have acted (realizing that other characters might have acted in other ways) and thought, 'How else could this person have acted?' So I am aware that the person's actions are *choices*, and that the person could have chosen differently.

"Readers, I'm noticing something else, too. It seems to me like Willie May's actions might fit a pattern. She throws herself into the chair. She says something disgruntled and honest about her job and about people. Together, these actions create an image of Willie May as the sort of person who asserts herself—the sort of person who doesn't hold back. I'd have to read on, of course, to see if my theory about Willie May is supported later in the text. It may just be that she's disgruntled and letting it out. She may normally be a much more docile (that means meek or passive) person, but I don't think so!

"The point is that a character's actions often act as a window to who they are, and sometimes there are patterns of actions that contribute to this image. As readers, we can look at these actions—at characters' choices and patterns of behavior—and grow little theories about what they are like as people. Then we read on and grow or revise those theories.

Then I stepped out of the role of reader altogether and said to the class, "Readers, let me just list what I did, and then I'm going to ask you to take over for me, continuing to read this character."

Notice the rhythms in my teaching. I shift between the role of reader and the role of teacher. Children can get confused when we do these role shifts. I've seen some teachers looking at a book and saying words that the teacher herself had made up. Watching, it looked for a bit as if the teacher's words were the author's words and the teacher was reading them from the book! This can be disorienting. So when I am reading, I hold the book clearly in front of my face. When I shift for a moment into musing about the book, my eyes are toward the ceiling and my voice takes on a musing quality. When I am not reading at all but am talking to the kids, the book is out of sight, and I lean forward and look the kids directly in the eyes.

You'll notice that I embed some additional specific tips into this demonstration. You may very well decide to highlight just one for now (perhaps that actions can be viewed as choices a character makes), saving the other, more advanced tips (that actions fit into patterns that reveal something about a character) to convey in small-group work with your more advanced readers.

In any minilesson, you will make one big teaching point, and then you will convey a whole bunch of little practical tips. Sometimes, teachers who haven't been taught a lot about minilessons seem to assume that the structure of a minilesson suggests that the one teaching point is the only instruction contained in a minilesson; the resulting instruction can become too lightweight, too flimsy. Notice ways in which Kathleen and I tuck little subordinate tips into the teaching component of a part. In this part, for example, I emphasize that theories are tentative—that readers expect to add to or revise them.

Teachers, you will need to decide which of these charts you want to make. There will be lots of times in your teaching when you make a quick list and decide not to turn that list into a permanent feature of the classroom. The chart shown above could just be a list that you talk through, and your real hope could be simply that many of your readers remember and use a couple of these pointers.

ACTIVE INVOLVEMENT

Invite children to listen as you read on and to develop ideas about a character, using all the tips you have given them.

"So let me read on. Will you join me in trying to read Willie May's actions so we can, together, come to understand her?" I backed up just a bit and resumed reading.

> Rob leaned on his broom and stared at Willie May. He liked looking at her. Her face was smooth and dark, like a beautiful piece of wood. And Rob liked to think that if he had been the one who carved Willie May, he would have made her just the way she was, with her long nose and high cheekbones and slanted eyes.
>
> "What you staring at?" Willie May asked. Her eyes narrowed. "What you doing out of school?"
>
> Rob shrugged. "I don't know," he said.
>
> "What you mean, you don't know? Don't be moving your shoulders up and down in front of me, acting like some skinny old bird trying to fly away. You want to end up cleaning motel rooms for a living?"
>
> Rob shook his head.
>
> "That's right. Ain't nobody wants this job. I'm the only fool Beauchamp can pay to do it. You got to stay in school," she said, "else you'll end up like me."

"Readers, take a minute to think about how Willie May's actions here tell us something about her. You might want to think about how she might have acted or spoken instead of how she acts and speaks here. Or are there patterns you're starting to spot in how she operates? Turn and talk to your partner."

I gave children a couple minutes to talk, and then I reconvened the group.

"Listening in just now, I heard some of you say that Willie May seems a little bossy, like Sistine. But then you were quick to point out that she also seems to care about Rob. She's encouraging him to stay in school so that he doesn't end up having to clean rooms for a living. A couple of you thought that being grumpy might be a pattern for Willie May.

"Let's skip ahead a bit, and you can add to or revise your theory."

To Grow Ideas About a Character, I . . .

- Notice the actions a person has made, seeing these as windows into that person.
- Notice actions that don't move the plot—they're often there to reveal the character.
- Realize actions are choices a character makes and examine what those choices reveal.
- Notice patterns of actions especially and think, "Why did the author have this character continually doing this? What might this mean?"
- If the actions don't seem to reveal anything, push harder to find something that could be significant. Try saying, "Maybe this suggests. . . ." Or "Perhaps it could be. . . ."
- Come up with an idea and then try to think more about the idea. Say, "This could be important because he (she). . . ."

> Willie May wants Rob to succeed and live a good life. She is a straight talker. She believe in him.

> W.m. thinks her life isn't great and that is why she is being grumpy but she is making Rob see how much she cares.

Willie May opened her eyes and looked over the top of her glasses at Rob's legs.

"Mmmm," she said, after a minute. "How long you had that?"

"About six months," said Rob.

"I can tell you how to cure that," said Willie May, pointing with her cigarette at his legs. "I can tell you right now. Don't need to go to no doctor."

"Huh?" said Rob. He stopped chewing his gum and held his breath. What if Willie May healed him and then he had to go back to school?

"Sadness," said Willie May, closing her eyes and nodding her head. "You keeping all that sadness down low, in your legs. You not letting it get up to your heart, where it belongs. You got to let that sadness rise on up."

"Oh," said Rob. He let his breath out. He was relieved. Willie May was wrong. She couldn't cure him.

"The principal thinks it's contagious," he said.

"Man ain't got no sense," Willie May said.

"He's got lots of certificates," Rob offered. "They're all framed and hung up on his wall."

"I bet he ain't got no certificate for sense though," said Willie May darkly. She rose up out of her chair and stretched. "I got to clean some rooms," she said. "You ain't going to forget what I told you 'bout them legs, are you?"

"No, ma'am," said Rob.

"What'd I tell you then?" she said, towering over him. Willie May was tall, the tallest person Rob had ever seen.

"To let the sadness rise," Rob said. He repeated the words as if they were part of a poem. He gave them a certain rhythm, the same way Willie May had when she said them.

"That's right," said Willie May. "You got to let the sadness rise on up."

After decades of watching teachers lead minilessons, my colleagues and I have realized that one of the major decisions a teacher needs to make is this: How will you act during the read-alouds that are embedded into your minilesson? Some teachers tend to write these sections of the text onto chart paper or display them using an overhead projector or document camera, and to stand while they read aloud, and their entire demeanor suggests the read-aloud has been incorporated into a class lecture. Others tend to sit on the edge of their seat, leaning close to the class, with children gathered close around the teacher's knees, as if the entire minilesson is an extension of a goodnight story or as if the minilesson is an occasion for sharing a special secret. As I mentioned earlier, I prefer this demeanor to the former, and have gone so far as to say that I'd like to banish overhead projectors from minilessons altogether.

This is a longer read-aloud than you'll generally embed into your minilesson. There will be times when you make the decision to do this, and of course this probably means that your read-aloud time that day becomes briefer and your entire reading workshop becomes longer because it incorporates some of read-aloud time. Certainly you don't want this to mean that children have less time to read independently.

In her "Ten Read Aloud Commandments," Mem Fox suggests that adults read aloud with animation. If you listen to your own voice, making sure it is lively, not flat, children will have an easier time understanding not just the words you read but also the message or mood the author intends to convey, the intonation with which characters speak, and their frame of mind.

"Turn and talk," I said again.

As children spoke, I moved around the room, listening in. I was curious to see whether children would hold onto the little tips I'd inserted into the minilesson, knowing it was a lot to keep in mind. As children spoke, I coached into their talking, trying to help them lift the level of their responses.

"Can you say more?" I encouraged.

Izzy said, "I still think she's grumpy."

"Well," Emma continued, "I think it's still more than that. I think that she cares about Rob. She listens, she tries to help. She gets him. Like his sadness. She 'gets' his sadness."

"Can she be both grumpy and good at reading Rob?" Izzy wondered.

"I think so," Emma said, nodding. "I mean, I hope so. Then we're both right."

"What might make her both grumpy and good at reading Rob?" I prompted.

Try to become accustomed to listening to what your kids can do and thinking, "How can I lift this up a notch?" In that way, your teaching will always rally kids to outgrow themselves.

> She is a kindred spirit. She gets the sadness. Sadness is in her too.

> She keeps it real. She sees the darkness in him and is concerned.

The girls looked stumped at first, then Izzy volunteered, "Well, maybe she's grumpy because she's sad."

"Oh, I know!" Emma exclaimed, jumping up onto her knees. "It's like your husband. How he's really good at reading people. Maybe Willie May is like him. So she can read people."

"Yeah, but what does that have to do with being grumpy?" Izzy asked.

Emma thought for a minute. Then she said tentatively, "Well, maybe it's the sadness. She has it because of her job and the people and so she sees it in Rob."

"Nice job," I whispered, and moved to another group.

Some of the teachers who piloted this work found that while their readers could easily grasp what characters were saying, they had a harder time understanding the feelings behind characters' words and actions. If your children are having similar struggles, you might build in a lesson designed to help children identify a character's internal thinking. You might suggest children act out a scene with one partner playing the part of a character, and the other partner assuming the part of that same character's internal thoughts. You could show children the way the external and internal dialogues sometimes conflict if you tell them, for example, about a time when someone gave you a gift you detested— yet you had to act thankful. My great aunt and namesake Lucy Lynn Linny gave me scratchy, frilly underpants when I was an eight-year-old tomboy, and I'll never forget how challenging it was to act thankful for that gift! You and a child could reenact such an episode, with one child being the recipient of the gift and the other voicing the recipient's internal thoughts.

LINK

Celebrate the inferences that children have drawn from the text and remind them that when they are learning to read *characters* well, they are also learning to read *people* well. Teach them that reading can develop a person's social intelligence.

"Readers, I want you to understand that what you are doing today is not just about *The Tiger Rising,* it is not just about this little scene in the laundry room. It's much larger than that. It's about how we respond to people in our everyday world. There's a thing called 'social intelligence' that essentially means the ability to understand people well, to glean what people are thinking and feeling. We need to use our social intelligence as we read characters, too. Avid, thoughtful readers tend to be people with a huge amount of social intelligence! They don't just sum people up with one idea or word, because they are really paying attention to characters' actions and choices and figuring out what these reveal. When we learn to understand characters deeply and well, we learn to understand people deeply and well. Let's add to our chart that paying attention to a character's actions is one more way we can grow ideas about characters.

"Before you go to your seats, fill in your logs. Then peek ahead to the section in your book that you'll be reading today. For now, please think especially about the main character. Think, 'What do I already know about this character?' Do that before you even get started reading, noticing actions, thinking of them as choices, and ask, 'What might these reveal?' Make Post-it notes about places in the prior text that serve as windows. Once you've written a couple of Post-its containing your insights on your character, read on. Please read with an eye to growing more ideas about your characters."

Strategies Readers Use to Grow Ideas About Characters

- We make a movie in our mind, drawing on the text to envision (or become) the character.

- We use our own experiences to help us walk in the character's shoes, inferring what the character is thinking, feeling, experiencing.

- We revise our mental movies as we read on, getting new details from the text.

- We notice when we feel connected to a character and use that feeling to deepen our understanding of the character.

- We read with our minds on fire and capture thoughts that lead us into grand conversations.

- We pay attention to the actions of our characters and see those actions as choices.

CONFERRING AND SMALL-GROUP WORK

Use Every Method to Help Children Talk Well About Books

During this portion of your unit of study, you'll want to help children to talk, think, and jot observations and ideas they develop about the characters in their books. Talking about something, like writing about it, can be an important step in the process of discovering how one feels or thinks. Most kids will talk any chance they get—about their weekend plans, about the new kid on the soccer team, about the math quiz they took. Talking is how many people process the stuff of our lives.

Some of you might have wondered, as I have, why children can talk so endlessly about some topics, but when we ask them to discuss the characters in a story, they look at each other with blank expressions. If this sounds familiar, ask yourself how much time you give kids to practice talking and thinking about books. As adults we forget that this does not come naturally and that children need opportunities to get better at whatever it is we want them to be able to do well. As we have worked in classrooms we have witnessed how painfully short the average class discussion time before, during, and after reading is. What if I said to you, "Think about *Pride and Prejudice*. How does Elizabeth Bennett's place

within her family affect her choices?" What if I said to you, "Have a thought about that. A deep one. Right now." Nothing coming to mind? What's wrong?

I am being a bit hyperbolic, but the point is that depth in thinking is not something that most *adults*, even, can achieve on demand, much less children who are learning how to grow their thinking from mere reactions and observations into something that resembles theories.

If you want to teach your children to talk well about the books they are reading, the most important thing you can do is lead rich conversations about books and do this often. The conversations can occur during conferences or read-aloud or partnership time, or they can occur while you and a student are walking down the hall together. You'll want to draw upon all the four major teaching methods to teach kids to lift the level of their talking (and their thinking) about texts.

Coaching is one of the methods of teaching that you can harness in your efforts to help children talk well about books. Kobe and Malik were talking during their partnership time. Malik began first, as he was apt to do, giving Kobe a quick "previously in" to catch Kobe up on the latest install-

---

MID-WORKSHOP TEACHING POINT

Readers Push Ourselves to Extend Our Thoughts Using Thought Prompts

"Readers, can I interrupt you for a minute? Before we read on, we're going to do something we don't usually do, but it's going to help us think even more deeply about our characters. We're going to read a bit more of *The Tiger Rising* and talk first about what we listen to—then about your independent reading books. I'm going to read a part in Chapter 7 out loud, the part when Rob and Sistine talk on the bus. As I read, think really hard about what this passage tells us about the characters. You can think about either Rob or Sistine—or both, if you want! As I read, jot thoughts on a Post-it note or in your reading notebook. Remember that characters, like people, are complex. They have different, sometimes conflicting emotions and motivations, and sometimes their actions don't reflect what they're feeling."

Then I began reading a part of Chapter 7, *The Tiger Rising*. It turned out to be an extraordinary day in almost every possible way. It started with finding the tiger and it ended with Sistine Bailey sitting down next to him on the bus on the way home from school. Her dress was torn and muddied. There was a scrape down her right arm, and her hair stuck out in a hundred different directions. She sat down in the empty seat beside him and stared at him with her black eyes.

"There isn't anyplace else to sit," she said to him. "This is the last empty seat."

Rob shrugged.

"It's not like I want to sit here," she said.

continued on next page

---

ment in his book. I noticed that Kobe was only occasionally looking at Malik as he spoke, and then staring off across the classroom. Malik finished catching Kobe up, and there was a prolonged silence.

Kobe shrugged and then took a big breath, as if to start in on his own long soliloquy. It seemed to me that he was signaling, "Well, if you are done telling me about your book, I guess it is my time to talk about my book." At that point, I said quietly to Kobe, "Aren't you going to ask your partner what he's been thinking about the book he just summarized?" Kobe did this, albeit grudgingly, and when Malik stated the big idea he was entertaining, I looked expectantly at Kobe, as if the ball was now in his court and I wondered what he would do with it. When he didn't pick up my cue, I said quietly, "Are you going to ask him to say more, or ask for examples?" Kobe's interest seemed to be piqued a bit. He followed my prompt and asked Malik, "Do you have any examples?" and soon they were off and running.

This sort of teaching is what my colleagues and I call coaching. The teacher interjects lean prompts into the child's talking or reading, and those prompts scaffold the child to do some new work. Even if it is independent reading time, you can ask two members of a partnership to pause in their reading and to have a little book talk together so that you can listen in and coach.

In the previous session, I mentioned that from time to time, during independent reading, I may decide to convene a small group of children and to ask them to talk about a character in the class read-aloud book (not their independent reading books). You'll recall that I recommend doing this because it is easier for children to talk well about the read-aloud text than about texts they are reading alone. After the children get a felt sense for what an insightful, deep conversation about a character feels like, I then ask them to try to continue talking in that sort of a way, only now about the main characters in their independent reading books. If you do that sort of work, this will again provide wonderful opportunities for you to coach in ways that lift what children are doing. As you move behind the small circle of children, you can literally whisper a question to one child, nudging that child to press for clarification. You can nudge another child to press a classmate to say more or to cite an example from the text. If you do this sort of coaching and the conversation goes better than usual, you will want to pause it at some point to extract transferable techniques from it. Point out what they did that you hope readers transfer to other books, other days.

You may want to convene groups of children who are reading within a shared band of difficulty because your expectations for their work with characters will be different for different bands of book difficulty. For exam-

MID-WORKSHOP TEACHING POINT

continued from previous page

"Okay," said Rob. He shrugged his shoulders again. He hoped that she wasn't going to thank him for saving her.

"What's your name?" she demanded.

"Rob Horton," he told her.

"Well, let me tell you something, Rob Horton. You shouldn't run. That's what they want you to do. Run."

Rob stared at her with his mouth open. She stared back.

"I hate it here," she said, looking away from him, her voice even deeper than before. "This is a stupid hick town with stupid hick teachers. Nobody in the whole school even knows what the Sistine Chapel is."

"I know," said Rob. "I know what the Sistine Chapel is." Immediately, he regretted saying it. It was his policy not to say things, but it was a policy he was having a hard time maintaining around Sistine.

"I bet," Sistine sneered at him. "I bet you know."

"It's a picture of God making the world," he said.

Sistine stared at him hard. She narrowed her small eyes until they almost disappeared.

"Okay, readers, take a few minutes to finish jotting your thoughts." I waited while they did so, and then voiced over, "Gather together two (or even three) partnerships, and one of you share your theories with your group and try to get a grand conversation going about that thinking." As children talked, I crouched alongside one cluster and then another.

After a few minutes, I said, "Readers, eyes on me please. You've done some sophisticated thinking, and you're coming to read characters in mature ways. The best thing I noticed is that you're not just forming an idea and holding steadfastly to it. Instead, you're challenging your own ideas, pushing yourselves to consider other possibilities. Emma, for example, who the other day called Sistine snotty, said just now that Sistine strikes her as very sad. She realized, while listening to this

continued on next page

ple, readers who are reading level K/L/M texts will probably find that their main characters are fairly static. Their feelings may change, but their traits won't. On the other hand, readers who are working with texts that are level R or beyond will probably find that their protagonists undergo changes, and those changes will be revealed in fairly subtle ways. Perhaps the character will have a different perspective toward the same place, for example, and this will reveal his or her changes. Perhaps the character will act in a way that contradicts an earlier action. Knowing the band of text difficulty will help you coach readers. You'll find more about this in the assessment sections of this book and in *A Guide to the Reading Workshop*.

Research-Decide-Teach Conferences

Of course, you could alternatively decide to lift the level of children's talk about books by following the more common research-decide-teach template for conferences. In such a conference, you might ask the child to share her thinking with you, and as you listen, you may note what the child does with automaticity. Perhaps the child had an idea and refers to a section of the text that supported that idea, and you note that the child is now grounding thinking in references to the text. That is a step ahead! You might also note what the child does not seem to be doing yet and this might lead you to form a hunch about an area you

---

MID-WORKSHOP TEACHING POINT

continued from previous page

passage, that Sistine is acting angry and tough, but Emma thinks that those are just the outside actions and that it is probably an act. Isn't that smart work—to wonder if a character's actions are just an act? She thinks maybe Sistine has grown that tough shell to hide her sadness. And then others in that group climbed onto Emma's idea and said that maybe Rob has learned to keep quiet to hide his sadness, so it is like everyone has their sadness stuffed inside.

"Josh came up with something interesting, too. He noticed that Sistine says things that don't seem to match what she wants. She *says* she doesn't want to sit next to Rob, but then she asks his name and almost seems like she's trying to be Rob's friend.

"Wow. What powerful thinking. There's a name for the sort of work you're doing. It's called inferring. That is, you're making a guess about something in the text that isn't explicitly stated. Remember how I mentioned back in Unit 1 that a guy named Paulo Freire said, 'Reading is not walking on words, it is grasping the soul of them.' That's what I saw you doing as you thought about Sistine and Rob, and I am hoping you can do the same sort of deep thinking as you read on and think about a character in your own independent reading book.

"Readers, I know you want to keep talking, and you are realizing how much thinking and talking we can do when we push ourselves to see characters as complicated. We are noticing that characters, like people in our lives, act in different ways with different people at different times. We also learned that the out-of-character moments are like cracks in an eggshell. It's like the author is giving you a glimpse into what's really inside the person and is letting you peek in at the character's real desires or fears. Those surprising actions can reveal powerful things about a person.

"So let's read on, making sure to mark passages in your independent reading book that allowed you to peek at your character, to get to know him or her. Also, remember to keep your theory about a character in mind, and expect it to get challenged. If you read with a careful, observant mind, if you take the time to notice moments when the character's deeper self peeks through, you will grow ideas that, like conversations, will reverberate in your mind long after you've put the book down."

---

could address in your teaching. First, you'll need to research your hunch, to inquire more. For example, if you notice the child's thinking tends to refer only to the single section of the book that she has read most recently, you might specifically nudge to see if she can easily reference other sections of the text that also support her idea. She may be able to make several references, but as you listen, you get the distinct impression that she compares texts in a sweeping fashion that overlooks details. You decide to compliment her on the effort to refer to evidence and to challenge her to expect the evidence to yield more.

In such a manner, you arrive at a compliment and a teaching point, both tailored specifically to the child. Once you name the teaching point, you may need to follow it up with some demonstration or some coaching, as you might in a minilesson.

I recently conducted a research-decide-teach conference after I listened for a bit to Izzy and Emma, who were discussing the end of Chapter 6 in *The Tiger Rising*. I knew I wanted to lift the level of their talk, and I knew that using the read-aloud book would set them up to talk more proficiently about their independent books. As I approached the girls, they had agreed upon the idea that Sistine and Rob would become friends and that Rob would stand up for Sistine. Then the conversation began to wind down. I wanted to teach them to talk with more depth and stamina, but before I could do so, I needed to understand the strategies they were already using.

"Is that the end of the conversation?" I asked, surprised. The girls started looking furiously through their notes, hoping to come up with a new trail of thought so as to please me. I intervened. "I know that you can come up with yet another topic to discuss pertaining to this book, but when I asked if the conversation was over, I meant the conversation about the relationship between the two characters. It seemed like one of you just threw out a thought about their relationship, the other concurred, and that was it. Do you have ideas for how you could talk longer and think more deeply about that?"

They seemed unsure, so I suggested they rewind the tape of their conversation, repeating the claim that Sistine and Rob would eventually become friends, and that this time they use the conversational prompts that I'd taught them to extend what each other said. This time when Izzy asked "What makes you think that?" I wanted to push the envelope a bit, so I challenged their premise, asking, "How do you know that Rob isn't going to go back to being quiet and allowing the other kids to bully him?" As I asked this question, I knew I was not really teaching them a technique that they could use another day—or at least, I wasn't sure what that technique was or how to make it transferable. Sometimes I simply join into a conversation to ratchet it up a little so that the participants can end up getting a sense for what it feels like to participate in a lively talk about books.

My somewhat outrageous challenge did, in fact, spark lots of energetic talk. "He's not going to go back to being shy now. He is finding a brave part of himself that he didn't know was there before. It's like, he was opening his suitcase a little bit." Emma mimed with her hands to show a suitcase opening a crack. "And, now that it's open, he's just going to keep opening it more and more."

"Wow," I interceded. "You two really were able to grow a spirited talk. I love the way you talked back and forth to each other. When one person made a claim about the characters' relationship, the other said, 'What makes you think that?' and you even countered, suggesting maybe it could go otherwise. Nice work. I hope you remember to talk back and forth to each other like that always."

"Can I give you one tip? You have been doing such thoughtful work thinking about the relationship in this story. And you are smart to know that almost always when you are thinking about a book, it will pay off to think about the changing relationships between the characters. But can I teach you one more topic of conversation that will almost always pay off?" This time, I explained to them that in books, the authors aren't just writing to tell stories. Authors like Kate DiCamillo and John Reynolds Gardiner are also writing to tell a truth. "The author wants us to understand a message, a big important truth about the world or relationships or human nature," I said. Then I added, "Often when you are reading, it pays to think about what the story might be trying to teach us, and this thinking actually helps a reader figure out what might happen next in the story. Like, in *Stone Fox*, some people might say that John Reynolds Gardiner told the story of little Willy to help us understand that we have to work hard to protect the most important things in our lives. If we know that might be the author's message, then we already know that little Willy will never give up before he has helped his grandfather, not even if the race seemed impossible or if his dog has died."

Then I suggested Izzy and Emma try asking the question "What might this story be trying to teach?" and then help each other grow ideas about the book.

Proficient Partner Conferences

Finally, you may decide that the best way for you to lift the level of a child's book talk is for you to engage in a book talk with that reader, with you functioning as the more proficient partner. Such a partner can lift the level of talk in much the same way that a more proficient tennis partner lifts the level of a tennis game.

You might have this kind of conference with a child who is struggling with book talks and tends to let his partners do all the work. Or you could meet with a sophisticated reader who doesn't have many other partners who can talk about books at her level. You can meet with children one-on-one or meet with both partners at the same time. As in a research-decide-teach conference, you often won't know the teaching point prior to the conference. You will decide what to teach after talking to the reader for a while. Guide the conversation in ways that will be helpful to that particular reader, and afterwards, try to step back into your teacher role and leave the child with one explicit tip to carry forward into her own reading work.

I knew as I entered into the conference that Fallon was becoming quite a strong reader as well as, of course, an avid talker. Just before pulling my chair alongside her, I glanced at my historical notes and saw a quick entry I'd made about the fact that she sometimes talked at length. I'd noted that her long-winded responses lacked precision and would lurch between sharing original insightful ideas and being just plain wordy. I kept that in mind as I approached her, already thinking that I might help her articulate her ideas and theories with more specificity. I find it helpful to begin a conference with a general idea of the reader's needs, which usually comes from my previous conferring notes. I often change my mind as I listen to what the child has to say and what I determine his or her needs are on that day, but it's useful to have a starting place.

"I'm going to partner up with you if that is okay," I said. I glanced at the cover of her book, and saw that she was reading *Esperanza Rising*.

She nodded at me while she finished her jotting. "Let me just get my last thoughts down. I think I have some good ideas about this!"

I allowed her an extra minute, then said, "Why don't we start with your telling me about what you wrote?"

"Okay. Well, I jotted that Esperanza is starting to change her mind about Miguel." She looked expectantly at me, as if eager for a compliment.

"Can you tell me which part made you think that? Was there a particular part in which Esperanza seems to be changing her mind?"

"Right, okay," Fallon said, beginning to rise to the challenge. "Well, first Miguel plants the roses from her father's garden. Then, Esperanza sees Miguel at the party, and sees how everyone respects him. It's like she always used to see him as her servant, and now she starts to see a different side of him."

I nodded enthusiastically. "Yeah, I think you're right about Esperanza's change of heart here. I remember that before the celebration, Esperanza was so angry about everything that she had to give up when she left her home in Mexico. And she thought that Miguel and all his family were beneath her because of the way they lived. But, then, like you said, she sees a different side of him. And it's almost like that was some sort of password between them. After he proves himself, she's different. It's like she's . . ." I looked up, as if searching for the words.

Fallon picked up the thread. "It's like after that she's decided not to think of Miguel as if he was her servant anymore. She dances with him and treats him like a friend. After that, she even seems to be less mad about having to work. It's like she thinks, if Miguel can do it, so can I."

Not wanting her to lose the starting premise that Esperanza is changing her mind about Miguel, I interjected, "So now Esperanza sees Miguel as . . . ," and again let my voice trail off, allowing her to land on a more precise description.

"She sees him as more than just a servant, like he's her equal, her friend. She sees that, in some ways, he is even better than she is. He's . . . admirable!" She bobbed her head eagerly, clearly pleased with this answer.

I nodded at Fallon encouragingly then switched into teacher mode. "That's how it goes. You talk or think or jot on and on in a blahdy-blah-blah fashion, and then if you push yourself, that can lead you to crystallize a really smart idea."

I told the rest of the class to wrap up their conversations. Then I said to Fallon, "Remember to get as specific as you can in your conversations. When you are talking about a character changing, you'll need specific examples from before and after the change."

TEACHING SHARE

Readers Look Hard to See Significance

Remind children to prepare for a book conversation, and then ask them to start their talks, focusing on character.

As children read, I said, "Readers, if you haven't already marked passages that are good windows to your character, mark at least one now. In a minute, you'll have a chance to have grand conversations about your ideas."

Then, after a moment, I convened their attention. "It has been interesting today to watch you reading not only *books* but *people*! Could you turn, and Partner 2, you do a quick 'Previously in . . .' to catch your partner up on your book? Then, read aloud the excerpt you've chosen because it gives a window to your character. Read the excerpt in such a way that you help your listener really picture the character. Add some gestures. Make your intonation show the character. Then show your partner the actions you noticed your character making and talk about the theories you have developed from thinking about those actions."

Rally readers for the work of finding more in their books.

After children did this for a bit, I intervened. "Readers, can I stop you for a minute? Some of you are saying, 'There's not that much to see in this passage.' I was at the beach the other day. It was windy and cold. I started to look for shells and sea glass, but even just a glance told me the beach had been strip-mined. There was nothing there. After a bit, though, I noticed this four-year-old friend of mine on his haunches, peering at the sand. 'What do you see?' I asked. It turned out that little guy had collected a whole bucketful of treasures. I realized—he had the eyes to see.

"Tonight, readers, as you continue reading, be sure you are looking for treasure. You have a theory about your character. Will you find ideas that go with that theory? Ideas that change it? Fill in your logs and give yourself an assignment to read tonight gathering evidence to support or develop one of your theories about your character." Pointing to our chart, I reminded students, "You can use some of the strategies we have listed here to grow ideas about your characters."

To Grow Ideas About a Character I . . .

- Notice the actions a person has made, seeing these as windows into that person.

- Notice the actions that *don't* move the plot—they're often there to reveal the character.

- Realize actions are choices a person makes; the person could have acted differently and made the choice to act this way. What do the choices reveal?

- Notice patterns of actions especially and think, "Why did the author have this character continually doing this? What might this mean?"

- If the actions don't seem to reveal anything, push harder to find something that could be significant. Try saying, "Maybe this suggests. . . ." or "Perhaps it could be. . . ."

- Come up with an idea, and then try to think more about the idea. Say, "This could be important because he (she). . . ."

- Have grand conversations with a friend or partner, sharing your idea with energy, giving examples from the text. Then hope your partner will challenge your idea. The goal of talking is for you to revise your ideas (and to help your partner do the same).

Expecting Complications in Characters

IN THIS SESSION,

you will teach students that readers notice complexity in characters by paying attention to times when they act "out of character."

erds. Jocks. Geeks. Girly girls. Kids learn very early to slap labels on one another, and on themselves. Even the youngest children habitually push their peers into the narrowest of definitions. "Steve's mean," they might say. Or "Annie is so shy."

But what about the mean kid who befriends a stray kitten and treats that kitten as a family member? Or the shy kid who tries out for the lead in the school play? People, as the saying goes, are often not what they seem.

When we look at people—real and fictional, alike—we see what we expect to see. Expect nerd, and that's what you will get. But this overly simplistic way of categorizing people is limiting on both sides. On the one hand, labeling people this way costs us the possibility of truly knowing and connecting with another person. On the other hand, being confined to such a narrow definition can be downright suffocating.

Those who love us the most, our families, often feel more at liberty than anyone to pigeonhole us into narrowly defined roles. I have a friend whose parents always referred to her as "pretty" while referring to her sister as "brainy." Well, it turns out the brainy sister didn't like school very much and weathered much disappointment when she didn't fulfill the dreams her family had for her. My friend,

GETTING READY

- Bring your read-aloud, *The Tiger Rising*, to your minilesson. You will reread a section from the end of Chapter 12.

- Prepare an anecdote to share with children about a time in your life when a person acted out of character, and instead of dismissing those actions as weird, you reflected upon those actions and therefore on the complexities of the person.

- Ask children to bring their reading logs to the lesson so they can study their partners' logs.

- Be prepared to channel readers to work in small-group discussions during the active involvement.

- You may choose to prepare the chart "When a Character Acts Out of Character, Think About. . . ."

- Bring the chart "Strategies Readers Use to Grow Ideas About Characters" to be reviewed during the lesson.

- Prepare the chart "Prompts to Grow Your Ideas."

- If you choose to confer with small groups, be prepared to read from books such as *Amber Brown Is Not a Crayon* and *Journey*.

the pretty one, went to fabulous schools and did well, yet still feels self-conscious about her intellect. No one fares well when viewed in terms of absolutes.

> ## Characters—like the people in our lives—are not just one way.

Novelist Anna Quindlen writes, "Books are the plane, and the train, and the road. They are the destination, and the journey. They are home." Reading, at its best, helps us to know and understand our world, our relationships, and ourselves. If we say simply that Anne Shirley is "unlucky," isn't that missing the point? We want to model for our children how to look at another person with openness and compassion, not rushing to decide what to call her and then moving on. Especially if we want children to read them-selves into books, we must pause to acknowledge the many different ways in which our characters can behave, under different circumstances, with different motivations. Characters—like the people in our lives—are not just one way.

I once met a third grader named Peter who was often at the center of disciplinary issues. In truth, Peter's exuberance and impulsiveness proved a challenge, and he had a reputation for being difficult. His teachers wrote this word—*difficult*—on his school forms to warn future teachers. Peter's classmates used this same word, or worse, to describe him. And, if asked, Peter himself would dismally say that he was a troublemaker. If we call Ramona Quimby "troublemaker," we are only seeing one part of her, just as many people in Peter's life saw him as just one thing. But if we encourage children to notice Ramona's sensitivity, her loyalty, her great capacity for joy—all the complicated, true aspects wrapped up in one character—might we also teach them to see the Peters in our rooms the same way? Might we also teach the Peters in our rooms to learn to see the wonderful, complicated depths in themselves?

MINILESSON

Expecting Complications in Characters

CONNECTION

Remind children that we read people by regarding actions as windows. Ask them to read each other by studying logs.

"Readers, would you bring your reading logs with you as you come to the meeting area?"

Once they'd convened, I said, "Last night, did any of you try to 'read' people in your life? Like at home, did you try reading your brother or sister?" A few kids nodded. "Well, before we continue, let's practice reading people, studying what a person does, and speculating what the actions might mean. To do this, exchange reading logs with your partner." After they did this, I said, "Partners, look at the reading log you are now holding and really quickly, in the blink of an eye, think, 'What actions does this log suggest the reader has and has not been doing? What choices do I see the reader making? What theories can I grow about this reader from considering the reader's actions, and choices?'"

After a minute, I said, "Readers, can I have your eyes? Give me a thumbs up if you noticed a pattern in your partner's reading—like you noticed that he or she reads more in one place or another, or reads some kinds rather than other kinds of books." Many did so. "That's wise. Remember, when trying to read a person or a character, it's especially important to notice actions that happen *more than once*, which seem like a characteristic *pattern*. After you see a pattern, you need to think what the pattern could reveal, what it could mean. You might ask yourself, 'How does everything I already know about this person connect with the actions I'm just now seeing?' Think about that for your partner." I gave them a long minute of silence and meanwhile did this

COACHING TIPS

There are lots of reasons for this connection. First, the connection ideally provides you with a vehicle for keeping lessons from previous minilessons alive—and that includes minilessons from much earlier in the year. For your teaching to matter, it needs to make a lasting impact. This will only happen if you revisit what you taught previously.

If you're worried about time, you could ask children to study their logs in partnerships when they first enter the classroom at the very start of the day, and then in the minilesson you could simply ask them to talk about their musings. But I think it is more likely you'll decide simply to give children just a tiny bit of time for scanning a partner's log. A lot can be seen in a minute!

Then, too, any one aspect of your teaching can always risk becoming ho-hum. Because minilessons are designed to follow a consistent architecture, it is important for you to be vigilant, making sure they don't slip from being patterned to being dull. I designed this connection after Kathleen and I said to ourselves, "We need to be sure we are varying our connections."

thinking myself. "Now think, 'What theory do I have that could *maybe* explain the pattern that I'm seeing?' Say to yourself, 'I'm thinking that perhaps my partner . . .' (finish that sentence in your mind.)" After a few seconds of silence, I coached, "Try saying also, 'Or, could it be that . . . ?' And finish *that* sentence.

"Partner 2, turn and tell Partner 1 your theory about Partner 1 as a reader. Start with, 'I'm thinking that perhaps you. . . .' Show your evidence and be gentle. If you have time, then share your alternate idea: 'Or, I'm thinking perhaps it could be. . . .' For now, Partner 1 just listen to this person say stuff about you."

Remind children of yesterday's discovery that when we read characters, we let their actions serve as windows to the sort of person that they are.

"You'll remember that we started out yesterday's minilesson talking about the fact that some people are good at reading people, and we said that those who can read people in real life can also read people in stories. To read people, it is important to see that actions can be windows to the person. So when you read your books, you paused from time to time, as we did when we read *The Tiger Rising*, to think, 'Let me use what just happened as a window to help me understand this person.' Remember that when you were growing ideas about Willie May, I coached you to avoid trying to pin her down too much. I cautioned you to resist trying to shoehorn her into just one single word—such as, *disgruntled*."

Name your teaching point. Specifically, tell children that characters are complicated.

"Today, I want to emphasize that it is important to keep in mind that characters are complicated; they are not just one way. And here's a key point: To grow nuanced and complex ideas about characters, it helps to think deeply about times when a person seems to act out of character."

Notice that the language I'm using with readers is tentative. The strongest ideas emerge out of lots of thought and reflection, after revising one's initial ideas. Teaching readers to be tentative with their theories teaches them to be more open to revision across their lives. Revision is, after all, the heart of much that is beautiful in our world.

I'm reading for longer period of time and fast. The books I'm reading I like so much I don't want them to end.

I can see I'm reading about 20 pages more and that amazes me. I am getting suggestions from Sam and from Jack.

You will not have time for the partners to reverse roles, with Partner 1 "reading" Partner 2. If you are really uncomfortable with this, you can sneak in some time later in the school day, outside the reading workshop. For now, though, remember this is just the connection, not the minilesson itself!

It is crucial that children recall previous minilessons, drawing repeatedly on all that we've taught. We keep yesterday's ideas alive by retelling them and by showing how today's teaching fits tongue-and-groove into yesterday's.

Notice in this teaching point as in so many, you help readers know a goal—growing nuanced and complex ideas that take into account the complexity of characters—and you equip them with particular techniques for reaching that goal—thinking about times when a character acts out of character. You have yet to give specific tips for how readers go about thinking about those out-of-character times. That is what the rest of your minilessons will do. You should be realizing already that when characters seem to act out of character, often this is actually because the theory of that character was too rigid, too simplistic. The person is actually not acting out of character so much as defying the label he has been assigned by someone else.

Teaching

Tell children about a time in your life when a person acted out of character, and instead of dismissing those actions as weird, you thought, 'Why might the person have done that?' and developed more complex, nuanced ideas about the person as a result.

"Sometimes in life, doesn't it seem like we can try to peg a person as being just one thing or another? Like I might say about a person, 'He's such a baby,' or 'She's spoiled.' But the truth is people are not just one way. To grow more complex ideas about a person or a character, it helps to pay attention to instances when the character seems to act out of character. Then instead of just saying, 'He's acting weird,' or 'That's really strange,' we can push ourselves to think, 'What might have motivated the character, the person, to act in this way?' That way, we can end up realizing that perhaps the character, the person, wasn't acting in such an odd way after all. Perhaps we just needed to expand or deepen our understanding of the person.

"Sometimes I work on my reading muscles when I'm thinking about the characters— the people—in my life. For example, last weekend my family convened in New Hampshire for a big family wedding. The night before any wedding in my family, most of the guests join us for a gala square dance. At the square dance, we always present a whole sequence of toasts, many of them rhyming ditties, created in the bride and groom's honor. At this particular event, my 89-year-old father stepped up to the microphone and began playing the role of the master of ceremonies. The wedding was put on by the bride's parents—my sister and her husband—but before either of the bride's parents could step into the role of MC, my father did so. After each cluster of cousins or sibling presented a song or poem, my father would add in his booming voice some commentary explaining who that group of presenters was and how they fit into the family.

Notice that throughout this lesson, I suggest that the people in our lives are, in a sense, characters. Notice, too, that many of the biggest ideas that we try to convey as teachers are actually conveyed as much through our word choice as through the content of our teaching. For example, notice that when talking about what it is that good readers tend to do, I refer to good readers using the pronoun we *not the pronoun* they. *Could any message be more important?*

Again, word choice alone conveys so much. There is a lot of power simply in this phrase: 'I'm thinking about the characters—the people—in my life.'"

"This wasn't my father's event. The nine of us kids are already married. My dad's a classy guy and doesn't usually push himself to center stage. Later, on the way home from the weekend, I thought about how it was *out of character* for Dad to act in that way.

"I could have just dismissed Dad, saying, 'He was acting a bit odd,' and shrugged it off. But instead, I tried to read him well, to think more deeply about this one time when he seemed to act out of character. I asked, 'Why might he have been acting like that?' Think about it yourself." I paused.

"You might be thinking what I'm thinking. See, it occurred to *me* that my dad is probably very aware that at age 89, he won't be there for many more family weddings. And he is no doubt aware that others will step in to fill his role as the head of the family. As I think about it, it makes total sense that he'd cling to the role while he can.

"Do you see, readers, that my father acted in a way that at first seemed out of character? I could have just shrugged it off, saying, 'That was weird of him.' But one way to grow richer, more nuanced ideas about people is to pay attention to times when a person acts out of character and to think, 'What might be behind this?' That way, we can grow ideas about characters that are more complicated. That's important, because characters—like people in real life—are not just one way."

Notice that instead of jumping to tell students the conclusion I came to, I unrolled the story in such a way that I hope they, too, are bemused by the way my dad has acted out of character, and they, too, are drawn to speculate what the reasons could be for his actions. Then, joining them in this mental work, I share the tentative theory I came to after I grappled with the question, "Why might my dad have acted so out of character?" I am always aware that if I sequence the teaching section of a minilesson just right, I support kids in actually joining me in the sequential journey of thought, the mental work, that I am spotlighting. The trick lies in not summarizing my thinking process, but in revealing it.

You'll find you own stories to share in the place of mine. For example, when fifth-grade teacher, Sarah Colmaire, piloted these lessons, she told her children a story about her childhood best friend, Maggie. Sarah explained that generally Maggie was a kind friend, but there was one way in which she was not kind. When she and Sarah played together, Maggie always insisted that she choose what they'd do together. Sarah was often confused by this, but accepted it, thinking this was just the way Maggie was in the world. One day Maggie's older sister Chelsea joined their playdate and was really bossy, deciding exactly what they would do and when they would do it! Maggie was silent and Sarah couldn't believe it! It took seeing Maggie with her older sister Chelsea for Sarah to realize why Maggie was usually so bossy—what motivated her to be that way.

I love that last sentence. "Characters—like people in our lives—are not just one way." This is one of those lines that I want to hit just right. I want to say it with a lilt, an intonation, that makes it likely that kids end up carrying that little bit of advice with them always. This means, of course, that I'll come back to this line repeatedly, like a theme song. Watch for it!

ACTIVE INVOLVEMENT

Set children up to notice, in a read-aloud, that the protagonist is acting out of character and to ask, "What does that show?"

"You and I definitely have some ideas about Sistine. We know that she's . . . what?"

Children called out, "Gutsy."

"Angry."

"Hates being in that town."

"So let's keep our theory about Sistine in mind, and pay attention—like thoughtful readers do—to whether there are times when Sistine acts *out of character*. If that happens, we could just say, 'What? That's weird!' But let's try, instead, to think, 'What might motivate Sistine?' and 'What might this show about sides of Sistine we'd never realized were there?'

"Readers, position yourselves in groups of four. The quickest way to do this is for your partnership to join the partnership that is near yours so you have a group of four. Remember not to leave anyone out. It can be a group of six. Are you ready? I'm going to reread a part of Chapter 12 and then, after I read a bit, you are going to talk in your small group about whether Sistine acts out of character, and if so, what that suggests."

Then I opened *The Tiger Rising* and began reading aloud from Chapter 12.

> When he straightened back up, he saw that Sistine had picked up the carving of her. He had left it lying on his bed, intending to work on it again in the evening.
>
> He held his breath as she stared at the piece of wood. It looked so much like her, with her skinny legs and small eyes and defiant stance, that he was certain she would be angry. But once again she surprised him.
>
> "Oh," she said, her voice full of wonder, "it's perfect. It's like looking in a little wooden mirror." She stared at it a minute more and then carefully laid it back on his bed.

You may want to recap all you've said by displaying a chart like this (you do not have time to make this right now):

> When a Character Acts
> Out of Character, Think About...
>
> • What might motivate someone (your character) to act this way? (What might be behind this?)
>
> • What might this show about the person that we might not know?

Notice that I return to a part of the text children have already read. I do this for two reasons: First, because this particular bit of text is a good illustration of what I am teaching and, second, because the task of understanding characters' complexities can be tricky business, and I know children will have an easier time of it if they do it by examining a familiar section of text.

"Readers, right now, turn toward your small group. Talk about what might have motivated Sistine—whom at first seemed to be angry about everything—to act in this way that at first seems out of character."

I stepped through the crowd of children sitting before me and then crouched alongside a group and listened for a minute. Wanting to ramp up the conversation, I whispered to Fallon, "Some people say that people are formed by parents and their home life. What do you know about Sistine's parents that could suggest why she would act so sensitive, so appreciative of something beautiful?"

I listened in as children talked. After a bit, Grace announced, "Rob is different from the other kids and so is Sistine. Maybe that's why she decides to be friends with him. Like when he first saw her, Rob thought she was even weirder than he was."

Josh added, "I think she was just trying to be nice for a change. Maybe she knew that he was holding his breath when she saw the whittled figures so she was real nice about them."

Sam added, "I don't know that she was trying to be nice. She's too blunt to be nice. I think it's that she respects Rob because he whittles. Sistine knows about art and about Michelangelo. She respects art. That's why she was so respectful of what Rob made. She knows he was the only kid who knew about the Sistine Chapel."

Josh continued, "They're both different from the other kids and they're both kind of artsy but she's a little crazy too. Like when Rob told her he knew where there was a tiger, she believed him at once, though it's kind of crazy for a tiger to be in a cage in the middle of nowhere and for no one to know about it."

Grace jumped in, "I agree. Sistine is the only person who takes Rob seriously and she even put her hand on his rash. I mean, that's so, ew. But she did. So she does crazy things, and she really takes Rob seriously. It's like once she's decided to be his friend she's really sincere."

Teachers, you will be pushing readers to see more. If you really want children to draw on information from earlier sections of the text, some will need a stronger scaffold. You could, therefore, move among the groups, whispering to one child in each foursome, showing that child a passage from earlier in the book and prompting that child to refer to that passage, using it to help the group think about why Sistine may be acting as she is, revealing a side of herself that we hadn't expected. Alternatively, if you want to prepare ahead of time for this, you can pass out little slips of paper to one member of each group, whispering to the recipient of the passage saying something like, "Aly, this might help your group think about Sistine in more complicated ways. Read it to yourself and try to find a way to insert it into your group's conversation."

Fallon said, "Yeah, Sistine respects art, and she respects Rob for being an artist. That's why she picked him to be friends with. She could sense he was different than the other kids in Lister. Like he had more depth to him. She gets the stuff he does."

Meanwhile, I was listening to a second group and heard Emma lay out her theory. "I think that Sistine just acts tough on the outside but inside she's really kind. Like she knew that Rob would be hurt if she made fun of his whittling so she was respectful instead."

Izzy jumped in, "Yeah, like she can be mean about the other stuff, but she knew that this must be special to Rob."

"Maybe she's got two sides, one mean and one nice," Malik wondered. "Or she's like—really moody 'cause she's always catching Rob off guard with her reactions."

At this point, I whispered to Emma that she might help the group consider *why* Sistine acted out of character, suggesting that sometimes people draw on what they learn from their parents.

Emma nodded to me and then turned to her group and with great confidence said, "Well, *why* do you think Sistine thought the figures were beautiful? Do you think it was because of her parents? I mean, they took her to see the Sistine Chapel." Emma said this last bit as if she was coming to a realization in that moment, as she spoke. "Her parents named her after the Sistine Chapel so they must have taught her to value art," she added.

"I think Sistine recognized art when she saw it," Kobe finished.

I convened the class. "Readers, I am stunned by what you thought. You're all coming up with insights about Sistine that I don't think you had when you were reading the book alone. Characters, like people in real life, are not just one way. Characters are complicated. Now, we're starting to see all the complex layers of Sistine and how she has more to her than she initially showed."

Listening to these children, what impressed me especially was the snowballing nature of their conversation. Even when one child disagreed with the previous child's ideas, there was a sense that their thinking took in each other's insights, becoming layered. Fallon's insight was well beyond anything she could have come to on her own, but because she comprehended the ideas that others shared, synthesizing those ideas with the book and adding her own original ideas, she ended with a dense and layered insight. Then, of course, it is interesting if a student can't respond in kind. As we listen in on kids' conversations, we're assessing comprehension. Later, in true Vygotskian fashion, we will try to help children do on their own what they were first able to do with support from each other.

As I say this—"Characters are not just one way"—I am aware that this will be truer for texts that are level N and above. Stories that fall within the level K/L/M band of book difficulty tend to feature characters who have one or two predominant characteristics, and these characteristics are described by the narrator or the characters. Still, if one looks closely and thinks deeply, even those characters take on layers of complexity.

LINK

Send children off to do their own reading, challenging them to notice when characters act out of character and to let those instances deepen their ideas about characters.

"As you read, I want you to author a reading life that allows you to see a lot in texts and that especially allows you to see that characters are complex. The work you have been doing, thinking deeply about Rob's actions and the way in which he seemed to act out of character, is the same kind of work you need to do with your independent book.

"Today and from now on, if your character surprises you, instead of simply saying, 'That's weird!' and letting the surprising part pass by you, try pushing yourself to really think, 'What might motivate my character to act in this way?' and 'What sides of my character might this reveal, sides I'd never realized were there?' Of course, you'll want to make sure that you are doing other work as a reader today, and I'll be coming around to admire that work. And remember you can always continue the work we've done for the past couple of weeks." I pointed to the chart.

Strategies Readers Use to Grow Ideas About Characters

- Slow down your reading so you can really attend to what is going on in the first few chapters.

- Remember to carry important things from one chapter to the next.

- Be ready to be confused. This book is not going to read like an Amber Brown book or even like **Because of Winn-Dixie**. It's going to be tough, but if you keep your thoughts and confusions in mind keep reading, it will all work out in the end.

You'll recall that throughout the first unit of study, you often talked with children about authoring reading lives in which reading works for them. So when you say, "I want you to author a reading life that allows you to see a lot in texts," you are harkening back to that earlier unit of study and keeping the content you taught earlier alive for your children.

It is very important to teach children the way in which a reading curriculum accumulates, leaving the reader with a repertoire of skills and strategies. Today gives you a chance to convey the cumulative nature of your teaching.

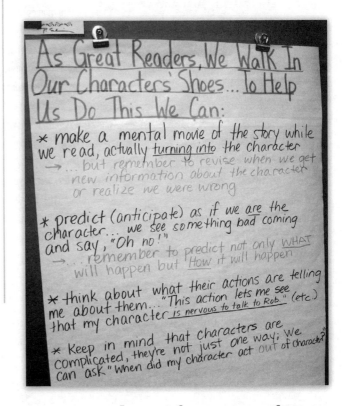

As Great Readers, We Walk In Our Characters' Shoes... To Help Us Do This We Can:

* make a mental movie of the story while we read, actually turning into the character
  → ... but remember to revise when we get new information about the character or realize we were wrong

* predict (anticipate) as if we are the character... we see something bad coming and say, "Oh no!"
  → ... remember to predict not only WHAT will happen but How it will happen

* think about what their actions are telling me about them... "This action lets me see that my character is nervous to talk to Rob." (etc.)

* Keep in mind that characters are complicated, they're not just one way; we can ask "When did my character act out of character?"

CONFERRING AND SMALL-GROUP WORK

Support Reading Skills that Transcend Any One Unit

Today's minilesson was an important one, and you will certainly do some conferring to be sure that readers are growing more nuanced and complex ideas about characters. Remember that if children are reading books in the level N/O/P/Q band of text difficulty, chances are good that their main characters are ambivalent. Amber Brown wants to be thirteen and also wants to be nine. She is starting to like her mother's new boyfriend but also resents him and is worried about betraying her father. There will probably be places in the text where the character or the narrator comes right out and tells readers about the character's traits and feelings, but readers will need to carry those places to other sections of the story where the character acts in those ways. You'll meanwhile want to keep in mind that once readers are working in the level R/S/T band of difficulty, characters will almost certainly be nuanced. Good guys won't be all good, and bad guys won't be all bad. And readers will often be expected to infer what the character is like as a person, often not only from noting the character's actions but also from noticing the character's interactions with the setting, with places. Terabithia reveals a lot about Jess and Leslie. I've written more about this in the assessment section in this volume and the next one.

> ### MID-WORKSHOP TEACHING POINT
>
> #### Readers Push Ourselves to Explain Characters Acting Out of Character
>
> "Can I give you one tip?" I said and waited for the children to pause and give me their attention. "When you find that moment when a character acts out of character, try putting a Post-it note there, on that moment, and try thinking to yourself, 'I wonder why the author *might* have made the decision to have the character do this?' and then jot at least one possible reason on your Post-it note. Ask yourself, 'What *might* have motivated my character to act this way?' and 'What side of my character *might* this reveal?' Jot your thought down and then think, 'What else could it be?' You see, sometimes recording one possible explanation gives your mind space to stop remembering that explanation and to think of another. Once you've written your first idea down, your mind is free to come up with other possibilities. You can go back to reading." *[Figs. X-1 and X-2]*
>
> After children resumed their reading, I said in a voiceover, "I just wanted to remind you that when you're reading and one of your characters surprises you, don't let just let this surprising section of the text pass by you. Instead, push yourself to think more deeply about your character by remembering that if a character acts in a way that seems odd, you may have discovered something about your character that reveals a different side of him or her. Be the kind of person who reads your characters really well."
>
> *continued on next page*

Although some of your conferring and small-group work will follow the day's minilesson, by the time you are midway into a unit of study, it will be important for you to be sure that much of your work also supports skills that transcend any one unit. In this section, I'll talk about two challenges you'll especially want to address. First, you'll have some children who will need you to help them develop into more resourceful and experienced word solvers. And secondly, you will also probably want to take advantage of the fact that you have a small window of time before your children progress into a nonfiction reading unit of study, so this may be your last good chance to move some youngsters up a level of text difficulty. It will be easier for them to tackle texts that are a notch harder now rather than waiting until the next unit of study, nonfiction reading, which will pose its own challenges.

Teach Readers to Figure Out the Meanings of Tricky Words by Relying on Context

My colleagues and I recently did an informal study of third graders across the fifteen cities and towns that we know best. We administered running records to thousands of readers and then studied those running records, looking for trends. One of the things we found was that an astonishing number of third graders decoded unfamiliar vocabulary but felt no need to generate any sort of a definition of the word and instead seemed to pronounce the word and then simply pass over it. We watched as a child encountered an unfamiliar word—say, the word *adoration* in the sentence "She watched with adoration as her big brother walked across the stage to receive his award." In most cases, the child could decode the word but then just continued reading on, seemingly oblivious of the fact that she had just said a word that meant nothing to her. Afterward, if we took the child back to the passage and said, "I noticed you worked hard to pronounce this word—*adoration*. What does it mean?" the child would inevitably shrug and say, "I don't have any idea." We realized, after gathering this data, that we needed to teach readers more strategies for figuring out the meanings of unfamiliar words.

The truth is that there are countless occasions when we are sitting with a child and that youngster nonchalantly breezes past a word that he or she does not really grasp. You'll want readers to understand that rather than letting those words simply slip through her fingers, it's really helpful to take note of the word, to act as if they've just found a small treasure. A person who is willing to work just a bit can make that unknown word her own. The reader can become word rich, if he or she collects the words that others overlook.

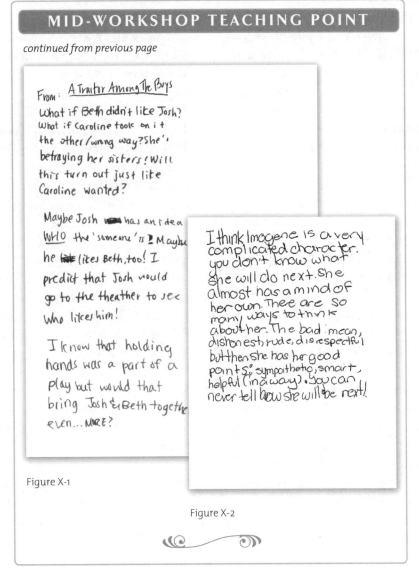

MID-WORKSHOP TEACHING POINT

continued from previous page

From: A Traitor Among The Boys
What if Beth didn't like Josh? What if Caroline took on it the other/wrong way? She's betraying her sisters! Will this turn out just like Caroline wanted?

Maybe Josh has an idea WHO the 'someone' is ? Maybe he likes Beth, too! I predict that Josh would go to the theather to see who likes him!

I know that holding hands was a part of a play but would that bring Josh & Beth together even... MORE?

Figure X-1

I think Imogene is a very complicated character. you don't know what she will do next. She almost has a mind of her own. Thee are so many ways to think about her. The bad: mean, dishonest, rude, disrespectful but then she has her good points: sympathetic, smart, helpful (in a way). You can never tell how she will be next!

Figure X-2

Of course, some children will not just breeze past words but will instead mumble tricky words under their breath or skip over them altogether, and of course if they skip past many words, the resulting text becomes full of gaps, like Swiss cheese. Readers do this either because they feel embarrassed that they are unfamiliar with the word or because they don't want to pause to figure out the word. It's important that you address this habit, either in whole-class lessons (if many children do this) or in small-group or individual conferences.

You will want to teach your children that readers use a variety of strategies to figure out the meanings of unfamiliar words. As most of your children will probably already know, readers first try to pronounce the word. Many readers find it helpful to "chunk" the word in meaningful ways to pronounce it, usually going back and getting a running start on the first chunk or two of the word as they progress to later ones, almost smashing the parts together. Remember to coach readers that after they've chunked the word into parts and pronounced a part or two, that is a powerful time for them to think again about meaning, going between the portion of the word they have said and the sentence's meaning, thinking, "What might make sense that starts like this?" Once a reader has pronounced the word, if that word is still unfamiliar, you'll want to encourage the reader to substitute a synonym for the word, and you'll say, "Check to see if that (substitution) makes sense in the sentence." You hope the reader will actually substitute the synonym, checking to see if the sentence now makes sense and sounds right. The process takes a few moments, but the more children practice this procedure, the more automatic it will become. Encourage the reader to own the word, putting it to use, integrating it into his or her own vocabulary. For example, you might say, "Now that you know that word, *adoration*, when can you imagine using it? Could you use it in any of the writing entries you've got going in your writer's notebook? Could you use it when talking about your social studies unit? Your church?"

You will find that some of your children can do this extremely easily. Give these children a passage with a few obtuse vocabulary words, and they will quickly be able to replace those words with new words that are at least the right part of speech (although children usually do not know parts of speech at this age) and will generally fit into the passage. Other children, however, will be utterly stymied by this activity. The latter group could certainly benefit from a bit more coaching!

But first, you probably just need to teach kids the process of trying to figure out what a word means and then using that information on the run during reading. To do this, gather a small group and begin with a clear teaching point. You might say, "I have noticed that you have difficult words in your books—and that'll keep happening even when you are my age. Sometimes, when you get to a difficult word, I have noticed that you drop your voices, begin to mumble and move past that word as quickly as possible." If you decide to demonstrate what it looks like when a reader does this, don't be timid about exaggerating a bit. You might, for example, read a sentence at full volume, and then when you encounter a difficult word, quickly drop your voice to a barely audible whisper and then bring the volume back up as soon as you are past the word. If it's humorous, all the better. Children will recognize themselves in your portrayal, but if you are being a bit goofy, they won't feel the sting of critique. You might then continue by saying, "We readers know that it's important to be able to read all the words in our books. And reading a word means being able to say it *and* knowing what it means. Readers use what we know about decoding words to figure out how to pronounce a tricky word, and I've seen you doing some good work so you can say the word. But even after you can say the word, readers need to figure out what the word probably means. To do that, readers use the context—that is, use what is going on in that part of the text—to figure out the meaning."

Model the process. Let's imagine, for example, that you decided to do this demonstration within the text *Amber Brown Is not a Crayon*. Opening the book, you might spot the sentence, "Her long blonde hair is perfectly combed, with a really pretty multicolored ribbon barrette," and you might think that *barrette* could be tricky for many readers of this series. You would then read the sentence aloud and deliberately stumble over the word *barrette*. You might think aloud, "Hmm . . . I should first try to pronounce this. I wonder if I can use any chunks at the start of the word— any parts of a word that I have seen before?" You might then notice that the first part of the word is *bar*. Then, you could repeat that first syllable and try to add the next part onto it, ultimately stringing the syllables together into the word *barrette*. Sometimes, simply figuring out how to pronounce the word is sufficient for the reader to recognize the word and know its meaning. However, sometimes the pronunciation doesn't help. You could then demonstrate how to go about using the context to discern the meaning of the word. You'll need to shush those helpful souls who call out the meaning. Say, "I need to focus here," and pretend to not hear their definitions. Make sure to show your thinking out loud. Ask yourself, "I wonder what that means?" Then read the sentences *around* the one in which the word appears to figure out a possible meaning. Your thinking might sound something like, "I notice that they are talking about hair so it must be something about hair. And they are talking about a girl's long hair; sometimes girls use clips in their hair. I'm thinking it means a hair clip. Let me try reading the sentence with the words *hair clip* to see if that fits." Then, substitute the synonym and reread the sentence, confirming that the new word makes sense.

Although you will want to show your readers that we juggle many strategies when we hit sticky parts in a text, make sure that your modeling is both explicit and brief. Children need to spend the majority of the small-group time independently practicing the strategies, so be quick and brief.

Of course, after a bit of demonstration, you will want to set readers up to practice the strategies you have demonstrated. You may distribute a passage with some tricky words in bold, and ask them to work for a few minutes on that passage, perhaps with a partner. Alternatively, you may immediately ask them to apply what they have learned to their independent reading books. "Readers," you might say, "it's time for you to work on this same strategy in your own books. Right now, skim your book and see if you can find a tricky word and put your finger on it. I'll help if you can't find one. Then, try to use what you know about being a flexible word solver to try and figure out that word. Remember to use more than one strategy." As children work on the words in their books, you will want to rotate from one member of the group to another, coaching each reader individually. When you do this coaching, listen to the child and compliment the child on any strategy that you think the child is beginning to use that will pay off, and then give the child a tip for how he or she can do even more with that one strategy or incorporate another strategy as well. You might, for example, help one child use prefixes and suffixes to speculate what the word might mean or help another weigh whether the tone of the text is such that the word seems to be a positive word or a negative one. Above all, encourage your readers to try more than one word-solving strategy and encourage them to not only aim to say the word but also to speculate about its meaning.

At the end of your small-group work, make sure to link today's teaching to ongoing work, reminding children that they should continue to use multiple strategies to figure out tricky words as they read. You may want to acknowledge that it can feel clumsy, pausing every time one encounters a tricky word, but remind readers that any new process—riding a bicycle or cooking an omelet—feels arduous at first. Tell your readers that the more they practice, the more natural the process will feel, until it's practically automatic.

Some kids find it useful to reread passages that contain words that were once tricky words. For these children, you could suggest that they leave Post-its at all the places in a book where they've done some good word-solving work, keep that book in their book bin (or baggie). A couple of times a week, these children could practice reading the marked sections. They might practice reading aloud those passages containing unfamiliar words to partners. So if the partner stumbles over lots of words, the other might say something like, "It's a bit choppy. Can you try it again?" The coaching partner could also say things like, "Whoa, slow down! You are going so fast it's hard to follow," or, "All that work on the tricky word messed this up. Can you go back and reread so it sounds smooth?"

Use Small Groups to Help Readers Tackle Books that Are a Notch Higher than Those They've Been Reading

Earlier in this section, I mentioned that you have a window of time to move children to higher levels of text difficulty while they are still reading fiction, before the upcoming nonfiction unit. Assess to see if some children may be ready. If you do move children up, remember that for a time, their baggies of books might contain some that are easier and some harder. For the harder books, it will help if you read aloud the first chapter or otherwise give a strong book introduction, and it will help if the reader is reading this book in synchrony with another reader, so their talk can be especially supportive.

Some of the time, you'll use small groups as a forum for moving a couple of readers up a notch. When I decided to move three readers from books at level R to those at level S, I channeled them to start by reading *Journey*, by Patricia MacLachlen, and doing so in sync with each other. I gathered the trio, and said, "You have told me you are eager to tackle books that are a bit more complex, so let's read one book together that will be challenging for you. I'll help you, and you can help each other, and I think if we pour a lot of effort into this one short, beautiful book, it will teach you how to read other books that are equally complex. I know you know to start by looking at the cover and reading the blurb on the back to get a feel for what this is going to be about, but before you do this, I want to remind you that books like this one will not contain straightforward, predictable stories like you read at earlier levels. Remember earlier when you read *Amber Brown* books? She had a problem, and in the book, she solved the problem."

"Yes," Isaac responded. "Her mother found a new boyfriend, David, that she wanted to marry, and Amber wasn't so sure."

"I'm sure all of you remember that everything worked out fine in the end. Amber realized her mother was going to marry David and she would have two families—one with her mother and David and one with her father. The books you used to read tended to go like that—the main character had one problem that you could put your finger on pretty easily, and that problem got solved. In the books you'll be reading starting today, there won't be one obvious problem, or one obvious solution. Today, you are going to read a story about another family, but you are really going to need to pay attention to what is going on in the first few chapters to set you up for what this story is going to be about. So I want you to think of doing several things:

> • *Slow down your reading so you can really attend to what is going on in the first few chapters.*
>
> • *Remember to carry important things from one chapter to the next.*
>
> • *Be ready to be confused. This book is not going to read like an Amber Brown book or even like Because of Winn-Dixie. It's going to be tough, but if you keep your thoughts and confusions in mind and keep reading, it will all work out in the end.*

"Here is a copy of the book *Journey*. Let's look at the cover, read the blurb on the back, and get ready to talk about what you think the book is going to be about. There is going to be a tricky vocabulary word in the blurb—*inevitability*. Remember how we look in and look around the word to determine its meaning. Let's see if you can do that work."

The readers inspected the cover and read the blurb.

"So readers, do you have some idea of what the book is going to be about?"

"The mother leaves the boy and his sister with their grandparents, but he doesn't know why she left?" Brianna replied.

"Did the rest of you have the same idea?" I pressed.

"Yes," Grace replied. "There were a lot of pictures on the front and back of the book. We are going to need to look for clues in the pictures that the grandfather takes and that will maybe tell why the mother left and where she went. It says, 'Journey learns to look and finds that, for him, the camera is a means of finding things his naked eye has missed.'"

"Great, I like how you went back into the text to support your answer. So what does *inevitability* mean?"

No one responded. The kids had puzzled looks on all their faces.

"See, I told you these books are going to be tricky and create questions or confusions that are not easily answered. I'll tell all of you that inevitable means something that must be done and is unavoidable. And yes, Journey's job and your job will be to find out why it was unavoidable that the mother had to leave.

"I'm going to read the first page to you. Do you remember that in *The Tiger Rising*, the characters got very complex because they had multiple problems and pressures (lots of problems and pressures)? Remember how Rob, at the start of the book, is alone in a new and hostile place, he misses his dead mother terribly and feels pressure from his father not to express his sadness, and he feels the pressure of knowing there is a tiger trapped in the woods. When I read this page from *Journey* to you, I want you to use a spyglass that lets you consider multiple pressures on the characters. I'll read the first page after the title page, which is called a *prologue*.

> Mama named me Journey. Journey, as if somehow she wished her restlessness on me. But it was Mama who would be gone the year that I was eleven—before spring crashed onto our hillside

with explosions of mountain laurel, before summer came with the soft slap of the screen door, breathless nights, and mildew on the books. I should have known, but I didn't. My older sister Cat knew. Grandma knew, but Grandma kept it to herself. Grandfather knew and said so.

Mama stood in the barn, her suitcase at her feet. "I'll send money," she said. "For Cat and Journey."

"That's not good enough, Liddie," said Grandfather.

"I'll be back, Journey," my mother said softly.

But I looked up and saw the way the light trembled in her hair, making her look like an angel, someone not earthbound. Even in that moment she was gone.

"No, son," Grandfather said to me, his voice loud in the barn. "She won't be back."

And that was when I hit him.

In the discussion that followed the reading, I led students to describe Journey as a boy who didn't want his mother to leave him with the grandparents. I led them to realize that characters will probably not just have one layer to their problems. What else could be going on here? The children thought that the grandfather seems to have a negative view of what the mother says about returning, and this makes Journey angry at the grandfather. And maybe Journey is struggling with the whole idea of living with people who won't tell him things. Then I prompted the readers to do similar work with the mother. At first, they seemed mad at the mother for abandoning her child, but I nudged them to realize that in the books they would be reading now, including this one, characters aren't all good or all bad. The mother is not going to be all bad. They described her as not bad so much as restless. And they saw signs that she cares for her children, because she said she would send money. She also told Journey she would come back.

I told the readers that before, they carried with them a sense of the characters. Now they will also need to carry with them confusions and uncertainties. What persistent questions were still not answered and needed to be carried into the book? The children listed several: Why did the mother leave? Would she actually come back? What do Cat, Grandmother, and Grandfather know about the mother that makes them feel that she would not come back?

Before I sent the students off to begin reading the book, I posted the things that they would need to remember as they began reading *Journey* and other books that were this complex.

TEACHING SHARE

Readers Grow Our Thinking to Spark Grand Conversations About Characters

Remind children to prepare for the conversations they'll have soon. Remind them to push their thinking. After a time, ask them to talk with their partners.

"Readers, in a minute, you'll have a chance to have a grand conversation. Your book talk will be a lot richer, though, if you anticipate the stuff you want to talk about and read in such a way that you are looking for treasures. You may be reading with tons of predictions flooding into your mind as you race ahead of the story, thinking, 'I bet such and such happens.' You may be growing ideas about your character and letting these ideas become deeper by noticing when the character acts out of character. In a second, I am going to give you another five or ten minutes for reading, but before you continue reading, reread any Post-it notes you've written so far, starring ones that seem to you like they could perhaps spark grand conversations. If you haven't already recorded an idea you'd really like to talk more about, do so now. Take a second to jot a thought you'd like to share with someone.

"If you already have a good thought recorded, or if you are just recording a thought now, see if right now, you can grow your thinking by jotting further thoughts onto your note. Push yourself to see more by looking more deeply at your idea and trying to uncover the treasure that might be hiding inside that initial observation or jotting. You could use one of these prompts to extend your thinking."

Prompts to Grow Your Ideas

"This is important because . . ."

"This makes me realize that . . ."

"The bigger idea here is that . . ."

COACHING TIPS

Usually a share session is the way to end a workshop, functioning as the bookend to the minilesson. This share, however, needs to be inserted into reading time, with the idea that readers will continue reading for another five minutes and only then meet with partners.

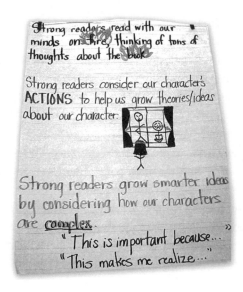

"Once you've recorded or extended your thought, get back to reading, but read with your thought in mind, carrying it with you, seeing if the upcoming story sparks more thoughts related to the one you are carrying. Remember, you're reading to prepare for a grand conversation, so grow some more cool ideas as you read, perhaps ones related to the idea you have already starred. Try to be the kind of reader who doesn't just pass by possible treasures but instead reads and jots with an eye for what is lurking beneath the surface."

After another five minutes of reading time, I said, "Get with your partner—and use the time well."

Attending to Objects that Reveal Characters

IN THIS SESSION,

you'll teach students that readers grow ideas about characters by paying attention to the objects our characters hold dear.

In his wonderful classic, *The Little Prince*, Antoine de Saint Exupéry explores the age-old theme of traveling far to cherish what is already close. Through the little prince's journeys to other planets, we see what happens when you abandon something you love only to discover that it cannot be so easily dismissed—that it matters above all else. Ostensibly, the object of the little prince's affection is nothing more than a vain, shallow rose. What's more, as he discovers on his journeys, his rose is just one of many. It is only when he looks closer at the other roses, after learning a valuable lesson from a wise fox, that the little prince can see what makes his rose so dear.

"You are beautiful, but you are empty," he says to the hundreds of roses before him. "To be sure, an ordinary passerby would think that my rose looked just like you . . . But in herself alone she is more important than all the hundreds of you other roses: because it is she that I have

watered; because it is she that I have put under the glass globe; because it is she that I have sheltered behind the screen . . . because it is she that I have listened to, when she grumbled, or boasted, or even sometimes when she said nothing. Because she is my rose."

In this session we want children to see the things their characters keep close and to really look, really think, about why those things might matter to the character. We want them to look at Rob's carvings and see not just little wooden figurines but treasures he can hold onto even if the people he loves leave him. Children know better than anyone what it means to keep objects and people they hold dear close. Even before they can talk, children recognize and cling to selected objects; they clutch a soft toy or blanket, caressing it until it grows worn. Later, children claim best friends, some imaginary, some real, all cherished. And they keep their most prized possessions in little treasure boxes close

GETTING READY

- Be prepared to reference *The Tiger Rising* in relation to the possessions that Rob holds dear. You can also use characters and objects from another familiar read-aloud.

- Produce oversized Post-it notes that are large enough for the entire class to see. These Post-its should relate to objects a character holds dear.

- Listen closely to partnership conversations during the active involvement section, because you will want to share one of these conversations during the link.

- Display the chart "Strategies Readers Use to Grow Ideas About Characters" for children to reference.

at hand, carefully stowed away under a bed or on the top shelf of a closet.

By now, of course, children feel as if they have become more expert as envisioners, predictors, and theorizers. You will have already begun equipping them with the thinking tools that can help them see and think beneath the surface, imagine what's not stated, make connections, dissect characters, and grow ideas. When you ask children to notice what is meaningful about the objects that a character has

> *Even before they can talk, children recognize and cling to selected objects; they clutch a soft toy or blanket, caressing it until it grows worn.*

imbued with importance, you'll hope that your children will draw on all the skills they've learned over the past month. You'll also hope children are accustomed to thinking about themselves and their own lives, and that they may listen to this minilesson and think not only about their characters but also about themselves, asking, "What are *my* prized pos-

sessions and what do they say about me?" One might think, "Why does my rabbit skin mean so much to me?" You'll also hope that children are thinking about the characters they know through reading. Why is that little wooden chair so important to Peter in Ezra Jack Keats' *Peter's Chair*? Why, in *Where the Wild Things Are* does the supper seem to matter—the supper that, in the end, was still hot?

Children may also join you in hearing stories about objects that mean a lot to people in the news. At Senator Teddy Kennedy's funeral, his nephew described how Teddy brought a bag of soil from the graves of his two brothers across the sea with him when Yitzhak Rabin died, and quietly, without ceremony, sprinkled the soil from his brothers' graves onto the soil, also, of Rabin's grave. That bag of dirt took on enormous meaning, first when Teddy carried it across the sea to a funeral held for a leader of a distant land, and then it took on yet more meaning when the story was told as part of a collage of stories, all combining to honor a great senator and humanist who'd just died.

The lessons from *The Little Prince* will apply to this session. "It is only with the heart that one can see rightly; What is essential is invisible to the eye," the fox tells the little prince when he is bestowing parting philosophical advice. When we ask children to look at concrete objects that characters cherish, we are, in fact, asking them to look at the *relationships* a character values and at the meaning and feelings and history behind the objects that matter. We are asking children to look, to see, to discover with their hearts.

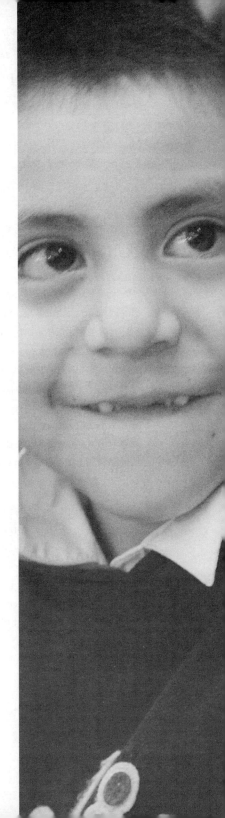

# MINILESSON

Attending to Objects that Reveal Characters

CONNECTION

Tell children about a time in your life when an object took on significance. Suggest that some objects are tightly packed with significance for people in real life and for characters in books.

"When I was your age, a new wing was built on my elementary school. Our principal decided to create a time capsule that would be opened fifty years later. A time capsule is a vessel—like a box or bottle—into which people put objects that mean a lot to them, objects that show something important about who they are so years later, people can open the time capsule and learn about the people and life in the earlier time. At my school, we put newspapers in our time capsule so that people would know what was happening in the world. We also put in pictures of ourselves, our town, and our school. As we did so, we were sure that our clothing would seem terribly out of fashion to future students. We included a copy of our school's poetry magazine. We hoped that these items would communicate something about who we were and what was important to us.

Right now, before you read on, think of the objects that matter to you. What is on your bureau? What objects did you take with you to college? What objects from your childhood do you still own? For this minilesson to resonate with you and your class, you will absolutely want to alter this connection so that it reflects your life.

"I know people say that material possessions are not important, but that's not always true. Often, possessions are little clues into what's important to a person. Some of these possessions have actual value, and some only have value to us: a framed picture on the kitchen table, for example, or a special book that was a gift from a loved one. A friend of mine keeps two shelves of comic books from when he was a kid. The comic books are a reminder of what was important to him; they help him keep that child-like part of himself in sight. And, now that he has a kid of his own, he hopes to share them with her one day. That way those comic books won't just represent his own childhood. They will represent a special link between that man and his child.

You'll have children in your classroom who have mascots, and the whole class will agree that those objects are emblematic of their owners. Personalize your minilesson by noticing the objects your students dangle from their backpacks or sit in the inkwells of their desks.

"As for me, I have a couple of letters from my grandmother in my nightstand drawer. My grandmother is not a very affectionate person, but in her letters she always writes,

'I wish I could give you a hug right now.' I find it very moving, because it's sort of out of character for her to say that, and I know it's a big deal for her to write something kind of mushy. The fact that I keep these letters close, right by the side of my bed, shows that I love my grandmother a lot, and I think of her often.

"Characters in books are the same way. When an author imagines a character, she often uses the character's most important possessions to reveal essential parts of the character. Think of Harry Potter, for example. The one object he has with him at all times, whether asleep or awake, is his wand, right? As a wizard (and a very special wizard at that) Harry has to be ready to defend himself with a spell. What else does Harry often have with him? Well, there's the invisibility cloak, right? There are a few other of these magical items that have been given to Harry by the people who are helping him in his quest. Harry's life is likely to never be boring. Because of who he is, adventure and danger often find him, and Harry has to be ready."

Much later, in the fourth unit of this series, you'll see talk of symbolism. That minilesson will build upon this one.

Name your teaching point. Specifically, tell children that readers pay special attention to the objects that characters hold close to their hearts. These objects often open a window into what the character is really like.

"What I want to teach you today is that paying attention to the objects that a character keeps near and dear is one way to grow ideas about what kind of person that character is. Those objects are often windows into the mind and heart of our characters. The possessions that a character keeps close almost always reveal something important about the person."

This teaching point builds upon the idea that characters and people reveal their personalities through their choices. Some children might not think of possessions as choices, but they are. The choice to give an object a position of prominence and importance is a choice that communicates a person's values and priorities in a powerful way.

Teaching

Using children in the class and the objects they hold close as examples, point out the way in which objects come to represent people's lives.

"This morning, I had a hunch that thinking about characters in this way would really pay off. When I came to school, a few of you were here early playing in the yard, and I watched you for a few minutes. I saw that Brianna, like always, was kicking her soccer ball around. You all know how that ball is practically attached to her leg? It shows how important soccer is to Brianna, and maybe how important sports in general are to her. I knew that I was onto something."

Demonstrate the process of mulling over the significance that objects have for characters by thinking aloud about the objects that are important to the protagonist from the read-aloud book.

"So I did some thinking about Rob from *The Tiger Rising*, and I jotted down my ideas. I want you to listen to how I use this question to grow my thinking. Notice that it's really a two-part question. First, I ask, 'What objects does Rob keep close?' Then, I ask, 'What does that make me think about him?'

"I asked myself, 'What does Rob keep close?' Well, for one, he has all the little figures that he whittled out of wood. I remember the scene when Sistine first sees the figures all laid out on the tray next to Rob's bed in the motel room. When I read that scene, it seemed to me that Rob felt both nervous and proud when someone else looked at his figures. Then, I asked myself, 'What does this make me think about Rob? What do those precious figures tell me about him?' And I realized that part of why these figures are so important to Rob is because his mother taught him how to whittle before she died, and when he whittles, he remembers her without having to talk about her. These figures help Rob feel close to his mother.

"Once I come up with an idea about what the objects might reveal about a character, I try to think more about that. Let me see if I can say more about that idea. Rob seems like a lonely character. He has a hard time talking about the things he wants and feels. So instead of saying how much he misses his mom, he does this thing that his mom taught him. Also, in a way, this 'village' of figures keeps him company in the bare motel room that he shares with his father. Maybe they help him not think about how dark and quiet his world has become since his mom died."

When thinking about the objects that Rob carries in The Tiger Rising, *I also name the processes I experience. I name the questions I ask myself and the thinking I assign myself to do. I'm trying to demonstrate in a way that leaves a path others can follow.*

Name what you have done in a way that is transferable to other texts, other days.

"Readers, that's where I stopped my jotting, but there's a lot more that I could say about what these whittled figures reveal about Rob. Did you notice how mulling over the significance of the objects that Rob cherishes really paid off for me? Now, I have some theories about Rob that I could think and write more about. Did you notice that I didn't just ask a question, answer it, and move on, as if I was answering the questions on a test? This isn't a test, and there's no right answer that you can write down before you race on to the next one. In fact, the longer you stay on one idea, the more likely it is that you will uncover powerful thinking. Earlier, when I was jotting about this, I pushed myself to write one more thing and then one more thing. That's how you make an idea pay off for you—by staying with it until you've pushed past your initial thinking and found yourself thinking ideas that surprise even yourself.

This minilesson is ostensibly about the objects that a character holds close, but of course it is actually about a way of thinking, and of writing and talking to help you think. If readers learn to mull over the possible significance of the objects a character holds close, hopefully they will learn that this process is transferable: They can think about the implications of almost anything a character chooses to do.

"I could repeat this process over and over again with the same character by thinking about other objects that play an important role. For example, I could think about the art book that Rob loves to pore over in the library or (especially) about the drawing of the tiger he carries in his pocket."

ACTIVE INVOLVEMENT

Prompt children to work so that one partner tells the other about an object he or she keeps close and the other helps the first discover the significance of that object. As children work, voice over possible questions to lift the level of their talking and writing.

"Readers, you are going to do something a little different today. You are going to work with your partners to practice examining the objects that a character keeps close; instead of thinking about the characters in your book, you are going to think about the characters in your life—starting with the main character. Start by asking yourself, 'What object(s) do I keep close?' Think about this for a moment without talking. Think about the special places in your home—the mantle shelf, the table beside your bed, the place where you keep your clothes. What objects do you keep in those special places? Perhaps you carry something with you in your backpack, in your coat pocket. Perhaps there is something you keep under your pillow. Right now, think of one object that you keep near and dear to your heart. We're going to do something with it."

I gave children a minute to think. "Now, turn to your partner. Partner 1, will you tell your partner about this object that is precious to you. Try to do your deepest thinking. Partner 2, help Partner 1 really think about all that the object might represent. If Partner 1 keeps Pokémon cards in her backpack, I don't want you to say, 'That shows you like Pokémon.' Go deeper. What might it reveal about what Partner 1 wants or needs in life? Okay, Partner 1, get started. I'll give you a few minutes for this."

You aim for your minilessons to be memorable. They are meant to make a lasting impact. So you will do everything possible to draw children in. One way to do this is to keep the minilessons varied. If every day you insert some thinking aloud into your read-aloud, and then you continue reading the read-aloud book, prompting children to do their own thinking, along the lines of what you have just done, chances are pretty good that many of your minilessons will flow past kids, with one feeling very much like another. You may want to pause and reread the minilessons that have been included in this series so far, noticing the various methods Kathleen and I have used to make them memorable. Those same strategies will be ones you use, too.

Here it might help to give children one or two more examples of someone who has a treasured possession. Make sure the examples are simple and that the thinking goes beyond the obvious. Is there an example from your own classroom? A child who keeps a special photo tucked in his pocket? You may want to reference the bag of prairie dirt that Patricia MacLachlan's protagonist cherished in What You Know First. *If you can talk about the examples that are familiar to the whole class, children will be nodding their heads and coming up with their own hypotheses.*

LINK

Share the work that one child has done, that you overheard, and in doing so give children yet one more example of what you have been trying to teach. Then remind them to do this often throughout their lives.

"Readers, wrap up your partner conversations. I heard some brilliant thinking just now. I heard David and Tyrell talking about the keys that Tyrell has in his backpack at all times. This is the first year that his parents have trusted Tyrell to be home by himself while they are working, so David thought the keys might be a sign that Tyrell is getting older and has more responsibility now. Then, David said something else that was really smart. He suggested that the keys might also represent the fact that getting older is not always easy. He said Tyrell probably gets bored being home by himself." Tyrell giggled and looked at the rug, both pleased and embarrassed by his classmates' scrutiny.

"Whenever you are thinking about a character—in your books, or in your life—remember that one way you can grow your thinking about that person is by considering the objects they treasure. Authors always include those objects for a reason. There is a reason why Kate DiCamillo gave Rob wooden figures and why J. K. Rowling gave Harry magical objects. These objects are always little clues about who the character is and what is important to him or her. Remember that writers include other details for the same reason—details about gestures or physical characteristics, such as Rob's shrugging or his rash. Don't rush over these details as you read. Instead, stop and ask yourself why the author included them. What can they tell you about the character?"

If you think your students will easily wrap their minds around the teaching point of this minilesson, you might want to tuck in some more teaching. You could add in the concept that the objects around a character, described in the same breath as the character are bound to be as revealing as the objects the character holds near and dear. Those first "meetings" with our characters are loaded with significance! Why does Willie May wear and fiddle with a butterfly hair clip as we first meet her? Could it be that the author is hinting that she cultivates metamorphoses? Why else would the author have chosen that deal to describe her?

CONFERRING AND SMALL-GROUP WORK

Plan for What You Might Teach

If you expect that a portion of your conferences and small groups will nudge children to entertain the notion that the objects a character holds dear reveal something about that character, then you'll want to take a moment before you circulate among your readers to think about examples from your own life. You might also think about other characters from books your class knows well and the objects that represent and shed light upon them. My sister is a pediatrician, and you can learn a lot about her by noticing that she never goes anywhere without her cell phone. She's *always* on call, always hearing from mothers and fathers of sick children. And Popeye, in the cartoon, always has—what? His spinach. Linus has his blanket. Snoopy keeps a typewriter handy, and Dora always carries her backpack. All of these objects help define the characters who carry them. You'll want to be ready to coach readers to ask, "Does this object confirm what I already know about the character's personality, or does it add a nuance that makes me see the character in a different light than before?"

Support Your English Language Learners in Understanding the Teaching Point

Pulling Rosa, Tyrell, and Gabe close, I pointed to the *Dora the Explorer* characters emblazoned across Rosa's pencil case. Before launching a dis-

> ### MID-WORKSHOP TEACHING POINT
>
> #### Readers Pay Attention to Subtle Details
>
> "Readers, can I interrupt you for a moment? I'm noticing that many of you are on the look out for objects your characters hold close as a way to grow bigger ideas about who they are. And some of you have noticed that it may not be that the character holds the object closely, but the object seems to have particular significance." Holding up the book *My Name Is Maria Isabel*, I continued, "When Rosa came to the end of *My Name Is Maria Isabel*, she noticed that Maria Isabel was wearing the same yellow dress she wore in the beginning of the book. Rosa decided that dress must be very important to Maria Isabel because she wears it in the beginning of the book and then again at the end. Rosa remembered that Maria Isabel was devastated when the dress got dirty. At the end of the book Maria Isabel is wearing the dress again when she sings at the holiday concert. When Rosa got to that part in the end, she didn't just pass by that detail about the dress. Rosa realized that Maria Isabel's dress might be part of her connection to her culture, and to her grandmother, who gave her the fabric for the dress in Puerto Rico. At the end of the book, Maria Isabel is finally being called by her real name *and* she is wearing the special dress her grandmother and aunt helped to make for her. In the same way that Maria Isabel's
>
> *continued on next page*

cussion about the significance of objects that a character keeps close, I asked, "What does Dora always carry with her?" knowing that this explicit example would make the teaching point clear to these three readers.

"Her backpack," Rosa and Tyrell said in quick unison. Gabe nodded his agreement.

"It has a map inside," Rosa added.

"A backpack," I repeated the information Rosa had just provided with deliberate pensiveness, "that has a map inside." I chose this example because I knew that all three were familiar with the iconic Dora, even though Tyrell and Gabe were probably not fans as Rosa was. "Hmm, I'm thinking, if I wasn't too familiar with Dora, I'd be able to tell a lot about her *just by noting* that she has a backpack—with a map inside—and other tools like a magnifying glass, a flashlight, and a rope. I'd be thinking, 'What kind of person carries a backpack with such things?' She's not a teacher, or there would be pens, books, and kids' work in there! She's probably a detective or an explorer, because *that* kind of person would carry those kinds of objects, right?"

As Rosa, Tyrell, and Gabe nodded, I repeated the day's teaching point more emphatically. "We pay attention to the objects that our characters keep close. Then we think, 'What do these tell me about this character? What kind of person would keep such objects close to them?' Let's think about the characters in your books and see if there are any objects that one of them keeps close."

Tyrell said, "Jack has a backpack too, for adventures," pointing to the picture on the cover of his *Magic Tree House* book.

Gabe's face lit up. "I remember that Elmer in that book *My Father's Dragon* had tons of stuff in his backpack too! He had gum and lollipops and other funny stuff."

"Why do you think he has those objects with him? What might that show about Elmer?" I asked him, hoping he would come up with a different idea than Tyrell. "Well, Elmer is always doing crazy things, and he uses what he has to get out of trouble," Gabe said.

"Do you remember a time he used an object to get out of trouble?" I asked.

"Well, once he gave these alligators lollipops so he could walk across their backs," Gabe replied with a grin.

"Hmm, so maybe those funny objects represent how creative Elmer is. Maybe those objects show how he is always prepared for unexpected adventures," I said, helping him make more significance out of his observation. Before I moved on to another group, I reminded them to watch out for *other* objects that characters keep close in their independent reading books.

MID-WORKSHOP TEACHING POINT

continued from previous page

name represents her connection to her culture, her two grandmothers, and her country, Rosa decided Maria Isabel's *dress* represents those things too. Because Rosa paused to think about the significance of the dress, she was able to grow bigger ideas about the character and the book as a whole. *[Fig. XI-1]*

"Readers, the important tip I want to give you is that readers don't just pay attention to objects that a character holds close, we pay attention to the key details that the author includes. As we know, authors don't just choose any old details for their stories! In a way, we can think of specific details as clues the author is leaving us. Those clues help steer us toward big ideas inside the book, or just the way Rosa used the dress as a clue to think more deeply about what her book was saying and how her character had changed. Even the names an author uses for his or her characters aren't accidental. What significance might we make of the fact that Sistine is named Sistine? Or the name Rob? Or Sassy? Or Opal and Gloria Dump from *Because of Winn-Dixie*? Remember, we are becoming the kinds of readers who see the details an author includes as clues! We don't just pass them by. We pause and wonder what kind of significance they might have. As you continue reading, you might be on the lookout for *details* that seem to act as clues."

I think Maria Isabel wearing the yellow dress again is really important because it shows her connection to her culture and grandmother and to herself.

Figure XI-1

As I moved to another group, I thought for a moment about the complex thinking that Rosa, an ELL student, was doing within the class. Her English vocabulary sometimes makes decoding difficult for her, but Rosa is literate in Spanish and she draws tremendous strength from that. She is familiar with story structure and academic concepts. Her comprehension work reveals these strengths.

Support Your Speedy Readers in Pausing to Think About Details and Stereotypes

Your conferences will not all align to the minilesson. This day, I knew I also wanted to work with a few children who seemed to me to be plot junkies, reading for what happens next with little attention to detail. As it turned out, my work with these readers still encompassed the discussion about objects a character holds close—but that became my means to an end, not my goal. I pulled Jack, Emma, and Izzy close, eyeing a graphic depicting the Peanuts gang from Schulz's Charlie Brown series on Izzy's T-shirt. I pointed to Linus, another cartoon character. "This guy was my favorite," I told the group. "Out of all the characters in the Peanuts gang, I liked him most because he was so smart, kind of like a philosopher." I waited for the group to peer more closely at the drawing of Linus on Izzy's T-shirt before sub-vocalizing, "But see the object he's carrying? It's a security blanket. That's odd, isn't it?"

I left a pool of silence after making this observation because I wanted to see what insights the students would come up with on their own. Thinking it over, Izzy said, "Maybe some smart people aren't always secure." To link Izzy's comment with the teaching point, I added, "When we study the details in a story, including the objects a character keeps close, we often realize something *more* than we previously knew. Like Linus may be smart—but he's *also* insecure."

The group began to talk about their characters and the objects they held close. For each character, they named an object, then moved on quickly. I wanted them to think more deeply. When Malik noted the frilly dress that Sistine was wearing when we first met her in *The Tiger Rising*, I asked him if there was, in fact, anything frilly about Sistine. "No," he smiled slowly. "Sistine is tough." Malik provided me an opening to extend the teaching point.

I said, "Sometimes, the objects a character keeps close are at odds with who the character really is. When we notice this, we might ask ourselves, 'Does this character rise above a stereotype?'"

To demonstrate this, I recalled the way in which Willie May is likened to a prophetess in *The Tiger Rising*. "In fact," I added, "Rob thinks that if God had to pick a person to talk through, it would make sense to pick her. But remember—the objects she keeps closest to her are cigarettes, eight ball gum, and a vacuum cleaner. Hmm." I wondered visibly at this. "Here is someone fit enough for *God* to speak through. She's remarkably

wise, like a prophetess, almost. If I had to choose the objects that a prophetess keeps close, I'm not sure I would choose cigarettes, gum, brooms, or a vacuum cleaner." Through my face and tone, I exaggerated my puzzlement, enabling children to recognize this as a glaring discrepancy. "The objects Willie May keeps close are at odds with who she really is in this story. We might ask ourselves, why does Kate DiCamillo choose *these* objects to represent Willie May? In a similar way as Sistine, how does Willie May's character rise above a stereotype as well?"

Of course, by discussing stereotypes and the incongruity between characters and the objects they hold close, I was pushing the conversation up a notch in terms of interpretive sophistication. The various teaching points that you and I carry around in our conferring bag will be adapted to fit the skill level of the students we're addressing, and in the process they might be extended, just as the teaching point of this session extended into a discussion of stereotypes in the conference described above. But if you approach your readers with a specific aim in sight, this extension is purposeful and strategic rather than accidental or tangential. My aim was to nudge Izzy, Jack, and Emma into thinking with more power and sophistication because these readers commonly focused only on the action of the story or problems related to the plot. I also wanted to push them to pause and ponder the subtle details inside texts that add layers of significance—and meaning—to their understanding of the characters in their independent reading.

TEACHING SHARE

Readers Find the Possessions a Character Holds Dear Revealing

Ask children to prepare for the conversation they are about to have. In this case, ask them to select, or further develop, their best thought to date.

"Now, meet with your partner and share some of the character work you did today. First, look over your jottings and over the section of the book you read. Pick the idea you had that you think is the strongest. It could be one that you jotted down or one that you just had in your head or one that you're just having right now. Take a moment to jot it down if you haven't already. And if you have already jotted it, take a second to let your idea grow by using thought prompts to push your thinking." I gestured to the chart of thought prompts.

Ask one partner to open the conversation with some thinking about character. Coach them in ways to make their thinking about character stronger.

After a minute, I said, "Partner 2, you start and share your thinking with Partner 1. If you don't find objects playing an important role in your book yet, perhaps because you are really early in the story, you can shift and talk with Partner 1 about other important observations you are having about your character. If the Listening Partner listens really hard, I'll probably see you getting into a grand conversation. I may even see you returning to the book to read parts aloud. If you return to passages in the book (and I hope you do), remember to read the excerpt in such a way that you help your listener really picture the character. You might add some gestures or make your voice match the character. And talk—really, really talk. You may never get to discuss the objects that reveal characters because you might get so involved talking about the significance of a certain passage or some other big idea you are having. The important thing is that you think deep and long, coming to new insights about characters and books.

"Remember to talk and listen with what we have been describing as 'a disposition for finding treasures.' What might the character's *name*, alone, show about him or her? What about the character's *relationships?* How might the character be changing? You can follow your thinking wherever it leads."

You should notice that although readers have been nudged in this session to think about something new—the objects that a character holds dear—the process that we ask them to go through is not new. Again and again, these sessions nudge readers to read and think, collect jottings, and then to pause to reread those jottings, selecting one as especially significant. The time you give students to reread their jottings and select one of particular significance also acts as a wake-up call to students who have not been jotting thoughts all along. Once a reader selects an important idea, you might help the reader develop that idea by using writing-to-think as a way to "talk the idea over." In this way, the student is essentially getting the conversation started on his own by simply adding another line or two of thinking to his Post-it, perhaps even sticking a second Post-it onto the bottom of the first. Or the reader can move the one Post-it to his reading notebook and begin writing long and strong down the page of the notebook. Either way, you may channel readers to use thought prompts such as, "To add on . . ." and "Furthermore . . ." and "This is important because . . ." and "This is giving me the idea that . . ." to extend their thinking. Finally, you give children the opportunity to extend this thinking by discussing their ideas with a partner.

Remind readers of ways they know to think about characters. Remind them to use these ways from now on.

When it was time to end the workshop, I asked for all eyes to be on me. "Readers, you already know lots of ways to grow ideas as you read, and especially how to grow ideas about characters. Right now, list across your fingers at least three ways you know for growing ideas about characters." I left a pool of silence and used that silence to do my own thinking, making my own mental list. Then I said, "I hope that today, you've added one new bullet to your list. As you read any book, and as you go through life, remember that the possessions that a person keeps near and dear—the journal, the lucky charm in a pocket, the ring that a person never removes—can help us grow theories about that person and may give us windows into their heart and mind." I meanwhile revealed that I had added today's strategy to our chart.

Strategies Readers Use to Grow Ideas About Characters

- We make a movie in our mind, drawing on the text to envision (or become) the character.

- We use our own experiences to help us walk in the character's shoes, inferring what the character is thinking, feeling, experiencing.

- We revise our mental movies as we read on, getting new details from the text.

- We notice when we feel connected to a character and use that feeling to deepen our understanding of the character.

- We read with our minds on fire and capture thoughts that lead us into grand conversations.

- We pay attention to the actions of our characters and see those actions as choices.

- We think about instances when the character seems to act out of character, and think, "How might these instances lead me to revise my initial ideas about the character?" Or "Might the character be changing?"

- We notice the objects that a character holds close and think, "What might the character's relationship with this object suggest about the character?"

Seeing Characters Through the Eyes of Others

n Joan Didion's book *The Year of Magical Thinking*, she writes about one of the most surprising parts of dealing with her husband, John's, death. "For forty years," she writes, "I saw myself through John's eyes. I did not age. This year for the first time since I was twenty-nine I saw myself through the eyes of others. I realized that my image of myself was of someone significantly younger." To some extent, we all rely on those around us—especially those very dear to us—to help us create an image of who we are. Even when we feel awful, a friend or family member reminding us that we are loved has

the power to make us feel better. I am loved, therefore I am lovable. That is a comfort.

We internalize what others' behavior toward us tells us about ourselves in both positive and negative ways. Who hasn't noticed a friend's chilly attitude and wondered, "Perhaps I said something offensive without meaning to?" We use the images of ourselves reflected in other people just as we would use a mirror, as a way of examining ourselves more fully and learning our own place in the world.

When we read, empathizing with a character and putting ourselves in her place, it helps not just to look inside the

---

GETTING READY

- You will draw upon your read-aloud book during today's minilesson. Find passages in the book that show the main character interacting with secondary characters. If you can't find a place in your read-aloud to support this, many picture books, including *Dancing in the Wings*, by Debbie Allen, can easily be used for your demonstration. Or you can use read-alouds from earlier in the year, such as *Stone Fox*.

- If you are using *The Tiger Rising* as your read-aloud, you can print several passages from the *Resources for Teaching Reading* CD-ROM. Distribute passages throughout the class, one for every child, so that each partner within a partnership has a different text.

- Display the chart "Prompts to Grow Your Ideas" for children to reference throughout the session.

- Bring the chart "Strategies Readers Use to Grow Ideas About Characters," which you will add to during the link.

- In Session XIII, you will reread a portion of Chapter 14 in *The Tiger Rising* to teach children how to use precise words when describing characters.

character at her feelings and motivations but also to imagine that character's view of the world. That landscape includes setting and, also, the other people who our character sees and interacts with every day. We ask ourselves, "When this character looks out at the world, how does it look back at her? What does she see in the mirrors of others' behavior toward her? And what significance does it have for this character and for my thinking about her?" I remember

> *The development of children's imagination directly aids the development of their compassion.*

reading Ray Bradbury's story "All Summer in a Day," which takes place on another planet, where the sun only comes out every nine years. The story is about a group of schoolchildren on this planet. None of the children remembers the sun, but they have learned rote facts about it from a text-

book. Only the main character, Margot, spent part of her life on Earth and remembers warmth and light and color. When the sun makes its brief appearance, the children play a joke on Margot and lock her in a closet. I remember being practically breathless with claustrophobia and outrage at being trapped in the closet while the other children played in a lone afternoon of sunshine. The way that the other schoolchildren behave toward Margot, the jealous cruelty with which they rob her of the one thing that she wanted— to feel, again, the air and sun on her face—prompts me to think about and empathize with Margot in new ways. The way they tease Margot and set her apart from their group makes me imagine the profound sense of isolation Margot must have had, the acute homesickness she must have felt. I'm aware how different she was from the other children because of her memories. I imagine all the name calling and insults, done with mock innocence on the children's faces. And I imagine that Margot would accept this treatment with silence, never fighting back or demanding that they stop.

Of course, if we have children who tease and bully, who refuse to imagine the impact of their own behavior on others, it will be difficult for them to imagine the impact that characters in a book have on each other. And, yet, if we have such children, isn't it even more important for us to help them learn to put themselves in another's shoes? To feel the sting of insults or glares or menace in another's stead? The development of children's imagination directly aids the development of their compassion.

MINILESSON

Seeing Characters Through the Eyes of Others

CONNECTION

COACHING TIPS

Once again, rally readers to take an active stance in their reading, making the most of this phase, studying characters, too.

You'll see that once again I'm rallying kids to invest themselves in the constructive process of making memory.

"You know, when any of us reads anything, we are given a text. Maybe it contains the directions for our cell phone; maybe it is a letter from a grandparent. Whatever the text is, we take it in our hands and we make a choice. The text can be, for us, just ink blobs on a page, or it can provide us with something useful. Everything a person needs, practically, is right there in words on the page, and it is free for the taking, but the stuff we need is not right there on the surface. Instead, we have to dig for it, to figure it out, to make it into something. The better a person is at doing that work, the more that person gets from words—from those ink blobs.

This connection conjures up the intensity of the work. Again and again we ask children to dig deeper. We ask them to probe the text, to push their thinking about the text, to talk back to their first impressions. This sort of work takes practice, and it is essential to building strong reading muscles.

"Earlier this year, we talked about how each of us is the author of our life. We acknowledged each one of us can decide to construct a life in which reading matters—or not. We talked about the choices you can make about whether you'll have time in your life to read. But today I need to add on to that message. Because you can spend all the time in the world reading and get very little from these texts, or you can spend that time reading and have your life changed because of what you see on the page. Today, as you read, I want you to author a reading life that allows you to see a lot in texts and that especially allows you to see that characters are complex. I want you to try to take the work we've been doing with *The Tiger Rising*, the ways we have thought deeply about Rob's actions, and try to do the same kind of work in your independent book, on your own. I'll help you.

One of the things I'm counting on is that people can resolve to learn—that we can aspire to be more than we are. I'm trying to rally kids to buy in.

"Readers, you already know that looking closely at a person's actions can give you deep insights about his or her personality. You've been doing such smart work in *The Tiger Rising*, thinking about Rob and why he behaves the way he does.

"You've been transferring this work to your independent reading books, too. As I walked around the room yesterday and listened to you talk with your partners, I heard many of you talking about your characters. For example, I heard David talking about his *Junie B. Jones* book. He told his partner about a scene in which Junie B. is acting quiet, which as you know, is *very* out of character for her! He said it made him think that Junie B. was preoccupied, as if something big was about to happen."

Name your teaching point. Specifically, tell readers that noticing other characters' behavior toward the main character can reveal important information.

If you scan all the opening passages across a sequence of mini-lessons, you'll see that I almost always compliment children on what they've been doing in a way that also summarizes what I've taught, and you'll see that as I do this, I accumulate more specifics.

"Today I'm going to teach you that when readers want to think deeply about a character, we can examine the ways that people around the character treat the character, looking especially for patterns of behavior. We not only notice how other people, other characters, treat and view the main character, but we also notice what others call the character, and the voice and body language people assume around that character."

Notice that my teaching points are often several sentences long. In the first sentence, I name the general goal of the minilesson, and in the second or third sentence, I spell out more specific strategies I will teach readers so they can reach the goal.

TEACHING

Offer children an example, from television or film or life, of an instance when a character creates a stir among other characters. Explain how the "stir" can be revealing.

"The other day, I was watching an old western movie on TV. The first scene began by showing the main character—a standard gunslinging cowboy—slowly riding his horse up the main street of a small town. As soon as the people in the town saw him coming, they scurried into the buildings. Shopkeepers closed their windows and closed their blinds. You've probably seen the kind of movie I'm talking about. The cowboy looked around at all this and calmly continued on his way. Before he'd said or done anything at all, I was thinking, 'He's got a reputation. I bet he's pretty tough. Maybe he even kills people.' Just by watching how the other characters behaved toward him, I began to grow a theory about him.

"You can grow theories about a character in real life, too, by watching how people act toward that person. For example, I had a colleague named Martin that I didn't like very much at first. He was always late to meetings and wasn't as generous sharing his teaching ideas as the rest of the teachers. I thought he was selfish. But then, one day, I noticed that the children in Martin's classroom seemed to adore him. They always looked happy with him. They would often spend their lunch hour in the classroom with him—helping him clean up and just chatting with him. If he walked by while they were at recess, they all called out to him and waved to him. I realized that he probably is a very good teacher, and there might be reasons other than selfishness for why he is late to meetings. Seeing how wonderful Martin is through his kids' eyes helps me to change my theory about him and understand him better."

Demonstrate applying this thinking to a familiar text. In this case, think aloud about how secondary characters in *Stone Fox* reveal more about little Willy.

"I'm going to show you how we can use this strategy in books, too, by noticing the way the characters in *Stone Fox* treat little Willy. I'm thinking about the last scene in the book, when Stone Fox helps Willy win the race. This is a really important action, and very out of character for Stone Fox. Here's a man who has won every race he has entered to win money to buy his people's land back. He also doesn't seem to associate with any people who aren't Indians. And then he helps Willy beat him in a race? Instead of asking myself what this says about Stone Fox, I'm going to ask myself what it makes me think about Willy. Remember, we can grow ideas about our main character by examining how the other characters behave toward him. Well, that scene makes me think that Willy is not like other people that Stone Fox has met. For one thing, Willy is a strong opponent. Stone Fox is probably not used to people being as good as he is, and I bet he's very surprised that a young boy with just one dog is so fast. He understands how much hard work and determination it took to get that good, and maybe he's impressed. Willy is the kind of kid who impresses even a person as stoic as Stone Fox.

Teaching children to think about how secondary characters are a window to the protagonist gives them a broader scope of the main character, her world, and the kind of power or impact she has within that world. When we watch stories unfold in the theater, or in a movie, we see facial expressions and notice body language which help us understand the relationships among the characters. We are privy to the reactions and ideas of secondary characters toward the protagonist, and all these observations help us form theories and may actually challenge our preexisting beliefs about someone. As we read, we must do that same kind of work by actively thinking about the relationships between characters, the power dynamics that may exist, and what those actions and reactions may reveal about the characters inside our stories.

You'll notice that when we want to teach children how to use a strategy, we often teach by demonstrating. We role-play that we are a reader, and then we use the strategy in front of children. Your role playing is meant to function as a how-to or procedural guide, so act out the sequence of steps you hope children will undertake. You are showing them how to proceed when using the strategy and modeling the kind of thinking that might be generated. In your role playing, show children the replicable steps to take whenever using the strategy. As best you can, try to make the thinking you are modeling sound genuine and in the moment, as opposed to scripted and rehearsed.

"When readers develop a theory about a character based on one part of the book, it's smart to consider other parts of the book, too. We want to know, is this part different from the other parts, or do they all fit together to support this one big idea? In this case, does the way Stone Fox treats Willy fit with how the other characters in the book treat Willy? Well, there's Doc Smith and the mayor. There's also the teacher and a couple of other adults in the town. And, yeah, they pretty much all help and support Willy. Even Doc Smith, who suggests that Willy take his grandfather to a home for sick people, or the mayor, who doesn't want Willy to enter the race, both come out to cheer on Willy. This definitely seems like a pattern.

"After I notice a pattern in the way several characters treat the main character, I try to reach for the words to capture the idea this helps me to grow. I've noticed that Willy is stubborn, he knows what he wants, and he expresses himself well. In fact, Willy has such a powerful way of expressing himself and going after what he wants that he convinces all the other characters, even Stone Fox, that he desperately needs to win the race."

Name what you have done in a way that makes it transferable to other texts and other days.

"Did you see how I noticed the way the minor characters treat Willy—especially thinking about places where there is a pattern—and used that information to deepen my thinking about Willy? In books, and in life, we can observe the way other people behave toward a person to imagine more about what that person's life and personality are like. We do this by asking ourselves, 'How might that be significant?' and 'What does that treatment help me to imagine about this person's life?'"

ACTIVE INVOLVEMENT

Offer children an excerpt of familiar text on which they can practice this thinking. Invite them to discuss their ideas with their partner.

"I'm going to give each of you a piece of paper with a very short piece of the text. Just a few lines. I want you to take a few moments to read it over. It will be a bit of interaction between Rob and another character—either his dad, Willie May, Sistine, Mr. Beauchamp, the principal, or the Threemongers. I want you to notice what's

In the classrooms that piloted these books, all six of the teachers spoke again and again about how this year, more than ever before, the read-aloud books lived with children long after they were done being read. I've come to believe this was the result of a few things. Teachers wore a love of reading and books on their sleeves and used each day to model that in their own reading, selecting texts that were well-written and spoke to the lives of children. Also, the read-aloud books continued to live in our lessons even after the units were done. Many minilessons revisited an earlier book.

This is not a typical active involvement. It is great to find new ways to work with readers because novelty ignites interest. The sheer fact that this is a new configuration will draw kids' attention. You and your colleagues may want to take on the topic of developing new methods for actively engaging children during minilessons.

happening in the bit of text I give you and also to think back in your mind to how that character behaved toward Rob throughout the book.

"After doing some thinking on your own for a few moments, turn to your partner, who will have a different slip of paper. I'll give you a little longer than usual—about five minutes—to discuss what each of you is thinking about your slip and then to make any connections between the two characters. As you're talking, you can also be bringing in thoughts about other characters in the book."

LINK

Send readers off, reminding them to add examining secondary characters to their repertoire as a way to grow ideas about characters.

"Readers, we've learned over the past few days that it is important to think deeply about a character. When you read today and always, for the rest of your life, push yourself to grow ideas about your characters. Notice your main character's actions and ask yourself what those actions say about what kind of person he or she is. Especially take note of patterns in the character's behavior and also note when the character acts in a way that seems surprising or out of character. I am going to add to our chart 'Strategies Readers Use to Grow Ideas About Characters' so that we all remember, from this day on, that another way to get to know a character is to notice how other characters treat, speak to, and view him or her. So, today as you read, you might try this strategy, and try to let it help you write, think, and talk more deeply about your characters. At the end of reading time, you're going to have a chance to get together with your partner and talk about your characters."

It is impossible to understate the importance of partner time for our readers. In the rush of many days, it is all too easy to abandon this crucial part of our workshop. Don't let that happen! Learning research shows that we learn to do first with another that which we will later be able to do on our own! Our readers will be more independent later if we first give them many opportunities to work with others.

Strategies Readers Use to Grow Ideas About Characters

- We make a movie in our mind, drawing on the text to envision (or become) the character.

- We use our own experiences to help us walk in the character's shoes, inferring what the character is thinking, feeling, experiencing.

- We revise our mental movies as we read on, getting new details from the text.

- We notice when we feel connected to a character and use that feeling to deepen our understanding of the character.

- We read with our minds on fire and capture thoughts that lead us into grand conversations.

- We pay attention to the actions of our characters and see those actions as choices.

- We think about instances when the character seems to act out of character and think, "How might these instances lead me to revise my initial ideas about the character?" Or "Might the character be changing?"

- We notice the objects that a character holds close and think, "What might the character's relationship with this object suggest about the character?"

- We pay attention to the way other characters treat, speak to, and view the main character.

CONFERRING AND SMALL-GROUP WORK

Assessing Readers

In September you were rushing around trying to do your best to get all of the readers in your class into just-right books. At that time we suggested your assessments needn't be perfect. But now you should be able to fill out your assessments with more details about each reader based on your observations, conferences, and small-group work. You may want to refresh your memory on ways to assess by rereading the sections on assessment from Unit 1 as well as the sections in this volume. Review your notes on your students too.

Can Some Readers Move Up a Level?

Look first at the readers with whom you were conservative during your initial assessments. You weren't sure whether you should put them at the higher level or not, so you chose to leave them at the lower level. Perhaps they read more difficult books with accuracy but not with fluency, so you decided a few weeks of reading easy books would be helpful—and no doubt it has been. But by now, you'll want to check again.

> ### MID-WORKSHOP TEACHING POINT
>
> #### Readers Study Relationships as a Way to Grow More Significant Ideas About Characters
>
> I stood up from a conference I had just had with Sam and began, "Readers, I want to stop you for just a moment. I wanted to share with you the work Sam is doing in *Wringer*. He is growing his thinking about the main character, Palmer, by examining how the secondary characters, Beans and Dorothy, act toward him. Sam noticed that Beans makes Palmer do things that Palmer doesn't feel comfortable doing, like leaving a dead muskrat on Dorothy's doorstep. Dorothy, on the other hand, makes Palmer feel safe so Palmer can be who he really is. As a result, Palmer actually acts like a completely different person when he is with Dorothy than when he's with Beans. [Fig. XII-1]
>
> "Then Sam took his idea to the next level. He asked himself, 'What does this make me realize about Palmer's relationships?' Now as he reads, he's keeping a theory in mind that the way Palmer acts with Beans is that he becomes the person he thinks his father would approve of, and the way
>
> > Bean's makes Palmer do things he's not comfortable with. Dorothy makes him feel safe and he can be himself.
>
> Figure XII-1
>
> *continued on next page*

If you decide to assess your readers by returning to the leveled passages you used back in September, remember, it goes faster if you bring four children together at a table, so that less of your time will be taken up with transitions. Convene children who are reading the same level of books and sit them with their backs toward each other so they are less apt to hear each other reading the text. The advantage of hearing several children read the same text and answer the questions is that you can compare and contrast their reading of that text as well as their answers to the questions.

You'll want to develop an eye and ear for readers who are ready to move levels. Children's reading logs will be your first source of information. Look to see if the reader is able to read more pages in the same amount of time than he or she was able to do earlier. Note how many books they are finishing in a week and compare that to previous weeks. Also check to see how many books the reader has read at a level compared to other readers at the same level. The more books children have under their belts at a level, the more practice they are getting. You can have children help you do this work by giving them a survey sheet and asking them to count how many books they have read so far at their current level.

Occasionally, you might decide to begin your conference by asking readers to talk about their experience reading a book. "Does it feel like you have to work hard throughout the book, on some parts of the book, or hardly ever?" If the reader responds that she rarely has to work hard, that might suggest the reader is ready for harder books. When the child talks about his thinking, ask the child to show you a part that supports whatever the child has shared. When the child turns to a page, take a second to estimate 100 words and ask the child to read them to you. While the child is reading, follow along, keeping track of errors and fluency. If you feel that the child is reading effortlessly, you may on the spot choose to grab a book from the next level. You can again estimate 100 words and do a quick running record. Then ask the child to retell what he has read. Some teachers have found it beneficial to pull one book from each level out of their library and use those selected books to assess children, but you can also read over the child's shoulder so you can even assess a retelling of a book you don't know.

When you decide to move readers up a level, you'll want to scaffold children during this transition by creating transitional book baggies. This is a baggie that has books from the current level as well as from the new higher level. Another way to scaffold for success is to suggest that for a time, reading partners read the same book. Two readers reading from multiple copies of the same book will provide a great support for comprehension. It is even more supportive for partners to read across a series. You can get them off to a good start by giving the partners a book introduction and guiding their reading through the first chapter, of the first book.

> ## MID-WORKSHOP TEACHING POINT
>
> *continued from previous page*
>
> Palmer acts with Dorothy is that he becomes the person he wants to be but is afraid of being. Sam used his thinking to make a prediction that Palmer is not going to be a wringer like his dad and like Beans because his relationship with Dorothy is going to help him see who he really wants to be.
>
> "By starting with his thinking about the main character, and then thinking about how other characters treat that character, Sam did some truly amazing work. Readers, keep reading, but in a little while I'm going to stop you so that you can meet with your partner to talk about how you are thinking more deeply about your characters. You might study character relationships just like Sam did."
>
>

You might designate a week every four weeks when you turn your attention to assessment. You'll want to mark that week on a calendar. Many schools have created a schedule for formal assessments that matches their report card schedule. You'll want to do everything possible to ensure that children aren't languishing at levels and to be sure that readers who aren't growing get extra support.

Lift the Level of Predictions and Ideas

Meanwhile, you'll also want to be ready to assess your students' work with any of the skills you've taught, what the student can do, and be prepared to help the student take his or her work another step. This will be easier to do when students' work is not full of problems. If the reader doesn't predict, for example, it is a rather obvious reaction to help that reader do so. But you'll also want to be ready to help readers who *do* predict take their work a step further.

For example, when some readers predict, they will think about what their main character is going to do next. And by "next" they often mean within the next couple of pages. One way to lift the level of this work is to push the reader to predict further into the book. You might say, "Now that you know so much about your character and you're getting the gist of the story, what do you think he might do later?" Then you'll want to coach students to look past the next couple of pages into the next chapter or chapters.

To help readers predict beyond just the next few pages, you might coach them to use what they know about how stories go, to make a prediction about how the character will solve the main problem. You might say, "We know in stories the problem is often solved and that the main character usually solves the problem. How do you think your character will solve this problem? What makes you think that?" Then coach them to use what they know about their character's traits to help them predict. Depending on the level of sophistication of your readers, you might decide to guide them toward doing this sort of work with secondary characters. You might say, "How do you think other characters will react?" or "What do you know about the other characters? Knowing that, what do you think might happen later on?" You might say, "What are all the inside traits that will help or hurt this character as he tries to overcome these struggles?" and "What are the outside factors that will help or hurt him on his journey?"

You can also approach conferences ready to nudge readers to develop more original or interesting ideas. If a child's ideas about a text sound curious or trite or unoriginal, you might take some time to gather more information, asking "Why?" repeatedly to push the child's thinking.

Imagine you're having a conference with a child about *Those Shoes*. You ask the child, "Why does Jeremy want new shoes?" "Peer pressure?" the child answers. It's not a wrong answer, but it seems automatic, somehow, not enough. "Why?" you might ask. Perhaps the child says, "People gotta have the right sneakers or they're laughed at." Again, you could ask, "Why?" This time the kid takes a little longer before answering and then says, "Because kids don't like to stand out. They like to fit in, and that means having the right shoes." Notice how a simple question can generate powerful thinking. Alternatively, you might say, "Say more about that" or "Maybe because . . . " The point is that just as we get children to search for more precise words, we can also get them to say more precise things in conferences so that we can best tailor our instruction.

TEACHING SHARE

Readers Pause to Ask, "How Will I Be Sure to Talk Well During This Book Conversation?"

Ask readers to name some ways they can prepare for their conversations and offer them another way. Then, after a time, invite them to begin talking together.

"Readers, you are going to meet with your partner in a few minutes and have a grand conversation. I wanted to give you a few minutes to prepare for your conversation. Let's think together about ways we could get ourselves ready to have a great talk." I waited a minute for readers to think silently. "Thumbs up if you have an idea. When I point to you, share out your idea. If someone already says your idea, put your thumb down."

I pointed to Aly, who said, "I could take my idea and write using prompts like, 'The thoughts I have about this is' or 'This is important because . . .'"

I pointed to Lily, and she said, "I could use the writing prompts, 'This makes me realize . . .'"

Again I pointed, and Jasmine said, "I could think of a memory from my life that connects with the story."

Kobe said, "I could reread my Post-it notes and find an idea I think is a good one."

I pointed to Sam. "I could push myself to grow a bigger idea by thinking about how the other characters affect the main character just like I did before."

After a few more children had a chance to share, I said, "Okay readers, I just want to give you one more tip. When you have an idea about a character that is based on one part of the book, it's smart to consider whether other parts of the book support your idea and how those parts fit together. Right now, reread your ideas and think about how to get yourself ready for a grand conversation. Remember, you want to bring ideas and questions that can spark a great talk. In a few minutes, you'll have a chance to meet with your partner and get started in a conversation."

The most important part of this may be the moments of silence. Don't skip past this! Give children a chance to think. Watch their brains work.

In the writing workshop, we often suggest that before a person writes, it can help to take a moment to resolve, to aspire, saying something like, "Today I am going to try to write with really honest words," or "Today I am going to try to let myself go as I write and to write tons more than I usually do." In reading, too, it can help to create occasions in which you ask readers to pause and to think, "What will I work on today so that my work is especially strong?" In this share, I'm asking readers to aspire to talk well. This nudges them to reconsider all they've been taught—which presumably means to refer to charts—and to create a little plan for themselves. You can ask children to say out loud what they aspire to do, as I do in this instance, or you can ask them to write a self-assignment on a special Post-it or piece of paper, leaving that in front of them as they work. Once again, this reinforces the notion that students are authoring their own reading lives.

Reaching for Exactly True Words

We can all recall passages from beloved children's books that have stayed with us over the years. One of my all-time favorites is a line in Cynthia Rylant's picture book *When the Relatives Came*, in which Rylant writes about that first night, when the house is chock-full of cousins, sleeping here and there throughout the house. She writes, "It was hard going to sleep with all that new breathing in the house." How I love that line. I read it and say, "That's it, exactly." Language works for me when it captures life, when it puts something into words for which there are no words. I cherish language that is precise and clear.

When we teach reading, we teach children to work in ways that are ultimately invisible. We can't actually observe children's reading, so we observe their talking and writing about reading. That's okay, because as children become stronger at talking and writing about reading, they become better at thinking about reading. The thoughts any one of us has in the privacy of our own minds are largely internalized conversations we've had in the hubbub of the world. For all these reasons, teaching reading has a lot to do with teaching children to put their fleeting thoughts into words.

GETTING READY

- You will be using your class read-aloud in today's minilesson. Identify a part of the book where characters' actions or feelings can be described in many ways that will allow children to reach for more precise words. If you are using *The Tiger Rising*, you can reread a part of Chapter 14 during today's lesson.

- Prepare the chart you may choose to title "To Make Sure I Am Using Precise Words, I Can Ask Myself . . ."

- Check your Post-it bins before today's minilesson because you can expect readers will be making lots of Post-its today.

- Session XIV requires that many of your readers' books contain at least half a dozen Post-its. If your children struggle to produce ample Post-its, especially ones that will set them up to do deep character work, you may find it helpful to teach a minilesson prior to the upcoming session that channels kids to look back over what they have already read, recalling and/or developing and writing ideas on Post-its. You may, alternatively, simply lead a small group today for children who need this support. If this is necessary for your class, see the extension to this session for a suggestion about that minilesson or small group.

- To prepare for Session XIV, look through your copy of *The Tiger Rising* and choose Post-its that students can look between, noticing which go together to synthesize insights about characters into interpretations of books.

Most of the time, when we help children read as well as they can, our focus is on the book or on the strategies readers use to interact with the book. We teach kids to read closely, to return to the text continually, to ask questions and search the text for answers, to carry questions and theories with them as they read on, and to entertain more than one idea. All of that is work that assumes the use of language but doesn't spotlight the language itself. It also makes

> *As children become stronger at talking and writing about reading, they become better at thinking about reading.*

sense to once in a while shine a spotlight on the language children use to talk and think about reading. If children use only simple sentences and the Dolch list of most frequently used words to convey their thoughts about characters and texts, it is unlikely that their thoughts will be complex and developed, nuanced and precise, vivacious and daring.

In this session, you'll say to children, "It is important to reach for the exactly right word, the true word." For instance, when a child says "hot," you'll ask, "Tepid, warm, or scalding?" just as you won't settle for "good guy" when there are more specific words to describe a character who might be anything from a bumbling, amiable type to a heroic, magnificent Adonis. You'll also suggest that often there is no one word that will capture an idea: People use figurative language to say what can't be shoehorned into a single word. Moments in your read-alouds when Dahl says about a witch's face: "It looks as though it had been pickled in vinegar!" or Rylant writes of October, "fat heavy pumpkins dot the farmers' fields," will be moments when you pause and celebrate picturesque speech—marveling at and repeating any turn of phrase that helps bring a reader's mental movie into precise focus.

In many schools, I find that children are far more comfortable retelling an incident than articulating an idea. When asked to write literary essays, many children's ideas are extraordinarily simple, almost crude. "Poppleton is nice," a child will claim. "Poppleton is a good friend." Then children switch to mining their book for examples that illustrate the idea, and they write with much more ease.

Helping a child talk in true and precise ways about Poppleton can be consequential. We want children who, in recognizing scarlet, crimson, ruby, or rusty as more precise forms of red, have a larger word repertoire—a repertoire that continually expands as they read. Ultimately, this increased word repertoire means access to a vast and varied inventory of *kinds* of ways, states, and things in the world around them. Of course, there are practical benefits to this. A child who can tell you about "a sudden sharp pain that increases when I bend," is far easier to help than one whose "tummy hurts" or another who merely grimaces and howls. There are enormous academic benefits, too—better reading scores, more effective college essays. But there are other benefits that are purely abstract, and we're lucky when we see them. In *Waking Up in America,* Natalie Goldberg describes a high school teacher of hers who one day turned off the lights and instructed the class to listen to the rain. Natalie describes how this single experience guided her to many ways of seeing, thinking, feeling, and even teaching. Thirty years later, she traced the teacher to thank him. The teacher was dumbfounded; she'd never said a word in his class, he recalled with wonder. He'd never known she even cared.

And so, too, when we initiate the conscious struggle toward more precise thought and speech in our children,

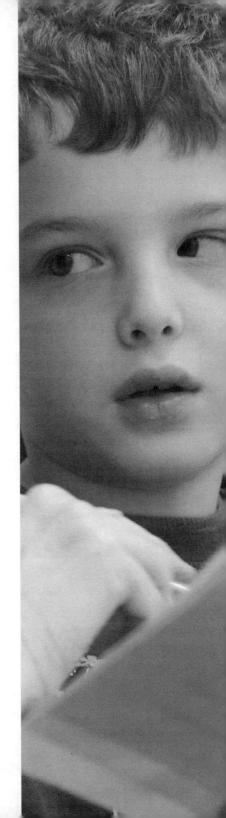

we probably won't get many outward signs when thoughtfulness and perceptiveness increase or ability to problem-solve or analyze takes invisible root. Whoever said lofty, long-term goals came with immediate gratification anyway? But knowing that reflective teaching has layered benefits—among them, the power to change the world—helps us plant the seeds with care.

Today, then, is one of many lessons throughout this series designed to help kids talk, write, and most of all, to think with precision, nuance, and clarity. Over the past few sessions, you've helped children grow ideas about characters. By the time you teach this session, kids will be generating ideas about characters, and now you will want to lift the level of that work. This session assumes that one way to raise the level of children's thinking is to help them use more precise language to convey that thinking.

MINILESSON

Reaching for Exactly True Words

CONNECTION

Celebrate that children are noticing the decisions that characters in books make, and the actions they take, and letting those decisions and actions act as clues about the characters.

"I remember one day when my son came home from school, slammed the door, threw his stuff onto the kitchen table, and then plopped himself on a chair like a sack of flour.

"Watching this scene, I formed a theory about Miles. 'You're upset,' I said.

"I'm telling you this because I know you do the same thing I do. You *read* people. I can tell that some of you notice little things that I do at the start of a day, for example, and you whisper to each other, 'It's gonna be a good day,' or, 'Watch out.'

"You read people not only in real life but also in books. You've been paying attention to what your characters do, and you've been using that information as clues, helping you to theorize about the sort of person a character is. In our read-aloud, you've seen ways that Rob, the main character, acts, and you've realized that others could act differently, and that has helped you grow ideas about Rob. The other day, we talked about the decision Rob makes to talk to Sistine on the bus, and we talked about the fact that other kids might not be so thrilled at that prospect of talking to Sistine. So we grew ideas about the main character not only from noticing what he does, but also from realizing that his actions are decisions and realizing that others could decide differently. When we really stopped to think about Rob's decision to engage in a conversation with Sistine on the bus, we speculated that perhaps this means Rob is lonely and eager for a friend. We decided that maybe Rob sees something in Sistine that he relates to.

One of the tricks in writing minilessons is to remember that we're aiming to reach youngsters. When I choose anecdotes and examples, I try to make them accessible to kids.

You'll notice, of course, that much of what I'm saying is review. The previous session's emphasis was on the fact that we read people just like we read characters, and I'm now essentially repeating myself. I do think that when we're trying to affect another person's actions, we need to be repetitive. I think, for example, of how many times I've corrected my son's grammar when he says, "Me and Jack." "Jack and I," I say, and he nods his head, acknowledging that somehow my correction hasn't yet managed to sink in. So, yes, repeat yourself.

"And I know when you are reading your own independent books, you are also noticing decisions your character makes, actions he or she takes, and you are letting those function as clues, helping you to figure out stuff about the people in your books."

Name your teaching point. Specifically, tell children that it helps to reach for precise words to convey something about a character.

"Because all of you are growing lots of ideas about your characters, today I want to teach you a technique that smart readers use to help us grow not just any ol' ideas about characters, but *wise and sophisticated* ideas. And specifically, I want to teach you that it can help to try to reach for the exactly, precisely true word (or words) to convey something about a character."

TEACHING

Tell kids to watch as you read aloud and then reach for precise words to talk about a character. Struggle as you do so to demonstrate specific techniques.

"So right now, I'm going to reread a little bit from Chapter 14 of *The Tiger Rising,* and you'll see me notice Sistine's actions and decisions (I do that always, just by instinct now). As I do so, pay close attention to how I come up with words to describe the sort of person Sistine seems to be.

By now you've become accustomed to the predictable structure of the method of demonstration I use during the teaching component of a minilesson. There is always a setup, a demonstration, and a debrief (think of these as shaped like a capital L). Moreover, the setup almost always contains a restatement of the teaching point and usually creates a bit of context that helps to show how or when I reach for a particular strategy. Then the setup tells children what their job will be during the ensuing demonstration. What should they be watching for? What should they expect they'll need to do later with whatever they notice?

"Notice, specifically, that I take the time to reach for the exactly, precisely true words to describe her." I read the first page of Chapter 14 and a tiny bit beyond that.

> "What's he doing out here?" she demanded.
>
> Rob shrugged. "I don't know," he said. "He's Beauchamp's, I guess."
>
> "Beauchamp's what?" said Sistine. "His pet?"
>
> "I don't know," said Rob. "I just like looking at him. Maybe Beauchamp does, too. Maybe he just likes to come out here and look at him."

There are several instances within these pages in which Sistine acts in a determined way, standing up for something she passionately believes in. My goal was to demonstrate for children how I tried on different words to describe Sistine before landing on a descriptor (of more than one word) that felt exactly, precisely true.

"That's selfish," said Sistine.

Rob shrugged.

"This isn't right, for this tiger to be in a cage. It's not right."

"We can't do nothing about it," Rob said.

"We could let him go," said Sistine. "We could set him free." She put her hands on her hips. It was a gesture that Rob had already come to recognize and be wary of.

"We can't," he said. "There's all them locks."

"We can saw through them."

"Naw," said Rob. The mere thought of letting the tiger go made his legs itch like crazy.

"We have to set him free," Sistine said, her voice loud and certain.

"Nuh-uh," said Rob. "It ain't our tiger to let go."
"It's our tiger to save," Sistine said fiercely.

Looking up from the book, I said, "So, I'm thinking that Sistine is *bossy*. She is a bossy friend. And I say this because she seems to order Rob around a lot. The tiger isn't hers. It's not even her *discovery*. Yet she talks about what she and Rob should do with it as if the tiger—and the decision—belong to her. This isn't the first time Sistine has been bossy. On several occasions throughout the book, she's told Rob what to do and what not to do. She's definitely bossy."

Then I paused. "Oops," I said. "My goal is to use precise words to talk and think about characters, and I've just said that Sistine is bossy. That's not the most precise word I could choose! And it doesn't really say much about Sistine as a person. It really just describes her behavior. I know Sistine is more complicated than her actions.

"Do you see, readers, that I am on watch as I do this work? Sometimes I catch myself using generic, general, nonspecific words to describe a character, or really, to convey any of my reading ideas. When I catch myself doing that, I say, 'Oops,' and then I press rewind on the tape of life, and I back time up so I can try again. Watch."

Notice that almost always, the passages that we read aloud with a minilesson are brief ones. It can be tricky to time your read-aloud work so you're always on the brink of reading aloud just the passage you need for your minilesson, so the solution is to do a lot of rereading within your minilesson.

It's absolutely essential to tuck how-to tips into the demonstration. When my graduate students compose units of study, their biggest challenge is learning to do this. Their instinct is to say, "Watch me as I . . ." and then to dazzle the kids with a fait accompli. That doesn't go far toward giving kids the know-how to do on their own what the teacher has demonstrated. One way to embed tips is to first show kids that you encounter difficulties and then demonstrate the step-by-step process you use to rescue yourself. That's what I'm doing in this minilesson.

This time, I thought aloud in a mulling sort of a voice. "Let's see. Sistine seems to me to be bossy. No, let me be more specific. Exactly what is she like? Um . . . controlling? Sistine is being bossy and controlling, yes, but she's much more than bossy. Feisty maybe? Hmm, . . . I'd say she's passionate. She's speaking up for something she believes in. She's fighting for that tiger with all her might. She's awfully fiery and determined, isn't she? Actually, she reminds me a bit of Willy in *Stone Fox*. Sistine isn't willing to let the fact of ownership get in her way anymore than she'll be stopped by the locks on a cage, or by the fact that the tiger, if it gets out, will surely turn on her. Sistine wants to "save" the tiger, she wants to "set him free." She thinks Beauchamp is being "selfish" and that what he's doing "isn't right." It seems to me that Sistine is on a mission. She's a person with a cause."

Name the thinking you used to avoid thinking in circles. Specifically, teach kids to self-monitor for vague language and then to rewind and try again. Teach them that more words are generally more precise than a single word.

Then, stepping out of the role of the child, I said to the kids, "Do you see how from two general words I generated a little list of other possible words, ones that are more precise descriptors of Sistine? As I think of a word, I consider it, thinking, 'Is this exactly true?' Then, 'Is this?' Then I take a few words that feel right and run with them, coming up with more and more to say that accurately describes this character. Conveying something about a character requires precision, and often that means going beyond labels, coming up with a list of words and then trying them on for size until you have the words that make a complex, fuller picture of a person.

"Often it seems to me that no one word sums up a person, because, after all, people are complicated. So sometimes I find other ways to capture what a person is like. Sometimes I compare a person to something. Like I might say, 'She is like a porcupine. She seems all prickly and dangerous, but really, underneath all those prickles, she has a soft belly.'

"So let me see if I can say something about Sistine that feels true. It seems to me that Sistine is passionate and determined and a real believer in justice. She doesn't let fear or rules or friends get in her way when she believes in something big. Something like freedom.

Notice how I demonstrate moving from single-word descriptors to almost a mini essay, thinking and then revising my thinking out loud. I am doing two things here: First, I am showing children how to move through their initial thoughts to land on thinking that rings true. Second, I am showing children that sometimes being precise means saying more words. Sometimes we need to speak at greater length to find an accurate, true depiction of someone or something.

When my sons applied to college, they each needed to select five words that best represented them. It's not an easy thing to reduce yourself to a handful of words. Try it.

You're probably listing the usual suspects: enthusiastic, hard-working, kind. The problem is, those words could be used for half your friends. So try again, and this time, try to capture the uniqueness of you. Reach for the precisely right words that capture your idiosyncratic ways. Instead of enthusiastic, are you zealous? Optimistic? Responsive? Then, too, you'll want to think between the words you've chosen. If you find yourself settling upon a list like this: resolute, industrious, patient, you may decide those terms all capture just one side of you, and that to create a fuller sense of yourself, one with more dimension, you need some terms that provide a contrast, perhaps irreverent or carefree or spontaneous.

"Do you see, readers, that when I set out to describe Sistine, I first did what you have been doing and paid attention to her actions? But then, when coming up with words that would describe her specifically, I tried several out to see which fit her precisely, just as someone might try clothes on to see which fit best. So I came up with a little list of possible words for describing her and then selected the ones from that list that work the best and used those words to talk at more length about Sistine, painting a fuller, more accurate portrait of her that felt right."

ACTIVE INVOLVEMENT

Read children a passage from the text and then have them describe the character in that passage using precise words.

"So let's try this. Let's finish this chapter, holding on to our new, precise image of Sistine, and see if we can say something equally precise about Rob. We've talked at length about both Sistine and Rob, and our descriptions of these characters—our ideas about them—have changed and grown. Listen closely as I read and keep your minds open to the most accurate pictures you might draw of Rob. Be sure to notice the tiny details that the author gives us."

I read the rest of the chapter.

> The tiger stopped pacing. He pricked his ears back and forth, looking somewhere past Sistine and Rob.
>
> "Shhh," said Rob. The tiger cocked his head. All three of them listened.
>
> "It's a car," said Rob. "A car's coming. It's Beauchamp. We got to go. Come on."
>
> He grabbed her and pulled her into the woods. She ran with him. She let him hold on to her hand. It was an impossibly small and bony hand, as delicate as the skeleton of a baby bird. They ran together, and Rob felt his heart move inside him—not from fear or exertion but from something else. It was as if his soul had grown and was pushing up higher in his body. It was an oddly familiar feeling, but he couldn't remember what it was called.
>
> "Is he behind us?" Sistine asked breathlessly.

In a minilesson like this one, you will see that although I convey one general teaching point, I also give learners a ladder of specific tips that they can use. Some of the tips are fairly accessible. A reader can listen to herself, guarding against the use of a very general term and, when noticing that she has used that term, can think, "Oh, no," and then rewind that bit of conversation, of thinking, and try it again. That's something most children can do, and you'll want to organize your strugglers to spend more time doing just this. On the other hand, some of the pointers in this minilesson are extremely advanced. Not many of your children are ready to reach for metaphors that capture the complexity of a character. This will fly right over the heads of half your class! But gather your more advanced children into a small group and help them tap into the power of this bit of advice.

You needn't rely on this particular scene. Molly Feeney, for example, gave this minilesson drawing on the scene in which Rob's father reads the letter from Mr. Phelmer, telling him that Rob has been suspended until his rash clears up. Rob says, "Yes, sir" over and over to his dad, agreeing with everything his dad is saying. When Molly asked her class to come up with precise descriptions of Rob, one group said he was a robot—mechanical. They quickly realized that Rob is part of the word robot and were delighted. When we ask children to think about language choices—to be accurate in their speech—their discoveries of words and word connections grow!

Rob shrugged; it was hard to move his shoulders up and down and keep hold of Sistine's hand at the same time.

Sistine said, "Stop shrugging your shoulders at me. I hate it. I hate the way you shrug all the time."

And that made Rob remember Willie May saying that when he shrugged he looked like a skinny bird trying to fly. It struck him as funny now. He laughed out loud at the thought of it. And without asking him what he was laughing about, without dropping his hand, without stopping, Sistine laughed, too. Then Rob remembered the name of the feeling that was pushing up inside him, filling him full to overflowing. It was happiness. That was what it was called.

"Let's pause there. Hmm, . . . I'm thinking about what we have learned in these pages (and earlier—readers are always drawing on earlier stuff as well) that can help us come up with theories about Rob. (I reviewed a couple of details.) Hmm, . . . what are some more precise words that could describe him? Stop and jot. *[Figs. XIII-1 and XIII-2]*

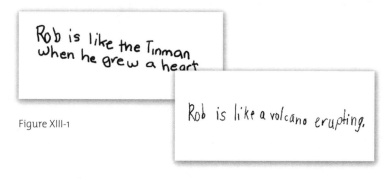

Figure XIII-1

Figure XIII-2

"Remember that sometimes, there is no one single word that will do it. Sometimes it helps to compare a person. Think for a moment about what you are trying to say. Could you make your point by describing Rob as being like another character in another book? As being like an animal? An object? Here are some questions you can ask yourself to make sure you are using precise words, words that come from the heart: *[Fig XIII-3]*

"For a second, talk with your partner and see if the two of you can come up with a way to describe Rob by likening him to something or someone else."

The children talked.

The active involvement section of a minilesson allows us, as teachers, a chance to teach through guided practice. That is, it allows us to provide scaffolds, which will be removed during independent reading. Notice the various ways in which kids' work is supported. First, I ask children to think about Rob. It's not an accident that I take on Sistine, whose character has been a bit less developed through class work, and leave Rob—the character the class has discussed more than anyone—for children to think about. Then, too, I select a passage that reveals Rob, so the children are set up for success. I read that passage aloud with as much expression and clarity as possible so the kids are able to envision and get back inside the scene.

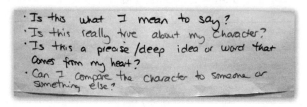

Figure XIII-3

As we proceed, I push students to remember everything they already know about Rob and draw upon that as well as on this passage. I give children a list of pointers on how to do this well, and I ask them to talk with a partner who is trying to do similar work. Then I share a copy of effective examples of what I hope they've done. In all these and other ways, I've provided scaffolds that make it likely children will have supported practice doing what I've just demonstrated.

"Readers, can I stop you? I heard Aly say that Rob is a bit like a turtle. He is in a hard shell, and he is kind of scared so he doesn't come out of it. But in this scene he is popping his head out, getting out of his shell. I heard Gabe and Rosa say that Rob is happy, and then they realized that *happy* is one of the words we retired today!

"Gabe and Rosa also realized that Rob is more than happy. They decided *overjoyed* was a better word, and then they realized that actually, Rob is practically bursting with joy. They noticed the line 'It was as if his soul had grown and was pushing up higher in his body.' They thought Rob was like a bottle of soda that bubbles over when you take the top off too quickly.

"Readers, these are such terrific, precise descriptions of Rob. *I* think of him as one of those wooden Russian nesting dolls. Have you seen those? The smallest one is solid and about the size of your pinky. It fits into a doll a bit bigger than it, which fits into one a bit bigger than it, and so on. There are about six or seven of those dolls nestled inside of each other and they remind me of Rob, with all of those different selves inside of him."

LINK

Remind children that characters' choices reveal who they are.

"So, readers, I know today you will be reading with your minds on fire, paying attention to lots of things in your books and capturing your mind work on Post-it notes. And I know that above all, you will always be reading the people in your book. Remember to pay attention to your character's choices because those reveal who that person is, and you can become aware of that if you pause and think, 'He could have chosen differently. It is telling me something that he made this choice.' Remember, too, that your ideas about characters will be more sophisticated if you take the time to reach for the precisely right word—and usually that means generating a little list of possible words, or of images, and choosing the one that fits your character just right.

"And meanwhile, I'm going to think again about Miles last night. He seemed upset, but could he have been depressed? Full of despair? Impatient? Like a stormy day? Like a thunderstorm? Hmm, . . . Off you go!"

CONFERRING AND SMALL-GROUP WORK

Help Students Reach for More Nuanced Language

As you immerse your readers in wonderful books and in your print-rich classroom, they will live in a sea of language. Some children seem to easily take in the words and expressions they encounter in texts and conversations, but many of your children will let book language simply wash over them. These children will rarely add new words and expressions to their own oral language. Research shows that the best way children can build vocabulary is through reading; you can accelerate that process by encouraging children to incorporate the words and expressions they encounter in texts into their own oral and written language so that they own that vocabulary. That is, you'll want your children to try on words just as you want them to try on anything they're learning.

How important it is to teach children to reach toward precise, exact words so that they can communicate the complexity of their thinking and convey exactly what they mean! It is said that Native Alaskans living in the Arctic Circle have twenty words for snow because in their world, snow is such a part of daily life no one word can convey all its distinct forms. For them it matters, on a survival level, that snow is described with precision. Just as one word wouldn't adequately describe all the nuances of snowy weather in the Arctic Circle, one simple word can't capture the nuances of a character's traits or feelings. For exam-

> ## MID-WORKSHOP TEACHING POINT
>
> ### Readers Use More than One Word to Convey an Idea
>
> "Readers, lots of times when I want to capture a feeling or an idea for which there are no good words, I find myself trying over and over to reach for the words to say what I mean. In between each effort, I write, 'In other words . . .' or 'That is. . . .' So I might, for example, write, 'I love my mother. In other words, my mother is at the center of my life. That is, my mother is like the anchor that holds me in place. In other words, my mother is the sunshine of my life.'
>
> "Right now, take the idea or feeling you have about a character in your book and try reaching repeatedly for ways to say what you mean. Between each effort, write, 'In other words . . .' or 'That is . . .' or 'What I really mean is. . . .'"
>
> As children worked, I coached into their work, suggesting they try this one way or another and celebrating when they took risks. After a few minutes, I intervened to reiterate what I hope they'd learned that they would take with them to another day, another text.
>
>

ple, we often hear children describe Rob as sad. Imagine if someone summed you up with that one word: You are sad. You'd protest, right? *Sometimes* you are sad, but really, it isn't sad so much as . . . what? Homesick? Frustrated? Yearning still to find your place in the world? The truth of the matter is that Rob, also, can't be contained within that one word. He is so much more than sad. Sad doesn't begin to capture the hollowness he feels over the loss of his mother. He is heartbroken, unanchored, desperately trying to hold all his feelings at bay. Likewise, *Stone Fox*'s Willy is often described as determined, yet he is so much more than that. He is resolute, unwavering, stubborn even. When we talk about our characters with specific and nuanced language, we are more likely to understand them better.

If you want to develop children's vocabulary, equip them with words you believe will matter, show them the endless source of words available in their reading, and encourage them to be risk takers. Push them to try on new ways of talking and thinking, to use unfamiliar words even before they fully grasp what those words mean. The wonderful thing is that as you support children's vocabulary, you will also support their thinking. Above all, you'll be helping them think with more precision—more specificity.

Teach Children to Reach for Precise Words to Talk About Characters

Realizing that she'd perhaps been so focused on struggling readers that she hadn't supported the strong ones enough, Kathleen spent a few minutes before the reading workshop looking through the bins of a few of her stronger readers. She noticed their books, their logs, and any Post-its they'd made as they read. Then she tapped four students on their shoulders and whispered for them to bring their books and join her in the meeting area.

Kathleen began the strategy lesson by getting right to the point. "I gathered you together because I want to teach you something that is going to help you read, think, and talk about your characters with more power and more passion. Earlier I studied the thinking you've been doing as you read" she gestured to their Post-its stuck in their books, "and I was so glad to see that you are capturing your thoughts. That lets me peer in on your mind work, which is really cool, and the great thing is it lets you do that, too. When I studied your Post-its, what I noticed is that you tend to write general ideas about characters. You seem to write your first thoughts. I've heard you *voice* pearls of insight, yet you don't tend to write those down. For example, I found a Post-it that said something like, 'The character is smart.' That says *something* about the character, but if that reader had pushed harder, she could have been much more specific. People are smart in so many different ways. What is *this* character's particular kind of smartness?

"Today I want to teach you that invested readers who are working hard to understand characters reach for specific language to describe them. Let me show you what I mean. In the book I'm reading, I could have written a Post-it that says, 'My character is smart.' Instead, I pushed my thinking and imagined a chain of more descriptive words that also mean 'smart.' Let's see. So far I've got stuff like: intelligent—wise—hmm, let me push harder. Sly, savvy, curious, precocious. What else? Worldly, know-it-all, brilliant, genius, practical?

"Just calling my character 'smart' could mean any ol' thing. Let's see, which of those words describes her best? I wouldn't say she's a genius. She isn't worldly because she's never really left her hometown. Hmm, . . . she's sort of older than the rest of her family and they go to her for advice. I *could* say she's wise and she's mature." Kathleen jotted that.

Kathleen paused to process how she came up with the most specific word. "Did you see that? I took a general word like *smart,* and I imagined different kinds of smart. Then I thought, 'What kind of smart is my character?' and reached for a more precise way of describing her.

"Now it's your turn to try this," Kathleen said, her small-group instruction following the same patterns as minilessons. "Look back in your books and find a Post-it where you described your character with general words that don't precisely describe him or her. Then, on the bottom of the Post-it, push harder to get more specific. Maybe you'll imagine a chain of words like I did and pick the words that can most precisely describe your character. Do that now, and I'll help as needed."

The students began flipping through their pages and quickly found Post-its they could revise. Kathleen leaned in toward Fallon, who had settled on a Post-it on which she had written, "Fran is kind."

"What are you thinking?" Kathleen asked.

"Saying that Fran is kind is sort of, you know, general. I can say it better."

"That's a good place to start. What question will you ask yourself to help you become more specific about Fran?"

"What kind of kind is Fran?" Fallon grinned broadly at her own wordplay. Kathleen gestured with a joyous thumbs up and left her space to continue. "'Cause she's, um, sort of a good person, caring, you know, the sort who'd be a good friend."

"Push harder, get more specific," Kathleen coached.

"And she helps people, too." Fallon jotted a few more precise words on her Post-it. *[Fig. XIII-4]*

"You can be more specific, Fallon. Remember when you talked about Sistine with such insight? Try to think that deeply about this character. Jot down some thinking and I'll see it later."

Kathleen left Fallon, who had flopped over on her belly on the rug, chin propped on her hands, biting her lip in thought. She moved to coach the other kids in the group. Josh was struggling to find other ways to say "Hazel is cautious," and didn't have anything written down.

Figure XIII-4

"Josh, are you stuck?" Kathleen asked.

"Yup. I don't know how to say 'cautious' in another way. That seems pretty specific to me."

"It's a good word, but can you say more? Make a word chain. I'll start us off. Cautious, worried—now you add one."

"Careful?" Josh said, unsure.

"Cautious, worried, careful, hmmm, withdrawn," Kathleen said using a gesture to suggest she was passing the word chain back to Josh.

Josh added, gaining momentum, "Scared, afraid, like, sort of on guard."

"Great! So now you've got more precise ways to say 'cautious.' Think about which ones best describe your character." Josh started jotting on a new Post-it as Kathleen moved on to the next student. *[Fig. XIII-5]*

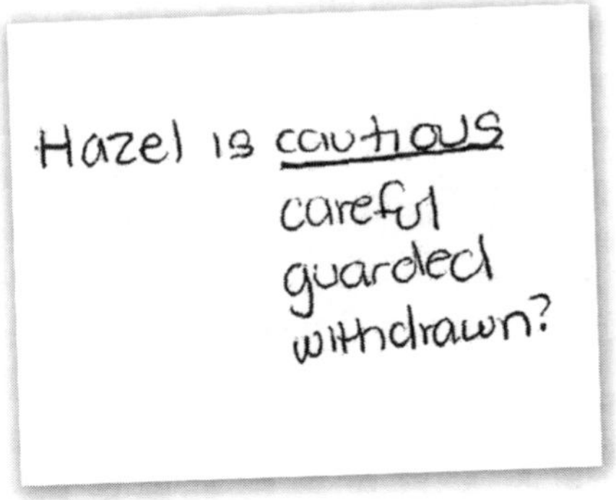

Figure XIII-5

After briefly coaching everyone, Kathleen reconvened the group. "Show the person next to you how you pushed harder so that your ideas about your character became more precise." The children talked for a moment.

As the children talked, Kathleen continued coaching, sometimes using familiar terms so that one word or two could convey a lot of meaning: "Be specific," or "Add more detail." Other times Kathleen herself used more specific and detailed prompts such as, "I'm having a hard time picturing her face. Can you say more about what she looks like? I get that she's sad, but does she have a quivering chin? A blank look on her face? Are tears forming in her eyes? What does sad *look* like for her? Is she dismayed? Bereft? Or just a little melancholy?"

Reconvening the group, Kathleen said, "So readers, remember this: Whenever you're reaching for the words to capture another person, whether that person lives in your story or in your life, instead of sticking with language that is general, such as 'She's nice,' or 'He's sad,' or 'She's funny,' it helps to reach for the most precise word possible. You might push your thinking by imagining a word chain and then, out of that word chain, picking the words that truly capture your character. Alternatively, you can ask yourself, 'What kind of nice/brave/smart/funny, etc., is this person?' Over the next few days, I'm going to be looking for evidence that you are working hard at becoming more precise."

Approach Your Teaching with a Pocketful of Ideas for How to Scaffold Children's Ways with Words

As you engage in this sort of teaching, you will, of course, teach kids some new words. Keep in mind as you do this that you needn't reach for the million-dollar words—for words such as *loquacious* and *petulant* and *abrasive*. When young people are coached by Princeton Review or Kaplan to develop their vocabularies in preparation for those all-important SAT exams, these companies always focus first and foremost on the words that are familiar to students, words that they know but do not yet control. This, of course, is the same philosophy that Donald Bear follows when supporting children's spelling development. He suggests working first with the parts of words that children "use and confuse." Your goal, too, should be to work within kids' "zones of proximal development," supporting next steps, not perfection. Channel children toward words such as *bold, cranky, lonely, observant*, or better yet, toward phrases such as "prickly on the outside, but soft on the inside" or "always watching with keen eyes and a sharp mind, ready to pounce."

When you teach students words, be sure not to teach the words in isolation. Show your children that they can take any word that suggests an emotion—sad, mad, glad—and then take that word up or down a notch or two. "What's a little more than mad?" you can ask. "What's even more mad than that?" With your help, kids will generate a spectrum of words such as *peeved, mad, angry, furious*, and *irate*. Some teachers have decided to equip their kids with language bookmarks. The youngsters in Erin Handley's class, for example, created slips of paper that named and illustrated an emotion, and some children would leave one of these slips of paper tucked between the pages of their book whenever they especially noticed a character feeling the emotion on that slip of paper. These slips, then, functioned almost as premade Post-it notes.

As you talk with your children, you'll sometimes notice them using new words in ways that feel just a bit forced and awkward. When I was working with Tyrell, someone entered the classroom—a man I didn't know. Tyrell saw the question in my eyes and said to me, "That's Mr. Roberts, the custodian." Then I watched Tyrell's eyes flick to his synonym bookmark, and he added, "He's valiant."

I had to hold back a belly laugh. It was charming to hear this young-ster use such an old-fashioned and venerable term to describe the young man who was trying to repair their broken window shade. But I masked my giggle and said, "That's so interesting; he's valiant. Why do you describe him that way?" Tyrell said, grinning, "That shade has broken ten times, and every time he comes to our classroom to try to fix it. He never gives up." Then he added, "And he stands on the tables. He's brave."

Teach Children To Use a More Expansive Vocabulary to Talk About Their Characters

Earlier you listened in on Kathleen's strategy lesson in which she helped fairly proficient readers use more precise language as they wrote, thought, and talked about their characters. It is, of course, important to tailor this instruction so that it also helps students who face more challenges as readers and as talkers. I convened a group that included Rosa (an ELL), Tyrell and Gabe (both of whom had been pushing themselves to say more about their stories and characters), and Kobe and Izzy (both of whom were able to read texts at a higher level than Rosa, Tyrell, and Gabe but who tended to think and talk in generalities about their characters).

"This morning while you all were at music, I was flipping through your books and checking out your Post-its to get an idea of what you've been thinking as you read. What I noticed is that you used certain words over and over and over again to describe your characters. So many of your Post-its describe your characters as 'nice' or 'sad' or 'happy' or 'mad.' While the words say *something* about your character, they don't say

enough because they aren't very powerful words. Besides, they don't show what you're thinking about the character. When I see the word 'nice,' for example, I wonder what kind of 'nice' you mean. Generous? Kind? Friendly? Welcoming? Sweet? What does 'nice' *mean*, anyway?

"Today I want to teach you that we can push our thinking so that we describe our characters. We can use stronger, more powerful words that reveal what we know and think about them. Let me show you what I mean. Imagine I wrote this Post-it about the Threemongers: 'The Threemongers are mean!' When I reread it, I realize it's a bit lazy; it doesn't say what I mean specifically enough. So I want to push myself to use more powerful, precise words to say what I'm thinking about the Threemongers. Let me see. I'm going to write some words that mean the same thing as *mean* but are more powerful. Help me do this." I jotted down some words on a chart and invited the students to pitch in.

"Nasty!" shouted Tyrell gleefully.

"Disrespectful," offered Izzy, with a rather prim glance at Tyrell, who said, "Well they are nasty!"

The students quickly added to the list so that after no more than a minute, it read:

> **Words to Describe the Threemongers:**
>
> | | |
> |---|---|
> | Nasty | Bully |
> | Disrespectful | Rotten |
> | Unkind | Rude |
> | Unfriendly | Snotty |

"Wow, that's some list. You know what I noticed? Some of these words can be used to describe a character that's somewhat mean, and some of them are for very mean characters. We can put these words into categories: somewhat mean and very mean. Let's do it together." I wrote the two headings on another piece of chart paper and invited students to call out their suggestions for categorizing the words.

"Bullying is super mean," Kobe said.

"Rude is just sort of mean. It's just like not that nice, but not really hurting anyone," Gabe said when I nudged him to join in the conversation.

After a moment, our list looked like this:

> | **Somewhat Mean** | **Very Mean** |
> |---|---|
> | Snotty | Nasty |
> | Unfriendly | Bullying |
> | Rude | Unkind |
> | Disrespectful | |

"So, readers, we've come up with a range of more words that mean the same thing as *mean*. Now, if I were to describe the Threemongers, instead of saying they're *mean*, I could write, 'The Threemongers are really nasty. They are bullies.' Doesn't that show more of my thinking about the Threemongers than simply saying they are mean?"

The kids agreed, Tyrell enthusiastically offering, "They're snotty, too. I hate them!"

"Now let's think about your work. As I said earlier, I looked through your Post-its and found some lazy, tired words like *nice, sad, happy*, and *mad*. I put a little star on the Post-its that had those words. Find one of the Post-its in your book with a little star on it." The students quickly located these. "So let's push our thinking. Reread the part where you jotted the Post-it that your character is nice, happy, sad, or mad."

After a minute, I stopped them, saying, "As you reread and rethink about your character, consider whether your character is just *somewhat* nice, mad, happy, or sad or *very* nice, mad, happy, or sad. Tell the person next to you what you're thinking." The students turned and talked about this for a moment, and I stopped them again. "Now, look, I made us some bookmarks that list a range of words that mean either somewhat nice or very nice—or mad, happy, or sad—that we can use to find more powerful ways of describing our characters. Find a word on the bookmark that does a better job of describing your character. If you think of a word that's not on the bookmark, add it yourself." The children did so.

"So, readers, when we're about to jot down a lazy, tired ol' word to describe a character, like *nice, mad, happy, sad*, and so on, remember that we can stop and push ourselves to use stronger, more powerful words that better describe what we're thinking about our characters. You can use these bookmarks to help you think of a range of words, and, of course, feel free to add more words to them or to make your own bookmarks for other lazy words you see."

TEACHING SHARE

Readers Share Our Talents with Others

Ask readers to notice their own reading talents and share that expertise with their partners.

"Recently, we talked about how valuable it can be to spy on yourself as a reader—to notice your patterns of reading, like how much you tend to read during reading workshop and when you slow down or speed up as you read. We also talked about noticing the sort of thinking you do as you read—whether you're the sort of reader who asks lots of questions about the text or one who predicts what will happen next, or the sort of reader who forms a really clear picture of the characters and the setting as you read.

"There's another angle we can take when we spy on ourselves and that's to notice what *gifts* we have as readers. That is, what ways of thinking come naturally to us. There's a saying, 'To whom much has been given, much shall be asked.' That's a lofty (fancy) way of saying that a person who has been given something—a talent, or a *gift*, as I'm calling it—has a responsibility to share it with others.

"All of us can think of things we do well outside of reading. I know, for example, that Jasmine, you're a talented knitter, and, Sam, you're an incredible hockey player. Most of us aren't in the habit of naming our talents as *readers*, but each of us has one or two or even three things we do especially well when we read. And just as it's important that we engage our outside talents and share them with others, it's equally important that we do the same with our reading talents. So right now, get with your partner and help each other name the thing each of you does particularly well when you read. Then, once you've figured that out, show each other how to do that thing. You'll be taking turns playing the role of teacher, so remember to be really clear as you teach. Try that now."

As the children talked with their partners, I walked around, listening in. After a few minutes I reconvened them.

"Readers, eyes on me, please." I paused. "I'm so amazed by all of your reading talents! I heard Kadija tell her partner that she has a gift for reading quickly without forgetting the meaning, and she demonstrated this by doing a quick read-aloud of a part of her book she hadn't even read yet and then summing up what had just happened. At first she wasn't sure

When you plan your teaching, you'll often find that one good idea leads you to think of another, another, and yet more. It's important to keep a teaching notebook to capture great ideas that you might otherwise forget. Another day, you'll feel empty-handed as a teacher and will be so glad you have compost out of which to generate new ideas. So record not only what you decided to teach, but also what you could have taught but didn't. On this particular day, I jotted this in my teaching notebook: "I could also have said to the kids, 'You can also spy on the kinds of characters that you choose to spend time with, the characters that you think about, not just when you are reading, but after reading time is over. Which characters do you let into your head? Are you a curmudgeon toward some characters? What, in particular, about one character intrigued you? What about another character turned you off? Remember our chart on things we do to grow ideas about characters? One of the items we added was 'Realize actions are choices a person makes; they are revealing.' That's true of characters but it's also true of people—of you. So notice those choices and use them to grow ideas about yourselves as readers."

how to show her partner how to do this, but then she realized that what she does automatically as she reads is make a list in her mind of key happenings and details. You can do that, too! And I heard Isaac say that he has a gift for imagining characters really well. The author throws out a few descriptors like 'red hair' and 'freckles' and from those two things he pictures a whole person from head to toe. These are such special gifts because they make reading both fluid and enjoyable.

"It seemed like many of you had a hard time naming *how* you do one thing or another well as you read. I'm not surprised. When something comes naturally, it can feel automatic. We do that thing without thinking about it. But I want you to get in the habit of being really active readers, noticing exactly what you're doing as you read. That way, you can continue doing that thing and also share it with other people—not just your reading partner but your family, your neighbors, your friends. So tonight and from now on as you read, remember to spy on yourself, noticing what you're doing as you read so you can share it with others."

From Inference
Toward Interpretation

 ART THREE

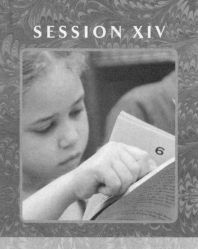

Synthesizing Insights into Ideas About Books

IN THIS SESSION,

you'll teach children that readers take time to organize the ideas we have as we read by pausing to search for patterns in our thinking.

 hroughout the last few lessons, but especially as this unit turns into its final bend in the road, you will need to be guided by a sense of what it means to grow ideas about a text well. You've already learned (and taught) that readers need to produce words that describe a character. The story will provide the actions the character takes, but the reader is often expected to see those actions as windows into the character and to infer what the actions reveal about the person. You will have taught readers that one way to do this is to be conscious that

GETTING READY

- Before you can embark on this minilesson, you will want to be sure that at least half your readers have a dozen or so Post-its in their current independent reading book and that those Post-its capture ideas (not just predictions) about the characters.

- Spotlight one child whose book is chock-full of thoughtful Post-it notes and prepare to celebrate that work with the class. Choose four Post-its that you will rewrite onto larger Post-it notes, visible for the entire class to see during the teaching demonstration. Try to be sure that two of the four Post-its you select obviously go together and two don't quite fit with the group. This will make it easier for the child whose work you will spotlight to demonstrate how she grows a bigger theory from her Post-its.

- Prepare a chart titled "Ways to Get Our Partner to Say More."

- Create copies of a sheet of Post-its about a character from a read-aloud your children know well. We suggest Post-its about little Willy in *Stone Fox*. [See the *Resources for Teaching Reading* CD-ROM.] You'll distribute whatever you decide to use to partnerships during the active involvement section when you ask children to try their hand at growing a theory.

- Bring big pieces of construction paper to help children create their theory charts during the link.

- Have a white board and marker ready.

- Ask children to bring their current independent reading book and a pen to the meeting area.

- Display the "Prompts to Grow Your Ideas" chart from Session X.

- As you continue to read aloud *The Tiger Rising*, you may want to steer children to think about who in this book does and does not have power (and how do you know), the various ways in which characters and people are stuck or trapped (both literally and figuratively), how the connections between characters are affecting their growth and change, and how characters are and are not voicing truths about themselves.

characters could have acted differently—that actions are choices and the choices are telling. You've also conveyed that as readers become more skilled, readers come to see characters as complex and resist trying to shoehorn a character into a one-word generic label. As part of that, you've helped readers realize that one way to get to know a character is to see how others view the character and to think about what those relationships reveal about the character.

> *Our job as teachers is to make sure that the amazing, jaw-dropping work that some readers do is actually within grasp for all readers.*

So what's next?

There is, of course, no one answer. There is no one highway along which all readers travel en route to becoming an expert reader, nor are all expert readers alike. Still, there is at least one fairly obvious next step for your children, and if you look closely at your youngsters' work, you'll see that this next step is actually what some of your children (the more skilled ones) have already been doing. That is, some of your readers—and these tend to be the ones who've made your jaw drop—have already progressed from growing insights about particular characters toward developing interpretations of their books as a whole. Our job as teachers is to make sure that the amazing, jaw-dropping work that *some* readers do is actually within grasp for all readers. And this means spying on ourselves as readers, yes, and also

spying on some of our children as readers, asking, in this case, "What is the difference between kids who are okay at growing ideas about characters and kids who are spectacular at this?" Once we can see the space that exists "from good to great" (to borrow the title of Jim Collins' best-selling book on leadership), then we have a plan that can guide our teaching.

Let's examine the thinking Sam did about *Wringer* in Session XII. Remember how he first noticed that the protagonist, a kid named Palmer, is really different when he is with Beans (who acts sort of like a gang leader, luring him to do troublesome things)? Then Sam went a step further, seeing a pattern, because Palmer is also different when he is with Dorothy (who brings out his kinder side). What Sam did was to see—actually, *to make*—a connection between two Post-its, or two observations. That's an important step for readers to make: to grow an idea that pertains to several instances in the book and that is more abstract because it applies across sections of the text. You'll see that the upcoming session aims to help as many children as possible do this same sort of thinking.

Sam didn't stop with his observation about Palmer's tug-of-war between the competing influences of Beans and Dorothy. He went further and linked that pattern—Palmer is different with one friend than another—to something else in the text, specifically, to Palmer's relationship with his dad (who seems to prefer his son's relationship with Beans to his relationship with Dorothy). All of a sudden, Sam has now developed an idea that relates to almost the whole book, and this is especially the case because the father and Beans both enjoy a particular form of "fun"—wringing the necks of pigeons. Sam's idea functions almost as an umbrella. The idea is so big, the whole story fits underneath it. Sam is able to use this umbrella idea to predict how the book will end, and this time his prediction will be based less on his knowledge of the plot and more on his sense of what it is that the author seems to be trying to say. Palmer will choose to not wring pigeons' necks like his dad did, like

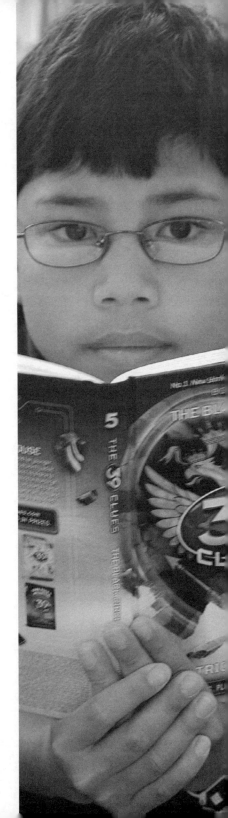

Beans does, because his relationship with Dorothy will help him decide the sort of person he wants to be.

Sam has begun to grow an interpretation of the book. He has answered the question "What is this book *really* about?" He's gone from thinking deeply about a single character to thinking deeply about the book as a whole.

When you think about helping kids grow ideas about texts, you'll be aiming to help youngsters do this sort of intellectual work on the run as they read. This is a challenge, but you'll be working with this challenge well beyond this upcoming bend in the road of your unit. In Unit 4, *Tackling Complex Texts*, you will again explicitly teach all of your readers to read interpretively. For now, in this unit, you'll move your readers along the trajectory of growing ideas about the books we read. Some of your children have yet to feel comfortable generating their own ideas about a text. You'll see these children either develop ideas that are not grounded in the text at all or, in the name of growing ideas, they will often do little more than retell the text, stating what is right there on the page, not replacing any of the author's words with their own. They'll generate a few timid ideas of their own, but these will feel safe, obvious: Dorothy is nice; she is a good friend. During the remainder of this unit, you'll be helping these readers go out on the thin ice of developing their own tentative, exploratory ideas. As part of that, you will continue to teach those and all readers to use conversational prompts as thought prompts, helping them to realize that just as one can *talk* to grow ideas, so too, we can *think* to grow ideas.

But a number of your readers will probably be ready for you to teach toward a new horizon, and so, you will begin the process of scaffolding children to read more interpretively. You'll first help them do as Sam did, seeing (or building) links between one specific idea (Palmer is different when Beans is around) and another specific idea (Palmer is different around Dorothy than around Beans.) In this session, you'll show readers a concrete process for sorting, combining, writing, and thinking between localized observations and ideas. The work you ask them to do today may seem to you to be overly concrete—and even simple. It should seem that way! Keep in mind that the work Sam did is a far cry from the work that the class as a whole has been doing, and it is especially a far cry from the work that your more concrete thinkers have been doing. Minilessons are meant to rally *all* kids toward work that you believe will have very large payoffs.

In this session, you'll suggest youngsters sort their Post-its rather like children in math class sort Unifix cubes. That is, when children are taught division, they are often given handfuls of Unifix cubes or buttons and told to share these with a couple of kids: "You get one, you get one, you get one. Now you get another, you get another . . . ." Just as the concrete task of sharing out Unifix cubes helps children grasp mathematical operations, so, too, today's session is designed to help kids grasp what it means to find ways to link one idea with another. You are teaching analytic thought.

During the upcoming bend in the road of this unit, you'll teach readers to grow large theories that speak to the whole of a text. You'll help them see that an idea about one character or one event or one part of the text can connect with an idea about another character, another event, or another part of the text. In this way, you'll help children learn to take their thinking up and down levels of abstraction.

Ideas aren't difficult to drum up; we have them every day. The challenge lies in finding an idea we can stand behind, speak about at length, one that says something important, that holds meaning and weight. You may want to liken growing an important theory to arguing for something that matters.

MINILESSON

Synthesizing Insights into Ideas About Books

CONNECTION

Celebrate with the class by spotlighting one child's book, brimming with Post-it notes, including some that show the child reading for precise language.

"Readers, before we do anything else, I'm going to ask you to thumb through your book, writing the page numbers for each of your Post-it notes. Write the page numbers right onto the Post-it notes. Do that quickly before we start."

After giving children a minute to finish that job, I held up the book *Crash* by Jerry Spinelli and said, "Look at Jack's book! It looks like a box of Post-it notes exploded all over it." Jack, meanwhile, sat beside me. "Of course, you and I know that a box of Post-it notes didn't explode. Jack's *mind* exploded."

COACHING TIPS

The work you're channeling kids to do today is multifaceted. You could ask them to number their Post-its after the minilesson, but we've found from experience that you may forget because you'll be giving them three other steps to take. Asking them to do it now is just a way to handle the logistics of the work you are asking children to do during independent reading.

One way to keep children engaged in your minilessons is to think about ways you can vary your connection. If you scan the ways we've started minilessons across this unit, you'll see that we attempt to use a variety of methods to bring children into the day's minilesson. Simply saying, day in and day out, "Yesterday, we learned. . . . Today, we will learn . . ." accomplishes many of the jobs of the connection, but a steady drumbeat of this will not enliven a workshop. Push yourself to really connect during the connection. Brainstorm anecdotes, save stories of what kids do, keep an ear to pop culture, and think about brief ways to engage kids at the very start of the minilesson.

I flipped through some pages and stopped and read a Post-it note, "'Crash is kind of *inconsiderate*.' Ooh, what a precise word!" I flipped to another Post-it note and read, "'Crash is mean to Penn because he thinks Penn is weird.'" I flipped to the next and read, "'I think he needs to listen to his sister.'" I looked at Jack. "Wow! All these great thoughts." Then I turned to the class. "So readers, here is my question: What is Jack to make of all of his Post-it notes?"

Liken the child's book of Post-it notes to your own jumble of disorganized, valuable stuff—in a drawer or a basket—and suggest that both you and the child are due for some organization.

"Jack's book reminds me of this drawer I have in my kitchen. It's full of stuff. When I open it up, it's hard to see what's in there, so last weekend I organized it. I found scissors, rolls and rolls of tape, glue sticks galore, tons of markers. I put them all in a plastic tub and labeled it 'Art Supplies.' I also found mittens and a ski hat, so I put those over our coat rack where we keep winter gear. I continued sorting and categorizing my stuff, and when I was done I couldn't believe the good stuff I found that I'd forgotten was there!

"Readers, I tell you this because I bet Jack doesn't remember what's on half of his Post-it notes. There are probably really good theories among these Post-it notes— ideas he has forgotten about. It's really smart to take a tour of your thinking, of your Post-it notes, and to sort over your thoughts."

Name your teaching point. Specifically, teach children that it's helpful to pause in the midst of reading a book to organize one's thoughts. One way to do this is to build piles of related thoughts or Post-it notes.

"So today, I want to teach you that when readers get about halfway through our books (or when our books are bursting with ideas), it is wise to take some time to organize our thoughts. One way to do this is to sort our Post-it notes into piles of ideas that seem to go together."

You'll probably notice that Jack's thoughts about Crash are not the most awe-inspiring thoughts ever. By choosing to spotlight Jack's work, I'm hoping that children will see what he does and think, "I can do that—no problem!" This session aims to teach children how to ratchet up their ideas into something more profound.

My bigger question is actually this: "Reading is like a river of thinking that flows through us. When reading is over, should something remain?" This is a question that preoccupies me a lot when I am thinking about teaching reading because often when we make products out of our reading or our children's reading, then reading suddenly becomes something other than reading.

There is nothing subtle about the categories I set up. I want it very clear that mittens and hats are not the same sort of things as glue sticks and pens.

TEACHING

Call on the help of the child whose work you spotlighted to demonstrate how to sort Post-it notes into categories that go together and then how to generate a new idea that grows from two or three.

"Before a reader can sort Post-it notes into piles, we need to remove them from the book—but of course, it is important to first record the page that each Post-it note references. Like the rest of you, Jack has added the page numbers to each of his Post-it notes. So far, Jack has removed a few of his Post-it notes. Watch the way he sorts and categorizes them, working in a way that is similar to how I worked when I made piles of stuff in my kitchen drawer. Before he does this, let's you and I read them and think how we'd categorize them." We did.

"Jack, which of these Post-it notes seem to you to go together?" I asked. *[Fig. XIV-1]*

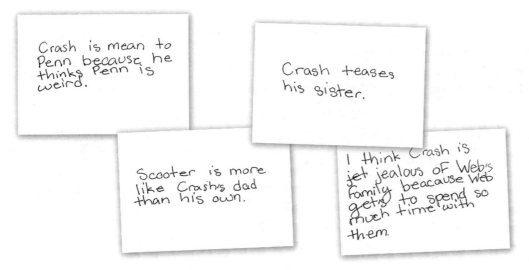

Crash is mean to Penn because he thinks Penn is weird.

Crash teases his sister.

Scooter is more like Crash's dad than his own.

I think Crash is jet jealous of Web's family beacause Web gets to spend so much time with them.

Figure XIV-1 Jack wrote his thoughts about *Crash* on Post-its.

Remember that I recommended in the getting ready section that you and the child select four Post-its that will be easy to sort into categories. Perhaps two have a clear relationship to each other, and the other two might each seem fairly distinct. In any case, you'll want to make this easy for children to understand.

Always remember that a demonstration will be light years more effective if children who are viewing the demonstration actually do the work alongside the demonstrator. This way, the children can compare and contrast how they'd go about doing the work to how the mentor does it.

Occasionally you may ask your class to read aloud some work together, using shared reading to get kids' voices engaged and to practice fluency. Hearing, seeing, and saying things together from time to time can benefit many readers. You may take a few moments to have the class read aloud Jack's Post-it notes so they have a chance to both practice fluency and notice Jack's work. If you decide to do this, use a pointer if you can.

After a minute, I indicated that Jack should show us the Post-its that he felt went together. Jack pulled a few from the lineup, setting them alongside each other.

I gestured to the small pile he'd made and asked Jack, "So those go together? Can you read them to us and tell us how they go together?"

"This one—'Crash teases his sister'—and this one—'Crash is mean to Penn because he thinks Penn is weird'—go together because they both say stuff about Crash."

I asked Jack, "When I asked *how* they go together, what I mean is, 'Do they give you a bigger idea about Crash? Or about the book as a whole?'" Then I reread them aloud, as if I pondered this question. I knew, meanwhile, that members of the class were mulling over the same question.

"Well, maybe that Crash is a bully?"

"Huh," I said, letting this idea wash over me. "What a thought!" I nodded and snuck in a quick gesture toward the chart "Ways to Get Your Partner to Say More" before adding, "Say more about that."

"He makes fun of people, and that's what bullies do."

"And. . . ." (I made a "Come on" gesture to show that wanted him to elaborate.) "What else do you notice about this?" As I asked this question, I again clued the class into what I was doing through a gesture to the "Ways to Get Our Partner to Say More" chart.

"He's making fun of people who are sort of needy—like his kid sister, and like Penn, who he thinks is weird."

"Wow, Jack, you just grew a new idea about Crash!"

When you ask the child to think more about the categories, the easiest way to help the child do this is to do it yourself. Listen to the idea yourself. Wrap your mind around it. Take it in. Even if you say nothing at all while you mull over a child's idea, there is a way in which others can watch the wheels inside your head turn, and the wheels inside their heads will turn along with yours. Do not underestimate the effect that you will have when you sit in the front of the meeting area and listen and think silently about what someone has said.

Ways to Get Our Partner to Say More

- Gesture to get your partner to say more.
- Nod or comment to show you're listening.
- Ask questions.
- "Say more."
- Repeat what your partner said.

Name the process that the one reader just went through in a way that will allow others to replicate the same process, applying it to their own texts to their own Post-its, and to thoughts that they may not even have recorded.,

"Readers, did you see how Jack laid out some of his Post-it notes (some of his thoughts) and read them over, scooping up several thoughts that went together? Then he thought, 'What are these thoughts saying or showing?' and he grew a bigger idea (a theory.) His bigger idea, that Crash is a bully, pertains to several relationships that this character has. It isn't just about one thing one person did. It applies to more parts of the book. In fact, his big idea really is practically about the whole book.

"Did you also notice how, as Jack's partner, I got him to say more?" I again pointed to the chart.

ACTIVE INVOLVEMENT

Set partners up to reread and categorize a few Post-its you will have collected from the class's work with the read-aloud, asking them to develop a new idea from the intersection of the ideas they placed into one category.

"Let's practice doing this, okay? You'll want to pause in the midst of your independent reading book, once you've gotten at least a third or halfway into it, to do this sort of thinking. Some of you are just starting your books, so to practice, let's go back and look at some of the Post-it notes I've been making as we've been reading *The Tiger Rising*. I've copied a few onto this chart." *[Fig. XIV-2]* (I distributed copies of the chart of Post-its to each partnership.) "I want you and your partner to reread these and draw arrows if you find some that go together. Then think, 'What are they showing about Rob?' And if you come up with a new idea, maybe even a bigger idea, like Jack did when he decided that two of Crash's actions, taken together, suggested he might be a bully, you jot it on your sheet."

Notice how I named, step by step, Jack's process for growing a new idea. You may even consider coaching the child beforehand so you are quite sure the child's work will illustrate the point you want to make.

Expect that this work will be more complex than it appears. Children will love doing this, but they will struggle in ways that surprise you, and nothing will be as quick as you expect. Certainly, you will not want to worry over whether children sort every Post-it into a category. You are asking them to draw forth a few Post-its that seem to speak to each other, not to sort each idea into its place on a game board.

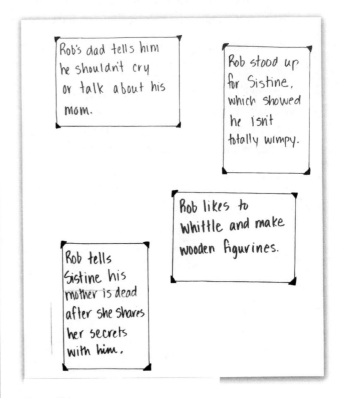

Figure XIV-2

Circulate, coaching to support children as they reach to develop big ideas.

I moved around, helping children to see connections, coaching into partnerships by saying things such as "Which Post-it notes seem to be saying similar things?" and then, when a child started to answer me, redirecting that youngster, saying, "Tell your partner about that."

Jasmine said to Lily, "I think the first and the third Post-it note go together because they both show how much Rob thinks about his mom but can't talk about it. He whittles figures out of wood instead."

I signaled Lily to encourage Jasmine to say more. Lily made a hand signal that said, "Come on, Jas," and Jasmine collected her thoughts before adding, "Maybe Rob uses whittling as a way to connect with his mom, as a way to remember her and feel like she is still a part of his life."

Lily considered Jasmine's observation, rocked her head from side to side, and then showed hers. "The second and the last Post-it notes also go together. They both show that Sistine might be someone that Rob feels like he can be friends with."

I leaned in and asked, "Is there any way you can see both your ideas fitting together?" Lily scrunched up her nose and looked down at her jotting.

Jasmine carefully scanned the piece of paper and said, "Well, what Lily said sort of goes with my idea because maybe his connection to Sistine will help him find a way to talk about his mom. Maybe Rob will be able to talk to her about his mom, instead of just thinking about her when he whittles."

I deliberately chose Post-its that could combine in various ways, not just one way. If they feel too complex for you, by all means write ones in which the connections are even more obvious. It usually makes sense to teach a process using very simple texts and then to show how that same process can be used with more complex texts.

Post-its From Tiger Rising

1. Rob misses the Tiger and just wants to think about it.

2. Rob has feelings, but he doesn't want to show them because he wants to be strong.

3. When Rob is around Sistine, words keep coming out even though he doesn't want them to.

4. I think it's good that Willy May is talking with Rob, and telling him to let the sadness rise up. I think this might actually help him.

5. I think Rob had the dream because the two major things that happened to him that day involved Sistine and the tiger.

6. Rob is experiencing freedom by his father letting him drink coffee and stay away from school.

7. Rob seems to be rising, like the title, "The Tiger Rising".

8. Rob and his father both seem to be opening up, but then they stop themselves.

Theory:

Rob is opening up and he seems to be becoming freer.

Celebrate that readers now have both big ideas and supportive examples. Ask one reader to share. Point out that this work resembles boxes-and-bullets work during essay writing.

"You all came up with amazing ways to connect these thoughts—Post-it notes—and grew all sorts of new ideas. What's really cool is that you now have a big idea, and some examples, or evidence, for that idea. Brianna has developed a theory that Sistine is helping Rob unlock his suitcase. And her evidence for this is that Rob runs after Sistine to tell her that his mother is dead. Brianna, can you say a little more about how telling Sistine his mother is dead is helping Rob unlock his suitcase?"

Brianna said, "He is starting to open up to someone, like he told Sistine the truth about his mom, but he had been keeping that locked up in his suitcase. He wouldn't talk about his mom at all, but then he does because Sistine gets mad at him for keeping secrets and runs away from him."

"And what other evidence do you have for your thinking that Rob is starting to unlock his suitcase?" I asked.

Brianna said, "Rob shows Sistine the figures he is whittling, and he decides to show her the tiger as well. He is showing Sistine more of who he is by showing her the figures, and he also is letting her in on the big secrets in his life."

While these Post-its about Rob may nudge readers toward the theory that Rob is developing an important connection with Sistine or toward the idea Rob uses whittling to express the feelings he can't express verbally, the paths readers will take to articulate these or other ideas will catch you by surprise. Welcome this. Of course, this doesn't mean that any old idea will do, but you'll want to take pleasure in the multitudinous ways readers' thinking will sprout from smaller ideas rooted in a text toward ideas in full bloom.

Notice that when readers have a big idea ("Sistine is helping Rob unlock his suitcase") and some evidence ("He tells her his mom is dead"), it is helpful to nudge readers to unpack how the passage cited actually provides evidence for big idea. This unpacking the evidence is a move that children will need to make when writing literary essays.

I encourage children to talk between their Post-its and their ideas, because it can be tempting to speak tangentially based on evidence found elsewhere in a text. While it's true that readers pull evidence for their ideas from a variety of sources in a book, including those not jotted down in front of us, right now I want children to think and speak based on their evidence at hand: Post-its.

"So class, do you see how you have a big idea, and if you talk between the Post-it notes and the big idea, you can show how they become evidence? It's like your boxes and bullets in an essay!"

Link

Tell children that readers sort and theorize about their thoughts—their Post-its, for now—once they are well into their books.

"Right now, look at how far you are in your independent reading book, and give me a thumbs up if you have read approximately half your book or more." They did this, and half the class indicated they were in the second half of their independent reading books. "Those of you who have not yet read half your book, fill in your logs and get started reading, remembering to grow really wise ideas as you read and to jot these on Post-its because we'll be doing amazing work with those ideas." I let those children disperse from the meeting area.

The reference to boxes and bullets is a reference to Breathing Life into Essays, *the third book in the* Units of Study for Teaching Writing, 3–5 *series. You do not need that series to explain to kids what you mean by boxes and bullets, but there will be many connections between essay writing and the work of this last bend in the road of this unit (and even more between essay writing and the upcoming nonfiction reading unit). Essentially, though, what you need to know is that in the essay unit, children plan their essays by thinking of their boxes (big ideas) and bullets (supports). [Fig. XIV-3]*

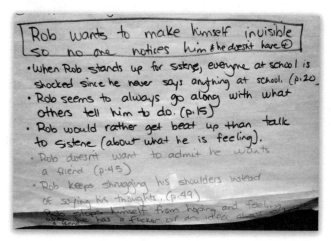

Figure XIV-3

Your children will be totally enthralled with the invitation to work together in the meeting area on extra challenging work, and especially to move their Post-its onto bright sheets of construction paper and to use marker pens to show their mind work as they think between their Post-its, growing theories. Your goal will be to get all of them engaged in this work, so you'll need to keep in mind the image of the circus man who gets plates spinning on the ends of sticks. You'll get one reader going, then another, then another. You won't be able to stay long enough to supervise what any one child does with your coaching, but know you'll cycle back to children often and know, too, that they can help each other. Also, the thing that matters most now is that they approximate what it means to look between Post-its, growing overarching ideas. The ideas they generate may not, in fact, be all you hoped they'd be, but remember this is Day 1 of this work.

"Those who have read half your book or more, I'm going to usurp (or take away) your usual choice of what to do during reading time. Come work here on the rug with me today because the work you'll be doing is challenging, and I'd like to be here to help you with it. Let me give you a sheet of paper for your Post-its. Reread your Post-its and locate some really meaty, interesting ones. For the work we're doing today, use Post-its that contain ideas about your character or about the book rather than predictions.

"When you have found four or five or six good ones, put them on what I'm going to call your Theory Chart." (I pulled out big, bright sheets of construction paper and started distributing one to each reader.) "Then you'll want to see if some of your ideas go together, and if they do, write some more words on top of them, or around them. You may decide to add arrows, or circles, or stars—anything that captures your thinking about how your ideas go together." (I held up my piece of construction paper to show what a completed theory chart might look like.) "Get started, and I'll come around and confer with you."

You'll notice that I rarely give assignments, because I believe strongly that choice is a crucial element of the reading workshop. However, there are times when I'll ask readers to try a strategy in unison. Today's workshop is one of those times. It is helpful that half the class is not ready to do this work. This allows us to provide the support that the remaining half needs more easily, and meanwhile those who are not yet midway through their books have extra incentive to create some really worthwhile Post-its.

CONFERRING AND SMALL-GROUP WORK

Help Readers Grow Ideas into Theories

As readers take on the work of this bend, as they learn how to take their nascent thoughts about their stories and characters and turn them into full-bodied theories or even into interpretations, you'll circulate, coaching individuals and small groups. You'll help children notice what their main character does and says and then grow ideas out of those observations. As you do this, it will be important for you to notice trends across your class so that your teaching can be tailored to respond to your children's work. If you anticipate the challenges children will encounter, you'll be ready to extend their work.

Some Readers Will Need Help Going from Observing a Character to Growing Text-Based Ideas

Some children will profit from help doing the work you have suggested in your minilessons. You'll need to take them step-by-step through the progression of work.

I pulled up my chair alongside Gabe, who was sitting among the children on the carpet reading *Liberation of Gabriel King*. Whereas others were fiddling with Post-its, Gabe was nose-deep in his book as had become typical of him lately. I didn't notice

---

MID-WORKSHOP TEACHING POINT

Readers Use Theories as Lenses

"Readers, eyes on me." I waited until I had their attention. "Class, I wanted to share with you the smart work that Jasmine was doing. Those of you who haven't been in the meeting area with us because you weren't halfway through your book, you need to listen up, too, because Jasmine's work can show you what you'll probably want to get started doing pretty soon.

"Jasmine's book, like Jack's, was bursting with ideas, so she decided she wanted to make something of all the thoughts she had on the run while she was reading. So she paused in the midst of reading and reread all her Post-its, including one that said, 'Juan (her main character) is home alone a lot,' and another Post-it that said, 'Juan seems like he is really poor 'cause sneakers is not a lot for a birthday.' Jasmine took those two Post-its out of her book and put them on her theory chart (I held up her large sheet of construction paper), and then she looked back and forth between those Post-its for a few minutes, and suddenly it was like a light went on." (With my hands, I gestured to convey that a light bulb of insight formed suddenly over Jasmine's head.) "She thought, 'Those three Post-its sort of go together.' Then she went further in her mind. She thought, 'Those three Post-its suggest that Juan has a really hard life.' *[Fig. XIV-4]*

"But here is the extra smart thing that Jasmine did. *She decided to look back over the book to see if her theory was really true or not*, and she ended up finding a lot more evidence, so she has put Post-its with the word 'Evidence' on them in a bunch of places across her book. And now she says *she is going to read on and see if her theory stays true as she reads further in her book.*

continued on next page

---

any Post-its jutting out of the margins. "Gabe," I said, peering over his shoulder. "Can you walk me through your thinking a bit? Show me a few Post-its you've written that reveal the ideas you're growing." During this unit, I had already conferred with Gabe on using his personal experiences and his knowledge of how stories tend to go to inform and support his reading work. He'd just the previous day been in a small group that aimed to help him use more precise vocabulary. I also knew that Gabe tended to be pretty diligent about jotting on Post-its, though he often needed an extra push to deepen his thinking.

Gabe looked up at me and waited a bit before saying, "Well, I did jot some notes, but I think I left them at home," he said. "Maybe I should go to my desk and read instead of doing this stuff with the Post-its 'cause I don't really have that many with me."

Because I could see that his book was bare, I knew that for Gabe to say he didn't have "that many" Post-its with him was an overstatement. He clearly didn't have any at all. "Gabe, I can tell that you are so into this book that it is hard for you to pull yourself away from reading on and on and on to get your thoughts onto paper. Is that what's been going on for you?"

Gabe nodded vigorously. "It is just *so* good," he said. I was glad to see that Gabe was becoming fluent enough to get that involved in his book and glad also that he'd chosen a book that was such a good fit. I wanted to praise that work but didn't want him to lose sight of the thinking that the Post-it work stimulated.

"I understand that. The same happens to me sometimes, and in life there absolutely will be times when you and I read books without ever coming up for air. It's great to see you reading so smoothly that you're getting caught up in the story like this, now. But in this class, we're working on getting stronger as readers, and the best way for me to help you get even stronger is to help you think more deeply as you read. To do that, I do need you to put your thinking out so I can see it, and so *you* can see it, and so we can work on making it even wiser. If it is hard to make yourself stop to think and jot, you could put Post-its at stopping places before you even start reading, and then whenever you come upon a Post-it, you could pause and to do your wisest reflecting. Would that work?"

Gabe nodded. "I was doing them before," he said. "I just sort of stopped recently."

"Yeah, maybe now that you're flying faster through your books, you just need a little bit of practice with stopping yourself every so often. How

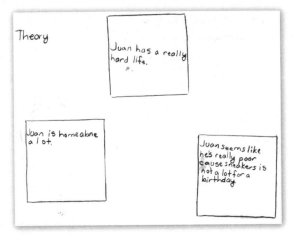

MID-WORKSHOP TEACHING POINT

continued from previous page

"I wanted to tell you that it is really smart of Jasmine to look between her theory and the parts of the book she has already read, thinking, 'Does my theory really seem true?' and it is also smart of her to read on, looking for ways the upcoming story confirms or changes her theory.

"Would you give me a thumbs up if you think you might be willing to try to do the same sort of work Jasmine has been doing?" Children so indicated. "Fabulous. If you read something that goes with your theory, mark it with a Post-it note. And as you read on, mark the places that support your theories, too, like Jasmine did." Then I added, "Some of you may even invent some way to get all the evidence listed underneath your big idea on your theory chart. I'm not sure how you could do that, but you are brilliant at solving problems, so I bet you will find ways. If you invent a solution, come and show me, okay, so I can share the idea with others."

Figure XIV-4
After doing this, Jasmine began reading her books and finding more evidence.

about if you take a minute or two right now to go back and flag three places where you had some good ideas about a character in your book. Jot your thought on a sticky note, and remember to write the page number." As Gabe did this, I briefly checked in with other readers at his table.

After a couple of minutes, I said, "Okay, Gabe, can you walk me through your jottings?"

Gabe put three Post-its side by side on his desk top. "The first thought I had is that maybe, it could be that Frita and Gabe have some of the same problems," Gabe said, showing me his first Post-it. "And my second thought is that Frita has a weird relationship with her brother Terrance. My third thought is that Frita is brave and helps Gabe to see that he can be brave, too."

"Wow. You've really been thinking hard about your characters. Now, let's do what readers do next, after we've read for a while and thought this and that about characters. Do you remember what readers often do next?"

Gabe said, "Reread our Post-its?"

"Absolutely. We look over our thinking, and then we can see if any of the meaty ideas go together. Readers do just what you are saying; we look across our jottings, our Post-its, our thinking, and as we do, we think, 'Is there a way to connect these ideas?' So, looking at your jottings, is there something that you think can connect them?" Gabe peered closely at his Post-its and scratched his forehead. "One thing that can help is if you notice some jottings that are centered on particular characters. You can think about how to link those," I added, to give him a strategy for looking at the Post-its.

"Well, these two (he pointed to Post-its 1 and 3) are both about Frita and Gabe. It seems like the two of them are connected somehow."

"That's so interesting, Gabe! It sounds like you're on to something. Now, try to push yourself to say something more, something even bigger about how they might be connected."

"They're friends, and Frita helps Gabe. Oh! Maybe she helps him because she relates to him, because they have similar problems. So now Gabe can be brave enough to face his fears."

"In other words . . . ," I prompted, hoping Gabe would put his idea into other words, saying it another time so the idea became even clearer to him.

"In other words, Frita has already faced her fears so now she can help Gabe do it, too."

"The lessons this teaches about life are . . . ," I said, pushing him toward a more interpretive idea.

"Umm. Well maybe it's that sometimes friends help us be stronger? And, like, better people?" he said with some of his old insecurity coming in. This kind of deep thinking about books was still relatively new for Gabe, and I knew he only needed practice to be as confident about this work as he was becoming with other things. *[Fig. XIV-5]*

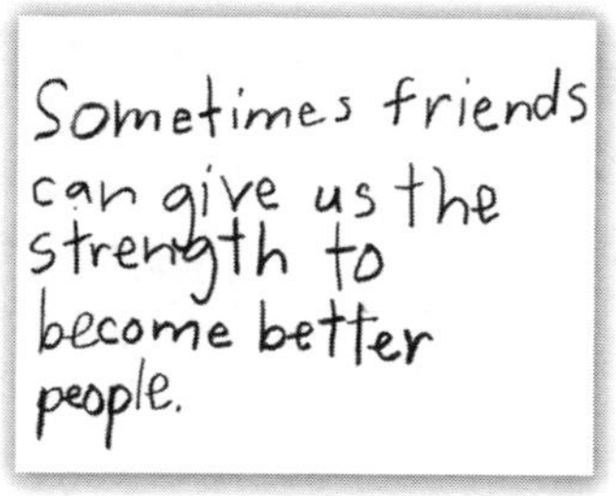

Figure XIV-5

"Gabe, wow. That's insightful. 'Sometimes friends can give us the strength to become better people.' Do you see how taking the time to jot down ideas—even quick, on-the-fly ideas—and then looking back over them for ways they connect helped you grow a theory that pertains not just to these characters and to this book but also to life? When we look across our thinking, our jottings, we start to see ideas that go together, and sometimes those ideas can help us build an even bigger idea. Super work. Write that down!"

Some Readers Will Think They're Growing Ideas When Really They're Paraphrasing the Text

As you work with children, you'll find that some will *think* they have no problem doing the work you've taught in your minilessons, but actually, they won't be growing original ideas so much as just paraphrasing the text.

Chances are good that many of them *will* have been successful at noticing several instances in their independent reading book that illustrate that a main character has shown a particular character trait. For example, one reader may have seen that her main character repeatedly helps a secondary character. This reader may then have deduced, "The main character is nice," or "The main character is a good friend." Meanwhile, another reader will have done similar work leading to the "big" idea that the main character is mean. Looking over the so-called big ideas that these children have generated, you may feel uncomfortable. Their version of big ideas may seem to you to be very similar to the smaller noticings that they've been collecting all along on their Post-it notes. Although the children may feel as if they have arrived at their very own insights, to you that insight may seem altogether obvious. If a reader deduces that Harry, the main character in *Horrible Harry*, is horrible, it'll be hard for you to be terribly excited!

It will help if you keep in mind that the child who decides that Harry is horrible may actually have accomplished something if he has located several excerpts from the text that all illustrate this one generalization. The ability to do this means the child is on the way toward being able to write a literary essay. Recognizing that the child has done one step is important, but you'll also want to extend that work. One of the most powerful ways to do so will be to teach the child that it is often provocative to think, "*Why* is the character this way?" Another way to word this is "What clues has the author given to suggest why the character is this way?"

You will also find that some of your children name what the characters did instead of growing ideas about the character. I recently convened a small group of readers, saying to Rosa, Izzy, and Tyrell, "I called you all together because as I was reading over your shoulders, I noticed you are recording the facts of the book, jotting down what the author has said about the character's activities, which is wise, but you aren't really growing ideas about those characters. It is true that readers need to notice what a character does, but we generally don't write that down because it's already written in the story itself. Instead, we write *our thoughts* about whatever we've noticed the character doing. It helps to recall what the character did or said (and for you all, that's what's on many of your Post-it notes now), *and then* to ask yourself, 'What's my idea about this?'"

Because the class all knew *The Tiger Rising*, I used this as the common text for this small group. Opening the read-aloud book to page 49, I said, "Listen really carefully to this part because you're going to turn and talk to your neighbor—first about what the author has said the character did. You readers are good at that! This is when Rob is talking to Sistine about his mother." I read aloud.

> "She's dead," he told her. The words came out in short, ragged gasps.
>
> "My mama's dead."

"Turn and tell the person next to you what the author has said the character did." I listened in. Rosa was talking about the whole book, so I asked her to focus on the part I just read aloud.

"Now, after recalling (but not writing) what the character did, I want you to do what thoughtful readers do and go a step further. Think about what sort of person this must be, or what ideas you have as a result of what you have seen the character doing. Now the challenge is to grow your own idea based on what that character did. The trick is to avoid just repeating exactly what is in the book. See if you can help me. I just read the part in *The Tiger Rising* where Rob acknowledges to Sistine that his mother is dead. If I jotted this on a Post-it—'Rob told Sistine that his

mother died'—would I be growing my own idea or simply restating what has been said in the book? Give me a thumbs up if that Post-it would have captured *my* thoughts and a thumbs down if I only wrote what was already written in the story." I looked around and was glad to see that the kids had given me a thumbs down.

"Will you three help me grow an idea?" Then I added, "Here's a tip. You can nudge yourself to grow ideas by using phrases such as 'This makes me realize . . .' or 'My thought about this is that . . .' or 'This shows that. . . .'" I pointed to the "Prompts to Grow Your Ideas" chart from Session X where I'd recorded those and other phrases. "Help me use one of the phrases to grow an idea about that part of *The Tiger Rising*."

Prompts to Grow Your Ideas

- This is important because . . .
- This makes me realize that . . .
- The bigger idea here is that . . .

I looked to the children for input, pulled out a white board, and placed my Post-it at the top. "Izzy, why don't you get us started? Tell me what I should write."

Izzy looked up at the chart and read, "This makes me realize. . . ." I wrote as Izzy was talking. "That Rob is. . . ." She paused.

I coached, "What words can you now use to describe Rob that you couldn't before?" I pointed to the sentence I had written.

Izzy started over and said, "This makes me realize that Rob . . . has changed."

To the small group of children, I said, "Now, let's add on to Izzy's thinking. Be more specific. *Explain* the change."

Tyrell said, after a pause, "Well, he isn't keeping everything inside anymore."

I coached, "How come? Always ask yourself why."

"He's got a friend," Tyrell smiled.

Rosa added, "Rob is happy now."

I stated back for her, "Rosa you're saying that when Rob told Sistine that his mother died it made you realize that Rob changed. And he's changed because now he's happy." Rosa nodded her head. I cupped my hand to my ear (this is a gesture that encourages Rosa, who you'll recall is an ELL student, to use her words), and Rosa responded, "Yes, he is now happy."

I asked, "How does telling Sistine about his mother's death show that he's happy?"

Rosa paused for a second and answered, "Because now he has a friend he can tell."

"Okay, let's come back together." I reread what we'd written so far.

This makes me realize that Rob has changed.

"Izzy, what should I write next?" As Izzy talked, I wrote.
"He's now opening up and talking about things that are hard."
I asked the group, "Why?"
I called on Tyrell. "Because now he has a friend to tell."

I then asked the children to study the work we'd begun with all the work they'd now completed detailing the difference. Then I asked them to stay right there and to grow ideas off of their own Post-its in a similar way by taking what the character did or said and then asking themselves, "What's my idea about this?" I reminded them that one way to come up with an idea is think, "*Why* is the character this way?" As the children worked, I coached them as I had done earlier.

TEACHING SHARE

Readers Enlarge Ideas by Taking into Account More Parts (and People) in the Text

Ask children to share their work of the day with a partner.

"Those of you who are far enough into your books that you can be looking across your Post-its to grow theories, you've done a very nice job. Right now, each of you find a reader who wasn't ready to do this work today and who has, instead, been reading, and show that reader what you did, explaining the hard parts, so that he or she will be able to do the same sort of work down the road. You and that reader might look at the Post-its together to see whether there are any emerging theories starting to develop."

Give children a tip about growing ideas by first listing some ideas about the read-aloud, then asking children if each is big or little. Then explain that often the key to a big idea is that it involves more than one character.

After a few minutes, I intervened. "I want to give you all one tip—and those of you who have not yet looked across your Post-its to grow theories, see if you can learn this even though it does not yet apply to you. It will by tomorrow.

"You are trying to grow *big* ideas. I'm going to say some ideas about *The Tiger Rising*, and I want you show to me with your arms whether the idea is a *big* idea" (I struck an Atlas-like pose with outstretched arms) "or a little one" (I pinched my fingers together).

"Rob likes to whittle." After giving children a chance to signal whether the idea seemed big or small, I pinched my fingers together to indicate this was a small idea. "Rob is hiding from his own feelings." Again I let the children lead and then joined them in signaling that this was a big idea. "Sistine is unhappy living in Lister." I let children make the small gesture. "Sistine and Rob seem to need each other because they both feel like outsiders." The children signaled a big idea. "Rob and Sistine want to be free like the tiger." The children stretched out their arms.

"You are right that it is not really a big idea to say 'Rob likes to whittle,' or 'Sistine is unhappy living in Lister,' and it absolutely *is* a big idea to say, 'Rob and Sistine want to be free like the tiger.'

COACHING TIPS

Whenever we can create opportunities for some children to teach others, we're wise to do so. This allows us to harness social energy toward the goals of increased literacy. Then, too, we all know that the best way to really learn something is to teach it. Enabling some children to function as teachers to others—in this instance, that would include children such as Gabe, Kobe, and Malik, who have not generally been thought of as the class's strongest readers—also helps those kids' self-concepts.

The work that you are teaching is part of the Common Core Standards. You'll revisit this work during Unit 4, so don't expect all your students to grasp all you are teaching.

Those of you who know my Units of Study for Teaching Writing *series may recall that children did similar work as they reflected on whether their story ideas were or were not focused. Then we differentiated between the two by asking, "Is this a big watermelon idea?" and "Is this a tiny seed idea?" Interestingly, then the goal was a tiny seed idea.*

"The trick is to learn how to grow big ideas, and I have one tip for you about that. Usually—not always, but usually—for an idea to be big, it needs to pertain to more than just one character. A fair number of you have ideas like this: 'Sistine is feisty' or 'Rob is lonely,' and those are important observations, but they will be richer and bigger ideas if you think not only about one character but between the characters. That is one way to make sure your idea links to more than one part of your book."

Ask children to try fitting more than one character into the ideas they are growing, to help make them big.

"Specifically, I'd suggest you spend a bit more time thinking about your main character *in relation to minor characters*. Let's think for a minute about Rob, and instead of just thinking about him alone—saying, for example, 'Rob is lonely'—let's think about how the secondary characters fit into this, too. Which other secondary characters do we know well from *The Tiger Rising*?"

Children called out, "The Threemongers," and "The principal, what's his name?" They suggested Sistine, too, but I pointed out that she is almost like another main character.

I added, "What about Rob's dad?" Then I said, "Let's consider these secondary characters—the Threemongers, Mr. Phelmer (the principal), and Rob's dad. Let's think to ourselves, 'How might these secondary characters fit with the idea that Rob is lonely?'" I left a pool of silence, and during that time I tried to think of a response to this thought.

"What are you thinking?"

Cries of, "Oh, oh! I know!" went up around the room, and soon the children had discovered ways that each of those characters contributed to Rob's loneliness. Mr. Phelmer suspends him from school because of his rash, which isolates Rob and makes him feel uncomfortable. The Threemongers bully and poke fun at Rob, making him feel he doesn't belong. And Rob's dad won't let him express his memories or his sadness about his mother.

Soon, the class had settled upon this big idea: "No matter where Rob turns, on the bus, at school, and even at home, the other characters are pushing him away."

"Yeah," Lily added. "There's no place for Rob to really feel free. Those other characters push his feelings into his suitcase."

"Readers, did you see that when we started thinking not only about the main character but also about how a few minor characters are in relation to the main character, we

I wanted to add that the other characters pushed Rob, himself, into a suitcase of sorts, but I kept that thought to myself, for now, sensing this wasn't the right time to bring that up.

started to see a pattern? We noticed a pattern in the ways that people were treating and responding to Rob, and that helped us grow an idea about Rob that *is* a big idea. Tonight, and from now on, as you read your books, when you are growing your very own ideas, try to make them into big ideas. And one way to do this is not only to think about the main character but to think about the relationships between the main character and the secondary characters, and especially about the patterns you see when you look at those interactions."

IN THIS SESSION,
you'll teach students that once
readers develop theories about
our characters, we read and
reread with those theories
in mind.

Seeing Texts Through the Prism of Theories

oland Barth, author of many books on school change and the founder of Harvard's Principal Center, often speaks to the principals who work most closely with the Teachers College Reading and Writing Project. Not long ago, he said, "You need to think about how many elephants in the room you have at your school—by this I mean, you need to think about the topics that are never brought to the table and publicly addressed but that are always on everyone's mind. The elephants in the room are the topics people talk about in hushed undercurrents in the bathrooms, the parking lot. A school's health suffers in proportion to the number of elephants in the room, the number of topics that everyone circles around without addressing."

Of course, the biggest elephant in the room of every public school in America is the question of time. There's never enough time to cover it all, and every teacher feels regret, guilt even, over all that we are not getting to do.

It is not only teachers who race at breakneck pace through the school day. Children do as well. Children move from one subject to the next, from one skill to the next, from one idea to the next. In reading, in particular, children can sometimes get caught up in "disposable thinking." On this page, a reader thinks one idea; on the next page, the reader thinks a different idea. But do readers ever see the ideas left behind on their pages as a trail of bread crumbs, leading them down the path to deeper insights?

The topic of time needs to be discussed. It needs to stop festering in dark corners and to be brought out into the light of day. And when the issue is brought into the light of day, I hope that we talk about not only all that is not covered but also about the cost of our hurried curriculum. We must stop to think about what is lost because of our penchant for always racing faster, reaching more places, covering more.

GETTING READY

- Prepare to tell a personal anecdote during the connection. The message of this story should convey that it helps to keep ourselves present, wide-awake, and flexible in the world and as we read.

- Keep *The Tiger Rising* or your current read-aloud text close at hand because you will be referring to it during the teaching section.

- Provide copies of an excerpt from *The House on Mango Street*, by Sandra Cisneros, or another familiar text. You will incorporate these in a demonstration of how our theories change as we read.

- In Session XVI, you will be revisiting Chapter 21 of *The Tiger Rising* to discuss the internal and external resources characters draw upon as they face obstacles along their journey.

It could be that the most important things that we are not getting to in the school day are not new topics, new subjects, but instead, qualities of mind. For example, in our overcrowded curriculum, have we found a way to teach perseverance, rigor, and depth? Are young people growing up knowing the joy of staying with an idea for a long time, long enough to understand what it means to take a creative idea to fruition? Could it be that Malcolm Gladwell's book *Outliers* has taken America by storm because his emphasis on the value of passionate, persistent hard work has struck a nerve with our hyperactive, fast-track culture? In this best-selling book, Gladwell cites example after example of people who became surprisingly successful and asks, "Where did these people come from? What contributed to this person's success?" And each time, the answer is that people achieve success not through raw talent or genius or luck so much as thorough persistent hard work. Before the Beatles became a smash hit in America, they took a job performing at a club in Hamburg, Germany, where they played eight-hour sets, seven days a week for a month. It was not inconsequential that before this group came to America, they had played together 1200 times. During all that persevering hard work, they'd taught themselves how to be a great band. What was their secret? Gladwell says, "They believed in hard work. They threw their heart and soul into something."

We cannot help readers to become sophisticated thinkers and readers unless we help them sustain their thoughts longer, linking one fleeting insight to another and another. Helping children learn to synthesize ideas is especially important because as they read more and more complex books, perhaps the single most important thing that children need to learn to do is to put together the pieces. In Chapter 1, the reader meets one character, in one place. In Chapter 2, the reader meets an entirely different character, in an entirely different place. The skilled reader needs to think, "How will these two characters' paths cross? Will the one character move in next door to the other? Will they attend summer camp together? Will the mother of one child meet and marry the father of the other?" Readers need to see that the actions a character takes toward the end of the book call into question the promise the character made at the start of the book, or hearken back to the good or bad omen that crossed the character's path at the end of Chapter 1. Reading, especially once readers are reading complex texts, requires a person to see (indeed, to create) continuities in the midst of discontinuities.

This session is one way to encourage children to understand that some of their thoughts and some of what they see in their books can fit together, forming an idea that has significance. An idea need not streak across the mind like a shooting star, with illumination that lasts just an instant. Instead, new ideas can illuminate a continued journey, helping readers to see new dimensions in upcoming texts.

In this lesson, we ask readers to carry an idea with them, using that idea as illumination—as a way to see more in the text. They will look with that idea as they continue to read on in their books. This, of course, will not be an entirely new concept to your children. Earlier, you taught them to carry predictions with them, and in the preceding session, your mid-workshop teaching point advanced this same idea. It should not surprise you to see that you return to this concept fairly often, reteaching it. In today's session, you will demonstrate, through your words and your example, that building an idea requires patience and faith. A reader reads on, looking at the upcoming text with an idea in mind, hoping this process will bring new light to the text and to us. There is a way in which this feels a bit like waiting to see a rainbow. We wait, look, hope, hold our breath, look again. As we watch, we hope it will come but fear that it won't. That's what it might feel like the first time you try this yourselves.

MINILESSON

Seeing Texts Through the Prism of Theories

CONNECTION

Tell children about a time in your life when you were open and flexible to the world around you and point out the possibilities that flexibility provides us in our lives and as readers.

"I was watching one of those famous dog trainers on TV the other day. I think he would say that I'm not a very good dog owner because I don't establish dominance over my new puppy, Emma. I don't keep my dog close at 'heel' the whole time I'm walking her. On our walks, Emma keeps her own pace, while I hold the leash loosely. Often, Emma stops to examine a particular spot, to chew on a pine cone, and I find myself enjoying a part of the world that I might not have paid any special attention to before. Some days, Emma catches a whiff of something and meanders off the path, with me following behind her. What I thought was going to be a brief walk can turn into an adventure.

"I see other dog owners sometimes, in a rush to take out the dog and then get right back home. They pull the dog along, looking straight ahead. I feel kind of sorry for all they're missing. They're not noticing that this year, for some reason, there are baby pine cones everywhere, nor do they see that a creature has burrowed its way under the old stump, or that there must be a dozen bird nests under the eaves of the shed. When I have a gentle hold on the leash, and a flexible idea of where I'm going, I experience so much more than I would if I had a very strict plan and stuck to it.

"Yesterday, many of you looked across your Post-its and developed theories that you wrote on charts."

You'll notice that this session relies on two different opening metaphors. I describe the flexibility that characterizes readers' thinking by likening reading to walking a dog on a loose leash, and then later I liken this tentative, open way of thinking to solving crossword puzzles in pencil. You may decide to select one metaphor only, trimming the minilesson a bit.

I love this metaphor—and don't love it, all at the same time. For me, it is always fun to bring the true details of my life into my teaching, and I do find that there are life lessons to be learned even in something like walking a dog. But on the other hand, I'm aware that this metaphor is not one I'll carry with me for a long while. Reading with a theory in hand really, truly, does not feel like walking a puppy. So whereas the metaphor allows me to make my point, it is not one that really adds to the message I am trying to say about reading. And I definitely am at risk of mixed metaphor. Is reading with a theory in hand closer to looking through a prism in hopes of perhaps seeing a rainbow (as described in the prelude), or is it closer to walking one's dog? You choose. You may not even mention the metaphor that doesn't suit you—or more likely, you'll mention it once and then dispose of it (a fitting thing to do in this disposable culture of ours).

Name your teaching point, specifically, that readers keep our theories in mind as we read on, looking for information that will change or grow our thinking.

"Readers, today I want to remind you that, as Jasmine showed us yesterday, once readers have grown a theory, a big idea, we reread and read on with that theory in hand. And I want you to know that we hold a theory loosely, knowing it will have a life of its own as we travel on. It will take us places we didn't expect to go."

TEACHING

Tell the story of a time when your mental flexibility allowed you to change your thinking. Remind children of since-revised theories they developed earlier in the read-aloud, highlighting ways those theories changed as the class continued reading and learning.

Gestures will help make your meaning more concrete for children. Imagine that your theory is a tangible object that you've got a hold of. When you talk about holding a theory loosely, you may want to thoughtfully look around, as if for other possible theories. Maybe you put it down and pick up a different theory instead ("Oh, this one works better. I'll try this one."), or perhaps you pick up another object and mush it together with your theory ("Hmm, . . . these two make sense when I put them together."). Many kids are visual learners; whenever possible, try to use images or gestures to help them understand these complex concepts.

"Do any of you have crossword puzzle lovers in your life? I do. One of my friends does them all the time, and my dad does sometimes. I even like to do them occasionally. And I've learned that to be successful at solving a crossword puzzle, it helps to think of the words that I fill into the blanks as *possible* answers, not final answers. In fact, I use a pencil to fill in the words so that I can easily change my first answers as I continue working. My friend uses a pen but writes with a very light hand so she can easily write over the faint letters. My dad, he writes his solutions as small as can be in the corners of the boxes until he's sure of them.

Over and over you'll be reminded that comprehension strategies are life strategies, thinking strategies.

"Crossword puzzle lovers know what readers know—that it's important to be flexible and open, to expect that as new information comes in, our initial ideas will change and grow. That's why we call these ideas we're putting down *theories*. Theories are important—grand even—like the theory of how this world was made or the theory of life on other planets. But theories are still open for questioning, for exploration. When all the information is in, all the information is at hand, then the theory becomes a fact.

"Yesterday many of you wrote theories onto theory charts, and I wish, in retrospect, that I'd given you pencils, not marker pens, for recording those theories. Except the beautiful thing is that because you recorded your ideas in big bold letters, this means your revisions will be big and bold, too, and we'll all be able to see and talk about and celebrate the fact that you are a person who lets your ideas have a life of their own. Your revisions will show that you let new information change your first ideas."

Notice that this second anecdote almost serves as an extended connection. You may hearken back to previous minilessons that focus on flexibility, such as Session IV, on predictions.

Remind children that the class didn't merely set out to prove their original theories about the main character in the class read–aloud. Instead, those theories have gone through several revisions.

"You know all about theories changing as one reads. Do you remember in the beginning, when we had just started reading *The Tiger Rising,* many of us were thinking, 'Rob's a wimp,' because he let the Threemongers taunt him? Then, as we read on, we learned more information that made us think differently about that.

"Did we just read on looking for evidence of all the ways Rob's wimpy? No way! Instead, we kept our minds open. We paid attention to new information we found along the way. And pretty soon we had revised our first theory—'Rob is wimpy'—to something more along the lines of 'Rob doesn't stand up for himself because he keeps all his feelings closed up tight and doesn't think about them.'"

Demonstrate the way you revise your theories as you read aloud a tiny text. Read a bit, devise a theory, and then read on, finding that the upcoming text challenges your initial theory.

"Let me show you what I mean by reading with that theory in hand, holding it loosely. I'm going to read a short excerpt from a book called *The House on Mango Street* by Sandra Cisneros. The narrator's name is Esperanza. Since the text is so short, I'm going to stop and jot a theory very early on. I'll be putting down the theory in pencil, because I know that as I read on, I'm looking for more information that will help me change my theory or grow my theory, making it even better. Be researchers and study what I do as I read and think because later I'm going to ask you to list the sort of thinking work you saw me do."

> Nenny and I don't look like sisters . . . not right away. Not the way you can tell with Rachel and Lucy who have the same fat popsicle lips like everybody else in their family.

"Even though I haven't read much, I'm going to stop here and put down a theory. It's okay if I think it might not be right. In fact, that's the way a theory is supposed to be. It's just a starting place. So, from the little bit that we know about Esperanza so far, I think that she feels like she doesn't quite belong in her family. Like, she doesn't fit with her sister, her family, and all. She's looking around at her friends' family, where they seem to go together, but hers doesn't work that way.

At this point, I could have also added, "Remember that just like you are reading on in your books with your theory in your mind, you can read back in your books with your theory in your mind. Of course, I don't literally mean that you will read backward. But you can think back to an earlier part of your book and see if your thinking about that part fits with or changes your theory in any way."

As an example, I could have told children that if I took the theory—Rob is wimpy—and read backward, I might have come to the part in the book where Rob is crying at his mom's funeral and his dad slaps him. That part could add to the theory in any one of several ways. For example, I could say that Rob's dad was acting like a bully in that part, and yet, true to his wimpy nature, Rob didn't stand up to him (just as he doesn't to the bullies on the bus). I could have ended by reminding kids to read backward with their theory in hand, as well as forward.

One reason I've read aloud such a small bit of text is that I plan to develop a theory, read on in ways that lead me to change it, and then read on in ways that this time invite the kids to change the theory yet again. So I need to be a bit stingy with the text, like a piece of pie that needs to be divided into three pieces.

"Now that I have a 'penciled-in' theory, I'm going to keep reading on with that theory in mind. Listen for how I find more information that might change what I'm thinking or make it bigger."

> Not the way you can tell with Rachel and Lucy who have the same fat popsicle lips like everybody else in their family. But me and Nenny, we are more alike than you would know. Our laughter for example. Not the shy ice cream bells' giggle of Rachel and Lucy's family, but all of a sudden and surprised like a pile of dishes breaking. And other things I can't explain.

"What I just read makes me change what I was thinking before. *Now*, I think that Esperanza feels connected to her sister Nenny in ways that go beyond just how they look; I think she's talking about bonds that are deeper and more important than looks. My new theory is this: 'Esperanza feels as if deep down, she and her sister are very much alike.' Then I thought, 'But what about that first thought I had about her not belonging to her family?' And I realized that my theory could change again to be 'Esperanza feels that although she and her sister appear to others to be different, the truth is that deep down, they are very much alike.'"

ACTIVE INVOLVEMENT

Give children time to discuss with partners their observations of your theory-building work. Then join them in naming what you did, reiterating your teaching point.

> "Researchers, what work did you notice me doing as I read the Cisneros passage? Turn to your partner and list the steps I went through to grow and revise my theory just now."

There are several read-aloud tricks that implicitly demonstrate how you changed your thinking as you read. When you read aloud the line "But me and Nenny, we are more alike than you would know," you might raise an eyebrow, your index finger, and the inflection of your voice slightly to convey the effect, "Aha! My thinking is changing here." Your thinking will again change when you encompass the first portion of the text into your idea. By acting out that your mind is changing, you help children see this as it occurs, and you help them change their minds, too. They are able to infer from your gestures, tone, and inflection what you will explicitly name after the read-aloud.

The theory you develop here is pretty sophisticated. If you are teaching third graders or children who struggle, and especially if you are teaching a class of third graders who struggle, you'll probably leave out the whole last cycle of revision (above) and settle on the original idea, "Esperanza feels that deep down, she and her sister are a lot alike."

Can you do what you have asked children to do? Try it. You need to become accustomed to taking a very small action that you'd be apt to do with automaticity, and spelling out steps within that flow of activity. One trick is to begin before the main action, so the first step is the action that leads into the new action, and either that step or the next ones involve initiating the new action.

After a few moments, I said, "Readers, turn your attention back up here. I heard one partnership saying that I made a theory that fit with the first part of the text, but then when I read on, that theory didn't fit at all anymore. The theory turned out to be wrong. When my theory didn't fit anymore, I put it aside and came up with a new one. But then I went back to whatever had prompted the original idea and made sure my theory was big enough to encompass the whole text.

"Did you see that my theory went through a series of changes? That's exactly what readers do when we have a theory and then hold that theory loosely while we read further, knowing it will have a life of its own as we travel on. It will take us places we didn't expect to go."

Help children practice reading with a theory held loosely in hand. Progress further in the text you've just read aloud, inviting them to listen with your theory in hand, revising that theory and then naming what they've done in ways that will transfer.

"Now I'm going to read the last bit of this short text, and I want you to take on my theory: 'Esperanza feels that although she and her sister appear to others to be different, the truth is that deep down, they are very much alike.' Let's keep *this* theory close as we read on. Remember to be open to new thinking that might change or fit together with our theory."

> One day we were passing a house that looked, in my mind, like houses I had seen in Mexico. I don't know why. There was nothing about the house that looked exactly like the houses I remembered. I'm not even sure why I thought it, but it seemed to feel right.
>
> Look at that house, I said, it looks like Mexico.
>
> Rachel and Lucy look at me like I'm crazy, but before they can let out a laugh, Nenny says: Yes, that's Mexico all right. That's what I was thinking exactly.

Hopefully by now you have seen repeated instances when instead of me just naming what I've done in ways that are replicable with other texts, I engage the children in this work and then follow their efforts by doing my own job of naming what it is I have done. When you write your own minilessons, you'll find that sometimes you can't really think of a way to support kids in doing the activity within a three-minute timeframe while they're sitting with you in the meeting area. When you are stumped over how to support everyone in trying whatever it is you have taught, a great way to nevertheless give children a chance to be involved is to ask them to be researchers, naming to each other what it is you have done. You may find yourself tempted to ask the class to do this in unison, with you calling on a few raised hands. I'd advise against this because although you may feel as if the class thereby gets a time to be involved (after all, for a moment it won't be your words that fill the air in the room, but a child's), the truth is that calling on one child or another means that 95% of the class is still simply listening to other people talk. Turn and talk is a way to engage everyone—and remember, if you'd like, you can vary it, calling, "Stop and jot," instead.

You might want to have your theory written out so that at this point, you can magically display it, allowing the kids to reference a physical manifestation of your theory as they read on.

You may want to look up at the class as you speak these last two lines, conveying that these sentences are ones that readers especially need to notice. This section of the minilesson is for guided practice, for scaffolded work, and you'll want to find little ways to set readers up for success.

"Readers, in your mind, use this new information to adjust the theory we started out with, that Esperanza feels that although she and her sister appear to others to be different, the truth is that deep down, they are very much alike. Ask yourself, 'Did I come to new information that changes the original theory? That supports the original theory? Does the new information make the original idea bigger?' I'll give you a few moments to jot down a few words or phrases to hold whatever you are thinking.

"Now, take a moment to talk to your partner. Try to start off the talk by having the partner who tends not to share quite as much doing the talking. Remember that it takes two people thinking and participating to get the most out of your partnership."

Name the work that children have just done in ways that transfer to other texts and other days.

After a few minutes, I interceded. "Readers, I heard many smart discussions just now. A lot of people seem to be saying that the last part of the text made you add on to the original theory. For example, Aly said that it's not just that Esperanza and her sister are alike, but that they are alike in ways that other people might not even notice or value, in ways that feel almost secret because most people wouldn't even notice them. And Josh said that Esperanza not only feels like Nelly. She also feels different from Rachel and Lucy.

"Both of those readers used the new information from the text to grow their theories into even better ones. The theories that Aly and Josh ended up with are not the same as each other's, and their theories are both grand, fascinating. If they were reading in their own chapter books, Aly and Josh would now each take their revised theories loosely in hand and read on, expecting what, class?"

In unison, the children chimed, "That their theories would change."

"And also," I added, with a twinkle in my eye because I knew full well I was adding a whole new spin, "they'd know that they might well grow whole other theories and end up holding two or three theories loosely in hand (and I acted out walking not one dog on a leash but two).

It strikes me that so many of our teaching points in reading—about being present, being open, being flexible—could easily function as life lessons for our children. Ask yourself if there are other opportunities throughout the day when you could demonstrate these concepts to children. We can say to children, "You know how in reading we are trying to carry one thought with us to develop a more significant idea, and we let that thought change and become wiser as we live with it? Well, in my art project today I'm going to try the same approach." We often draw parallels to life during the reading workshop. We can do so also during other parts of the day.

Like adults, some children feel very comfortable sharing their ideas. Others require more prompting and encouragement. As you circulate among reading partnerships, one thing you might look for is that both readers are using up more or less the same amount of "air time." If you discover that one child dominates conversations, this is something you could address in a conference or in a whole-class minilesson. I find that it helps to tuck reminders about sharing talk time into my minilessons. Most children do want to be fair and take turns talking, but they forget and fall into familiar habits. Brief reminders as children go off to talk can be very effective.

LINK

Remind readers to read, growing ideas, and then to read on, expecting their original ideas to be revised.

"Whenever you are reading, this is how growing an interesting, unique theory goes: You pause to reread your notes and to review your thoughts, and you come up with a theory that pertains to many parts of the text. Then you hold this theory as you reread, perhaps, and certainly as you continue in your book. Your initial theory is most likely not your final one, but it gives you a starting place. As you read on, you're expecting that the information you encounter and the new ideas you develop will help you to grow an even better theory. Usually you end up adding more words to your theory. You may change your original thought so it pertains to more parts of the text (including the secondary characters) or so it is more true. Then you again read on, holding your newly revised theory in hand. I'm hoping you can do that work as you read today. Off you go."

CONFERRING AND SMALL-GROUP WORK

Help Readers Grow Ideas

As you confer with your children today, you'll help many of them do the work that you taught in yesterday's minilesson—that of rereading their Post-its and trying to grow a more umbrella-like idea, one that applies across instances in the text. You'll help others to carry the idea they have developed with them as they read on, letting that idea become more true and more specific or letting it spark new ideas. You should worry if your conferring and small-group work adhere only to the content of any one day's minilessons. Instead, always plan to use your interactions with kids to keep the work you have taught earlier alive.

Some Children Will Develop Localized Comments About the Text Rather than More Overarching Ideas

Some children will find it easy to generate passing comments as they read and harder to articulate an overarching idea that pertains to several sections of the text. Kobe and Malik organized their Post-it notes from their reading of *The Hundred Penny Box* together (this, again, is a book that was a bit easy for them, but it is also a provocative one). While doing

> ### MID-WORKSHOP TEACHING POINT
>
> #### Readers Expect a Flimsy Theory Will Grow
>
> "Readers, something terribly important just happened in a conference I had with a reader in the class, and I would like to tell you about it. I noticed that Josh didn't have any theories written down on his chart, even though he is more than halfway through his book. When I asked him about that, he said that he was struggling to come up with one. He felt like none of the ideas he had were good enough.
>
> "I know from talking to you that some of you have felt the same way; you think a theory has to be a big, complicated idea, and the ideas you have don't seem good enough. But remember what I told you in today's minilesson: A theory is a starting place. Don't worry if your first theory seems a bit flimsy. It will become more substantial.
>
> "In *The Tiger Rising*, we, too, had a flimsy idea about Rob. We were thinking that he was wimpy. That's a pretty obvious idea, but it gave us someplace to start, someplace to put our feet. As we read on and thought more, we used our theory to help us go deeper. And one way to use a theory to get oneself further is to ask questions. For example, we might have asked ourselves, 'Is *wimpy* really the right word to describe his behavior?' Or we could have asked, 'What seems to be making Rob act like such a wimp?' My real point is that it is just fine to start with a very obvious theory and to know it will grow and change. Anything is okay as a starting place. Think of how insubstantial a seed seems compared to a large plant. But, of course, the plant would not be possible if not for the seed taking root.
>
> "If your idea seems small or flimsy, have faith that you can grow it into something more."

this work, they invented a chart that used plus signs and equal signs to show how one idea plus another idea led them to a new idea. Of course, they had developed this tool with some encouragement, and I celebrated it as if they'd created the idea out of scratch. Although I was glad they'd made a tool that encouraged them to accumulate their ideas, when I actually studied the work they'd done with the tool, it seemed to me that despite the plus signs, the boys hadn't actually added together their ideas. Instead, they had restated the text. As I listened to them, I glanced at the books they were holding to see how far along they'd gotten in the book, since sometimes readers retell rather than grow ideas when they are still at the start of a book, but Kobe and Malik had read quite a bit of the book.

Taking hold of the page on which they'd used an addition sign to link their Post-it notes, I read the sequence of work as I might read a sentence. *[Fig. XV-1]*

"Boys, what I am noticing is that your first idea—'Aunt Dew is annoyed . . .'—is pretty much the same as the big idea you come to. It restates your original thinking. Reread what

Figure XV-1

you have written and see if you can spot how you repeat yourself." The boys read their work over. I asked them to tell me what they saw, and they agreed. They then added to their big idea verbally. Now their big idea was that Aunt Dew doesn't want to throw away her stuff, including the Hundred Penny Box, *because* those things are important to her.

Although that is actually not the most impressive idea in the world, I said, "I think you are on to something! And this is something that is important to the whole text, to the whole of the story. Your idea is central to the story, isn't it? I can't imagine reading this book and *not* thinking about the significance of the penny box to Aunt Dew. The author wanted the reader to think about this because she chose it as the title to her book. So you are the kinds of readers who know how to determine what's worth growing a theory about. This is huge!"

I then suggested that Malik and Kobe might record and then read over the big idea they'd developed about *The Hundred Penny Box* and discuss the idea among themselves briefly. "Sometimes when people talk about an idea—like when we talk about an idea we discover in *The Tiger Rising*—the idea grows," I pointed out. I knew the chances were greater that the idea would grow if I endorsed the idea, if I backed it. After they discussed the idea for a little bit of time, I interrupted and repeated what Kobe had just said and then added a transitional phrase: "Aunt Dew is

annoyed that Ruth is throwing stuff away because that stuff matters to her. *This is important because. . . ."* I gestured to the boys. Malik continued the sentence, "Because the pennies mean a lot to her."

"And, " I coached.

Kobe added, "The pennies represent her whole life." The boys exchanged glances, and laughed.

Again I said, "And. . . ."

"And Ruth didn't realize they were important, and throwing them away was kind of like wiping her out," said Malik.

I prompted, "What I'm trying to say is? Aunt Dew . . . Ruth . . . the pennies. . . ."

"Aunt Dew would have nothing if she didn't have her box full of memories." *[Fig. XV-2]*

Figure XV-2

Flabbergasted that once again, with heavy coaching, Malik had ended up expressing a beautiful, sophisticated idea and capturing the idea in a metaphor, I repeated his words and then restated the teaching point of the conference. "It is important to reread your own thinking and monitor for inadvertent repetition. If you want to push yourself toward new thinking, there are a cluster of prompts such as 'This is important because . . ." and "What I am trying to say . . ." that can help, as can talking with someone else." I then left Malik and Kobe with the job of being sure they paused again while reading their wonderful book and, this time, that they tried to do similarly deep thinking, only without my help.

Some Children Will Need Support to Find the Significance in Their Post-Its to Develop Theories

Years ago, in my son's second-grade classroom, there was great interest in rocks and minerals, so the students started a collection of rocks, stones, and pebbles and displayed them in the classroom. They would sort through the collection of rocks during choice time and write Post-its that revealed the ways they were grouping them. The Post-it near one cluster of stones said, "These are smooth." Another said, "These have lines."

Many students treat their Post-its in the same way. They are not a collection of pebbles but of thoughts about characters. Some readers do as my son did and sort their Post-its into categories and then simply name an attribute that fits that category.

For example, Jasmine and Lily were reading *Anastasia Krupnik* by Lois Lowry. Anastasia is a ten-year-old who has an up-and-down year of fourth grade. She falls in love, finally gets to know her grandmother, discovers she's no longer going to be an only child, and deals with the death of her grandmother.

When Jasmine and Lily put their Post-its together, they found that most contained jottings about Anastasia's mom. [Fig. XV-3]

When they looked over their Post-its to develop a theory about the character, they wrote, "Anastasia's mom's feelings." In other words, Jasmine and Lily named an attribute, or categorized the Post-its in much the same way as my son categorized rocks, coming up with a label that named a category for the Post-its rather than using them as a resource for growing ideas about the character.

To help readers move from supplying a one-word or one-phrase label for a group of Post-its toward using those Post-its as seed ideas for growing theories, we can teach readers to reread their Post-its, searching for and making significance. We can teach them to ask themselves, "Why is it like this?" or "What makes it this way?"

For Jasmine and Lily, these questions were very helpful. In our conference, I complimented them on coming up with a label for their Post-its. "Now, though, your work is to push your thinking by asking, 'Why is

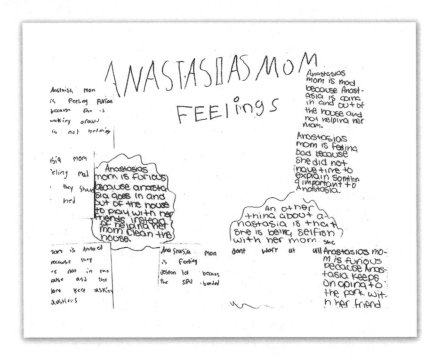

Figure XV-3

it like this?' Look over the Post-its about Anastasia's mom's feelings and ask yourselves, "Why is it like this?" or "What's making her mom this way?" When you do this work, you're likely to actually make a theory about the character. So, let's push our thinking. What's making her mom this way?" I looked at both of them and they looked at each other.

"Maybe she's tired because she's having a baby?" Jasmine said.

"And she's stressing out and getting crabby and frustrated," Lily added. "Maybe she's just tired out from raising a kid like Anastasia. She's overwhelmed 'cause she is pregnant and taking care of Anastasia."

Jasmine said, "She needs more help and she's crabby because she's tired. That's what happens to grown-ups."

Once they batted this idea back and forth a bit, I stopped them. "Readers, I noticed that you didn't just push *your own* thinking to grow a theory, you were pushing *each other's* thinking. You were passing the theory back and forth between you, each adding a bit to it. Now, I think you're ready to go back to your Post-its, and instead of writing 'Anastasia's mom's feelings,' you can write the theory you've grown about

Anastasia's mom. Just remember, for this time and always, that it helped so much when you thought of the significance of your Post-its, when you asked yourselves, 'So what?' or 'Why is it like this?'"

Some Children Will Benefit from Learning to Use Writing (Specifically Thought Prompts) As a Tool for Revising Their Theories

When you approach children who are, you hope, reading with their theories in hand and expecting those theories to change through this work, you may find that children aren't quite sure what you mean by "expecting their theories to change." One reason they may not grasp what you mean by letting an idea morph is that they may not have a method for doing this. Many children are accustomed to having an idea, then locking that thought in their minds, and then recording what they've already thought. It is a great thing to help these youngsters learn that they can let the pen take them to places they wouldn't have journeyed. You may, then, want to anticipate that some children will benefit from you helping them write to learn. You'll probably find that some of your children take to writing like a fish to water, while others struggle with it and still others actively resist, perhaps complaining they have no more to say or their hands hurt or they can't write fast enough. All of this may be true, but don't let them break you down. Be persistent. The more you work with resistant learners, the more they grow.

I gathered a small group around me and told them that I saw they'd each developed a couple of different theories about their books and they were now reading forward, mining their stories for parts that supported their theories. I told them that one reason I'd gathered them together was that they were each reading particularly wonderful books, and with books like those, I thought they could perhaps generate even more complex theories. Then I told them that one way readers often make theories about books more complex is by using writing to develop ideas. I asked them to go to a clean page in their notebooks and to write one of their theories at the top of the page, keeping the other theory or two close at hand. I explained to the group that I was going to call out thought prompts. After I said a phrase, I wanted them to record what I said and use it to help themselves keep writing and keep thinking. I knew my interjections would not be timed to allow them to finish every previous thought, so I let them know that when I threw out a phrase, they'd need to stop what-

ever they were writing (and thinking), skip a line, and quickly record whatever I said. "You'll be writing fast and furious," I said. "I won't stop for you to catch up."

I asked them to reread the thought they'd recorded at the top of their page, and then I extended their thought by saying, "To add on. . . ." I made sure the lilt in my voice rose in a way that helped to convey that they were going to say more about their first thought.

As children wrote alongside me, I peeked at what they were writing, knowing that what I saw would help me choose what I'd call out next, and letting their pace influence my timing. At some point, I noticed a few children would write just one sentence and then wait, so I said, "Keep your pen moving and your mind moving 'til I call out something else." When I noticed children's thinking becoming repetitive, I was especially apt to insert a thought prompt. "This is making me realize. . . ." or "This is true because. . . ." or "On the other hand. . . ."

At the top of Emma's page was her theory that Leslie (in *Bridge to Terabithia*) is having difficulty fitting in with the other kids at school because she is so different. Then Emma had written, "To add on . . . Leslie is new to the school and no one is really accepting of the new kid especially when she isn't like the other girls. She is more athletic and would rather play with the boys but they don't want to play with her because she beat them all in a race and it's like they can't handle it. The girls don't like the way she dresses and her short. . . ."

I called out, "This makes me realize. . . ."

Emma pushed up her knobby red plastic bracelet and continued to scrawl: "This makes me realize that the other kids in school don't know what to do around her. It's like she makes them uncomfortable so they push her away."

After a few other thought prompts, I lifted the entire enterprise by saying, "This may fit with my other theory (the one you've kept close at hand) because. . . ." Then I added a parenthetical tip. "Take your other theory and try to connect it with what you are writing right now." To get them started, I said, "Let me say the prompt again. This may fit with my other theory . . . because. . . ."

By now Emma was, in fact, writing fast and furious—and in ways that struck me as pretty impressive, given the fact that she'd entered the year as a child who read fast but didn't think in response to books with any sense of fluency. She wrote, "My other theory is that Jess isn't the kind of son his dad wanted, so both kids aren't fitting in somewhere. Jess's dad wanted a tough kid because his dad doesn't know what to do with a son who'd rather draw and play with a girl." Then Emma reread her first set of ideas, in which she'd written about peers rejecting Leslie, and now she added, "It's like Jess's dad is pushing Jess away just like the kids are pushing Leslie away. And when his dad does that it makes Jess feel like he isn't a part of the family."

I called out, "The bigger idea I am having now is. . . ."

Emma recorded my thought prompt and kept writing: "The bigger idea I am having now is that both Jess and Leslie are on the outside in some way and their friendship makes them feel less alone. But I think Jess has it the worst because feeling on the outside of your own family is worse than being on the outside of friends."

After I prompted, "In other words . . . ," Emma wrote, "In other words, Jess and Leslie are left out, Jess at home, Leslie at school."

After I interjected, "My new theory is . . . ," she wrote, "My new theory is that it is because Jess and Leslie are left out that they go to each other." [Fig. XV-4]

I gathered the group back together, and we shared out our new theories, and then I restated the techniques I hoped they'd begun to learn, pointing out that they, too, could draw from the chart of prompts and that the most important thing was for them to understand that their big ideas would change, becoming more true.

Leslie is having difficulty fitting in with the other kids at school because she is so different.

To add on she's new to the school and no one is really accepting of the new kid especially when she isn't like the other girls. She is more athletic and would rather play with the other boys but they don't want to play with her because she beat them all in a race and it's like they can't handle it. The girls don't like the way she dresses and her short

This makes me realize that the other kids in school don't know what to do around her. It's like she makes them uncomfortable so she they push her away.

My other theory is that Jess isn't the kind of son his dad wanted, so both kids aren't fitting in somewhere. Jess's dad wanted a tough kid because his dad doesn't know what to do with a son who'd rather draw and play with a girl. It's like Jess's dad is pushing Jess away just like the kids are pushing Leslie away. And when his dad does that it makes Jess feel like he isn't a part of the family.

The bigger idea I am having now is that both Jess and Leslie are on the outside in some way and their friendship makes them feel less alone. But I think Jess has it the worst because feeling on the outside of your own family is worse than being on the outside of friends.

In other words, Jess and Leslie are left out, Jess at home, Leslie at school. My new theory is that it is because Jess and Leslie are left out that they go to each other.

Figure XV-4
Emma uses thought prompts to nudge her thinking forward.

TEACHING SHARE

Readers Share Thinking About Books to Grow Ideas

Ask students to share their work of the day with their partner.

"Get with your partner and look over your Post-its and, if you have them, at your theory charts. As you look at your theories or your Post-its, decide if they are big or small ideas and talk with your partner about how you might grow your ideas into even bigger or more complex or more true ideas. If you finish that work, you can continue reading, seeing if your book teaches you more about your big ideas."

As children worked with their partners, I pulled close to a group of youngsters who needed some extra support with this work.

As you listen in, if you hear a situation you suspect several students are coping with, convene a small group and work through that situation together, modeling the process students can use on their own.

"I just heard Tyrell say to his partner that he couldn't find any good Post-its, and I thought maybe the rest of you could use some help, too."

Tyrell said, "I can't tell if my Post-its are little or big. They seem in the middle. And sometimes I forget what I mean."

"Let's all of us work with Tyrell's Post-its for *Jake Drake, Know-It-All* and try to decide if his ideas are small or big, and then see if we can work together to grow a big idea that is like a theory." I turned to Tyrell, who was kneeling awkwardly near me, his big shoes stuck out behind him, and said, "You read us a Post-it, and we'll all decide if it is big (I stretched my arms out) or tiny."

Tyrell sat up a little higher on his knees so his classmates could see him and pointed to a Post-it in his book. [*Fig. XV-5*]

> Jake has a friend who also likes computers. I can't believe he likes that much games on the computer.

Figure XV-5
Tyrell isn't sure if this is a big or small idea.

One of the quickest and easiest ways to form small groups is to cast your eyes and ears quickly around during the active involvements in minilessons, mid-workshop teaching points, or teaching shares. You can literally hear as well as see the readers who are struggling.

I considered pointing out to children that one reason they were having a hard time finding Post-its that "went together" and that led them to bigger ideas about the character or the book was that they tended to be doing lots of predicting and questioning. I'd taught them to do this, of course, and it is certainly important mind work for readers, but the truth is that it doesn't set readers up to develop theories as much as other kinds of thinking will do. But I decided to keep these thoughts to myself for now. They might confuse matters, and in any case, I had very little time.

I mused, "It is about two characters, but I'm not entirely sure that saying two characters like the same thing is a big idea. I'm just not sure. What do you all think?"

Tyrell, quick to dismiss his idea, replied, "Small."

I asked, "Thumbs up if you agree." Most of the thumbs went up. "Tyrell was wise to try growing an idea about two characters, wasn't he, but sometimes the ideas we come up with won't really carry big messages. Let's listen to the next Post-it and be ready to give the signal for big (I stretched out my arms) or small (I pinched my fingers together)."

Tyrell turned to his next Post-it and giggled as he read, clearly enjoying being in front of the group. [Figs. XV-6 and XV-7]

When Tyrell shared the thought "I don't think I can hold six cans of soup," I was tempted to show children that a seemingly teeny tiny thought such as that one could actually be grown into a bigger thought by just adding another sentence to the initial thought. Had Tyrell thought, "What does that let me know about Jake?" he might have thought something such as "Jake is always doing the impossible." This would be an idea that functions almost as an umbrella—the idea big enough that the whole story fits underneath it. But for now I thought that would be too much to do during this one time.

I don't think
I can hold
six cans of
soup.

Figure XV-6
Tyrell and his classmates decide this constitutes a small idea.

I think Kevin
and Marsha are
jelous that
Jake Knows
more than
them.

Figure XV-7
The votes are mixed of whether this constitutes a big idea.

His classmates signaled this was a small idea. I put that Post-it close to the other small thought, but not on top of it. Then Tyrell read, "I think Kevin and Marsha are jealous that Jake knows more than them." This time, one lone child stretched out his arms with confidence while the others, including Tyrell, just sat, unsure.

"So we aren't sure what to make out of this idea. Is it big or small? It might help if we compare it to Tyrell's other thoughts and think if it's similar or different." The children agreed that indeed this thought was bigger than the others. It was an important observation that could be the beginning of a bigger idea.

Laying the Post-its beside each other is important because sometimes when we lay tiny ideas next to each other, we may be able to look across and see something significant. At this point I wasn't sure if this was something I would be able to teach into or not, but it was a possibility.

There was another idea that was clearly a big one—"Jake feels all trapped because kids see him as a know-it-all." [Fig. XV-8]

Then I suggested Tyrell continue working alone and that the other children take a second to glance at their Post-its and see if they, too, had recorded some important thoughts. I coached one child, then another, asking, "Is this a big or small idea?" "Is this an important thought about a character or is it just stating what the character did once? If so, then what does the action make you think?"

If the work of the small group blossoms into work the whole class could learn from, share that.

I reminded the group of what we'd learned so far about growing big ideas. "Remember, one way to grow big ideas is to look at those ideas that seem to go together, and think, 'What are these saying or showing about the character?' And then we can push the idea further by thinking not only about one character but between characters."

The children turned to their partners and talked. I listened in and coached by saying, "How does that fit with another Post-it?" Or "How does that affect other characters?" Or "Why does he feel that way?"

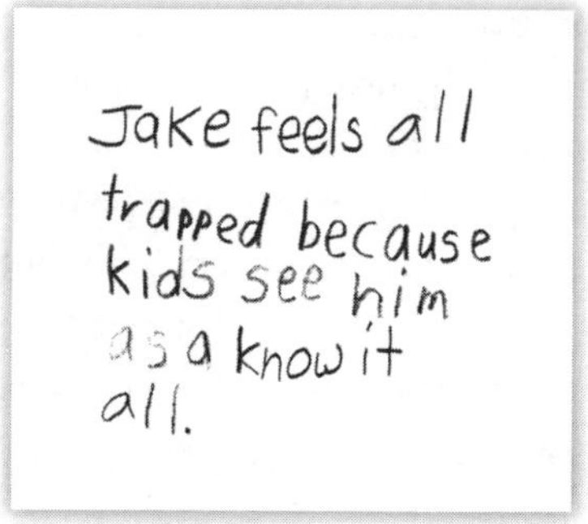

Jake feels all trapped because kids see him as a know it all.

Figure XV-8
Everyone agrees *this* remark is a big idea.

End the day by sharing work others have done, along the same lines as the challenge you've just worked through together. Remind children of what they can take from this day into their reading lives forever.

Then I called for the attention of the whole class so that a few children could share the bigger ideas they'd developed. "Kevin and Marsha's jealousy hurts Jake. This shows that jealousy can make people do mean things." "It's good to want to do well, but it is not good to care more about winning than friendships." I ended the share session by saying, "The work we have just done with Tyrell's big ideas is work that I know all of you will do tonight as you read—and always. The powerful thing about recording your ideas is then you can reread them, and you can think, 'How does one idea, and another idea, lead me to an even better idea?' It is like following a trail of bread crumbs to a magical new place."

Bringing a Narrative Frame to Theories About Characters

IN THIS SESSION,
you will teach children that readers use what we know about narratives and characters in general to examine the specific motivations of our own characters.

Anyone who writes or reads fiction knows that characters are driven by struggles and motivations. Without these, there is no story arc, no journey. As readers, we read wanting, above all, to go on a journey. We want to stand by as our characters slay not just dragons but inner demons, as they protest injustices and fight for change. We want to cheer our characters on as they make connections and as they take steps toward realizing their dreams. We want to rejoice when our characters experience victories. We want to learn lessons and change and grow alongside them. We want to share our characters' motivations and struggles because doing so gives us insights about other people and, especially, about ourselves. And when we're done reading, at the end of the journey, we want to challenge ourselves, just as our characters have challenged themselves, to think about and live differently in the world.

When Rob struggles not just with the Threemongers but also with Sistine, with his dad, with himself, we think, "Rob is the kind of person who struggles to stand up for himself," or "Rob has all these feelings deep down inside that he can't let out," and this leads us to think more universally: "Often people struggle to face their feelings and their fears." Likewise, when we read about Rob's friendship with Sistine, about his carvings, about that tiger he is keeping a secret, we think, "Rob wants to connect with someone," or "Rob yearns to feel more alive," and this leads us again to think universally, to theorize that "People desire connections—with other people, with their feelings, with themselves."

As we think and talk and write about characters' wants and struggles, we often discover that the two are linked, that what characters most struggle with is often linked to what they yearn for above all. Rob wants to connect with a friend, with his dad, but doing so requires that he first connect with

---

GETTING READY

- Prepare to demonstrate your thinking aloud about the desires and motivations of a character from a familiar story. We've chosen Willy from *Stone Fox*, which will work beautifully.

- When you confer, bring a small stack of familiar books with you that help you make your teaching points.

- Before Session XVII, you will need to have completed Chapter 25 in *The Tiger Rising*. You will reference a section of this chapter in the minilesson.

his feelings—that he open his suitcase. Likewise, when Rob faces one of his struggles, when he stands up to the Threemonger boys, he is in fact acting on his desire for a friend. He wants to connect with Sistine, and the desire for that friendship is so large that it outweighs his fear.

In this session, you'll teach children that when we read, we aim to grow theories that encompass that which is central to the story. Of course, there is no *one* thing that is central to a story, but there are aspects of a story that are clearly

> We want to share our characters' motivations and struggles because doing so gives us insights about other people and, especially, about ourselves.

marginal or tangential to it. One of the best ways to channel children toward growing ideas that are central to a story

is to help them recognize that most stories are constructed around a story arc that links together a protagonist's motivations and struggles. If you can help children to take these into account as they think about a story, this will function as your previous instruction did when you channeled readers to attend to subordinate characters. Your teaching will nudge them to look not just at a single incident but rather across the text at multiple incidents, searching for patterns of behavior, of thinking, so that when Rob stands up for Sistine, children will think, "Why is he standing up to those bullies now when he hasn't *before* now?"

This is where the hard work begins. This is where children will have to think about all they know about Rob—about his motivations, his desires, his fears—to land on the idea that Rob *must* stand up to the Threemongers, not just for Sistine but for himself. And perhaps through this work, children will come to ideas that encompass not only more of the story but also more of the world. Perhaps they'll come to think that it is not really the Threemongers who are Rob's worst enemies; they're just mean boys. It's Rob *himself* who is his worst enemy, who is preventing himself from making the connections he needs—that all of us need—to live meaningfully, to be happy. Once Rob realizes that—and this moment of standing up for Sistine is the start—he can face his own fears, of letting his feelings rise, of allowing himself to miss his mother, to want a closer relationship with his father, and to have a friend he can count on.

MINILESSON

Bringing a Narrative Frame to Theories About Characters

CONNECTION

Tell children that experts know which features of a subject merit attention, and direct their gaze to those features. Give examples from your experience, drawing a parallel to reading. In a story, the protagonist's wants, struggles, changes, and lessons merit attention.

"Readers, you all have been thinking about ways to grow your observations into bigger ideas, and many of you are using the process we talked about yesterday to do so. You are pausing sometimes to look back on your jotted notes, sorting them into ideas that go together, and trying to create ideas that are big ones, that are theories. Today I want to approach the idea of growing ideas from a different angle by helping you think about things that are worth paying attention to as we read.

"I've been reading a popular book, *Blink*. Malcolm Gladwell, the author of this book, suggests that experts on a subject can look at something related to the subject and, in the blink of an eye, generate important and surprisingly accurate insights about it. As an example, one marriage expert can observe a married couple in conversation, and then he can predict with 95% accuracy whether the couple will still be married fifteen years later. The secret is that he is an expert who knows which aspects of the interactions between married people are especially noteworthy—especially predictive.

This minilesson is a variation of Session III in Literary Essays: Writing About Reading, *a book in my* Units of Study for Teaching Writing, Grades 3–5.

Gladwell's books have tons of implications for those of us who teach. Read them with this in mind and you'll be intrigued, as we have been! The theme of this book has resurfaced for me constantly. For example, I do find that after years of work with young readers, one can draw conclusions about them with surprising speed and accuracy.

"I've noticed something similar when I watch the Westminster Kennel Club dog show on television. I love to put myself in the judge's place, eyeing the flat-coated retrievers, the golden retrievers, and the English setters. But inevitably, I am still checking out a dog's coat, shape, and proportions when suddenly the judge signals, 'Walk him.' Then, before I've had a chance to really take in all that new data, the judge moves on to the next dog! Expert dog watchers, like expert marriage analysts, can make judgments in the blink of an eye! Malcolm Gladwell says that a good part of the secret lies in the fact that experts on a subject know which features merit our attention. They don't have to give equal attention to all the parts of a subject the way nonexperts do."

Name your teaching point. Specifically, tell children that our reading experiences become even richer when we pay attention to characters in general, as well as when we zoom in on a character's particular motivations and struggles.

"Today I want to teach you that expert readers believe that when thinking about stories, it can deepen our reading to pay attention to characters in general and to their motivations and struggles in particular."

Teaching

Tell children that expert readers ask questions about the desires and motivations of the characters in our books. Demonstrate this by reflecting upon a read-aloud text or character that children know well.

"One way to be insightful about people and characters is to think, 'What does this person seem to desire? What motivates him?' That is, when you are good at reading people, this means you understand what drives a person. This is true in life, but it is especially true in stories. Writers create characters who have big desires or motivations.

"Usually, the main character in a story, the protagonist, has desires that lead him or her to go after something, and predictably, the character ends up struggling to reach that goal. Usually, something gets in the way, there are obstacles, and the main character has to try, try, try to reach the goal.

Readers sometimes feel overwhelmed and paralyzed by the task of thinking, writing, and talking about a book. Faced with so much information, often readers don't grasp how to select important parts on which to focus. This is in part why we find children who jot or talk about an element of a story that seems inconsequential. It's important to help such readers know what features merit attention. This is one reason why this unit was devised. The entire unit directs a reader's governing gaze to characters. Of course, in a fiction book, the decision to notice characters doesn't exactly focus a reader's attention, so you'll see that I suggest there are certain aspects of a character that especially merit attention. Specifically, I hope readers attend to the protagonist's traits, motivations, struggles, changes, and lessons. I also hope readers attend to conflicts between characters and to changes in relationships.

You'll remember that actually my list of features that merit attention is bigger than this. I also want readers to pay attention to repeating images and to patterns in the protagonist's relationships with subordinate characters. But for now, it seems enough to help children see the value of reading with an eye toward the most central features in a story arc—a character's motivations and struggles.

"Listen as I do this thinking about a character from a book I recently read: *Lance Armstrong: It's Not About the Bike*. Actually, he's a real person, but I just read a biography about him, the story of his life, and I realized that not surprisingly, the story of his life sort of follows the story patterns we usually see.

"Let's see. What are the main character's, the protagonist's, desires? Hmm. Lance Armstrong wants to be the best bicyclist in the world. He wants to win the Tour de France, a really hard bike race, more times than any other cyclist in history."

"So now, the harder part to think about: What are some of the obstacles my character has to face and overcome to achieve his goal? Well, Lance Armstrong had cancer and was very sick. He could have died, but instead he fought to recover. He began to train himself back into shape after almost dying, even though people thought he was crazy to even try. He had to find a trainer and doctors that would believe in him. Lots of people accused Lance of cheating by using steroids to get stronger, but he had to ignore the distractions and keep on fighting. He had many drug tests to prove he didn't use steroids. Then, to make history by winning the Tour de France more often than anyone else, he had to focus only on the race—had to train like crazy, eat a very restricted diet, and be away from his kids for months at a time. He had to put together a team to ride with him, even though lots of cyclists were wary of him because of his illness. Even so, he pulled together an amazing team." Then I paused, and said to the children, "Do you see how the character in my story, Lance Armstrong, had a really big motivation and then he ran into one obstacle after another? Do you see how so many stories are like this—a big dream and a character try, try, trying?

In this teaching demonstration portion of the lesson, I chose to use the story of Lance Armstrong because the overarching details of his life are familiar to some children. I recognize that Lance Armstrong's story is not fiction, and therefore, it may require a bit of work to transfer the ideas here to fictional texts. In any case, the familiarity of Lance Armstrong's story provides an opportunity for me to demonstrate how a reader can apply the story code to more deeply understand the characters in their texts. Because I'm not using an actual text here for the demonstration, I can more easily and efficiently use a text during the active involvement portion of the lesson without making the minilesson so text-dense that the text distracts from the teaching point.

Notice that as a reader, I am asking myself certain questions about the character. I begin by asking, "What is it that Lance Armstrong wants?" Then, when I come up with an answer or theory, I push myself to ask another question that somehow relates but that can give me even more precise information. I ask, "What are the obstacles he had to overcome, and how did he get past them?" By inquiring about the actions and circumstances of Lance's life and pursuit of his goals, I am guiding myself into a deeper analysis of the main character, becoming an even greater expert on the story and furthering my expertise as a reader in general.

"Readers, I want to tell you one more thing that shapes most stories. You know characters have motivations and that as they set out to make their dream come true, they run into obstacles. They have to climb every mountain, ford every stream. But here's the other thing. To get past the obstacles, the character has to draw on what's inside of him. As readers, we have to get to know what's inside of the character by asking ourselves, 'What resources does the character have deep inside that helps him or her reach goals?' About Lance Armstrong, I would ask myself, 'What does Lance have deep inside of him that helps him overcome the obstacles he faces?' There are no answers spelled out on the page. Readers make up those answers based on all we know about the story. For me, I think one resource Lance drew upon is a very competitive spirit. He wants to be the best, no matter what, and that competitive drive makes him take on challenges. I also think he is able to be incredibly focused. Nothing gets in the way of his dreams, not cancer, not people who are against him, not his desire to spend time with his kids! So at this point, I have a theory about my character and about the book I have been reading that I think is central to the story."

Name what you have done in a way that is transferable to other texts and other days.

"So, readers, did you notice that when I wanted to grow ideas about the book I have been reading, I didn't just put my mind anywhere—say, on his bike—and then try to come up with ideas? Instead, I drew on my sense of the features of stories that tend to matter most. I know that it pays off to think about the protagonist and, specifically, about the protagonist's motivations and struggles. So first I asked myself, 'What does my character want?' Then I asked, 'What are some of the obstacles that get in the way of his wants, and how has he been dealing with them?' Finally, to get really close up to my character and the story, I asked myself, 'What resources does my character draw upon, from deep inside, to meet the challenges and reach his goals?' When I thought about these things and began to find answers, I came up with theories about the book I read that seem really central to it."

This upcoming portion of the teaching is optional. I could simply leave it at the idea that it is important to consider characters' motivations and struggles. As you teach, you'll keep an eye always on kids' engagement and will adapt your teaching to maintain that engagement. So you may well enter this minilesson intending to teach all of it, and midway through, you may scale down your plans. That's how teaching goes, always.

In truth, we know that to meet challenges, characters draw on resources inside themselves (including strengths they probably didn't even know were there) and also on resources outside themselves. In this example, Lance Armstrong draws upon his competitive instinct, his laser-like focus, the support of his teammates, trainers, and doctors, and the love of his kids. Those relationships help him to reach his goals. I've decided to leave this out of the minilesson this time, but it might find its way into a conference at some point.

Active Involvement

Invite readers to consider a character's motivations and struggles, working within a familiar text. Set them up to talk about their ideas with partners.

"Let's try this powerful thinking work together by considering a story we know well, and thinking about the main character's—the protagonist's—desires, and thinking also about whether that main character encounters difficulty en route to meeting those desires. Let's think about Willy in *Stone Fox* in this close-in way.

"So remember, think first about what the main character wants. Let's see . . . um . . . little Willy wants. . . ."

The kids were up on their knees, dying to call out, so I gestured for them to share, and they called out variations of this sentiment: "To save his grandfather and the farm!"

"So, little Willy's biggest desire is to save his grandfather and to save the farm. That's what motivates him. Now, the harder part. What are some obstacles he faces, and how does he deal with them? Think about how little Willy runs into obstacles and has to try, try, try to overcome them. Turn and talk to your partner about this."

I listened in as children mentioned obstacles such as "At first Willy isn't sure how to save his grandfather, and the obstacle is that his grandfather lost his voice and can't say what is wrong. So, little Willy solves that by hand signals," "I guess it's that Willy needs money bad, so he decided to enter the race to get the prize money, but he didn't have the entrance fee? He ended up using his college money, right?" I shared these out to the class by rephrasing them a tiny bit.

"Readers, we're thinking about the obstacles Willy faces, how he has to climb every mountain, ford every stream. You mentioned that Willy has to learn what's making his grandfather sick, he has to figure out how to communicate with him, he has to raise money to enter the race, he has to win the race, and so on.

"Now, here's the next thing. We know that characters draw on what's inside of them to overcome obstacles. So, to meet his challenges, little Willy has to draw on what he's really like inside. That means that by watching how he deals with the hard stuff on the outside, we get to know what's inside little Willy. Do you think that's true? Think about it for a moment. What resources did little Willy draw upon to overcome his challenges? Stop and jot your thoughts about that."

If you are teaching a fairly advanced class, you may want to instead invite children to reflect on The Tiger Rising. *This work will be more nuanced than work focused on* Stone Fox.

You'll notice that I frame or prompt kids' thinking throughout this active involvement, and then I invite them to speak out to the group, to turn and talk to a partner, or to jot their ideas.

As children turn and talk, I take the opportunity to listen in and gather information about their thoughts. I share their ideas back with them strategically, choosing to share things that reinforce the line of thinking of the lesson to keep the lesson concise and streamlined.

Notice that I shift gears by asking readers to stop and jot at this point. My original plan was to have them turn and talk again, but I felt like I needed to calm the lesson a bit, especially after the last turn and talk, which was particularly exuberant. Including a stop and jot opportunity during the active involvement portion of the minilesson also provides artifacts of a reader's thinking. I collect these and then, after the lesson, I can take a closer look at them to see how the work is going and what readers understand and what is confusing to them.

After a moment, Kobe looked up, and I signaled to him to read aloud what he had jotted. He read, "Little Willy keeps trying. We can see that he never gives up."

"Little Willy keeps trying. We can see that he never gives up," I repeated. "That's so true. Another way of saying this is that little Willy is persistent. He's determined."

Lily chimed in, almost interrupting, to say, "Little Willy is brave, too. He gets the doctor, he goes to the bank to get money. He does things that kids don't usually have to do. He's brave."

"Whoa. Did you see how that line of thinking took us on quite a journey, and it started with paying attention to what little Willy wants, to what motivates him, and it got us to a place where we understand little Willy a lot better. We did this deep thinking by asking these questions: What does the character want? What are the obstacles in the way and how does the character overcome them? What resources does our character draw upon from deep inside to overcome the obstacles? And, by doing that, we have a much deeper understanding of little Willy and probably a deeper understanding of the important issues in the book."

LINK

Send readers off, ready to read with attention to key parts of the text—in this case searching for characters' desires and for what they draw on to overcome obstacles. Ask readers to remember that characters in books travel through a life that is uncertain and often complicated, where they make mistakes and have wants and needs—just like real people.

"Readers, you've shown such incredible insight today. You've grown such big ideas. It's not always easy discovering a character's motivations, especially when those motivations aren't ones you can imagine for yourself, or when the motivations seem like they might harm, not help, the character. In a minute, you'll turn back to your independent reading books. Whenever you read, today and always, remember to notice what motivates your characters—what drives them to do things—and also what they draw on to overcome what gets in their way. Remember that characters, like real people, are fallible. They don't always know right away what's best for them. In fact, often that's part of the journey they go on, right? They need to struggle to figure something out, and along the way their wants and goals may change. Look out for that as you read!"

Little Willie keeps trying. We can see that he never gives up.

CONFERRING AND SMALL-GROUP WORK

Keep Mentor Texts at Your Side

One way to make your conferring and small-group work more effective is to carry a small stack of familiar books with you as you work with youngsters. You'll need to choose texts that you love and that you know the children will love also—texts that can stay alive in your classroom throughout the whole year. Ideally, you will think ahead of time about ways in which those texts might be useful when you want to demonstrate a teaching point within a conference or a small group. When it is time to say, "Watch me . . ." and "Notice how I . . . ," you'll reference one of these familiar, beloved texts.

You'll find that if you love a text, you and your children can return to that text time and again, each time finding more and more in it.

To imagine how you'd use these touchstone texts, think for a minute about how you have used *Stone Fox* within this unit (now that it is no longer the read-aloud text). Of course, it was important that the text was already familiar to the class. You could hone in on just one part, knowing that readers had enough contextual knowledge to understand that one part. To use the books in your short stack in this same way, you'll want to read them to your class

as literature, for the sheer power of those texts. Only if the texts have traction with your class and affect your readers can they be candidates for the role of touchstone texts.

Once you have identified a text or two that will join your short stack, "spy on yourself" reading it. To do this, aim to be an alert, thoughtful reader but not to be a professor of literature. What do you see yourself noticing, doing, asking, thinking, assuming, drawing from? Once you have articulated something that you do and determined the skill that this illustrates, then your challenge is to think about how you can help children go from what they are already doing to more skilled reading—closer to what you are able to do. You'll need to start by putting yourself in a youngster's shoes, deliberately pretending to read like many of your youngsters read, so you can show children a step-by-step process they can use to make that reading better.

It takes a bit of practice to learn to catch yourself in the act of reading and to do the backward work of resurrecting what you've done to make sense of the text in hand. As you read with these goals, you may want to mark particular places in the text with Post-its so that when you are later

---

MID-WORKSHOP TEACHING POINT

Readers Consider Characters' External Resources, Too

Voicing over as the class read their books, I said, "Readers, in a few minutes you are going to have a chance to share some thinking and ideas about your character with your partners." After a minute or two, I said, "Readers, before you turn and talk, think in your mind about what is motivating your character. What does she really want? What does she desire more than anything? Push yourself to consider *why* your character wants this thing so badly. Now, think in your mind about what is getting in your character's way. What struggles does your character face on his or her journey? Jot some of your thoughts down. When you have your ideas in your mind, put a thumb up." [Figs. XVI-1 and XVI-2]

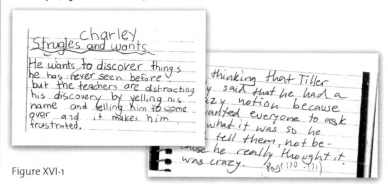

Figure XVI-1

Figure XVI-2

continued on next page

teaching an individual or a small group, you can find, on the spot, an example you are apt to need. You may find it helpful to pencil your own reader responses into the margins. Later, as you confer with a child, you can lay your own process of thought bare by showing the child the thoughts that *you* had as you read. Your stack of books might support teaching points already covered in this or other units of study, or they may inspire brand new teaching points. Teaching points will also occur to you as you see a child struggle in a conference. Knowing the mentor texts in your short stack inside out will help tremendously. As a teaching point occurs to you during a conference, you should be able to mentally rifle through your selection of mentor texts for the specific place in the book that is just right to illustrate this particular teaching point.

You won't want to mark just a few preselected passages that you can cite in your conferences and small groups. Instead, the whole goal during one-to-one and one-to-four teaching will be to tailor your teaching in response to what kids show you. To be in a position to do this, you'll want to anticipate a host of different ways in which you could conceivably use each of these texts. Because you will have imagined a score of teaching opportunities within any one of these texts, it will be easier for you to ground your conferences and small groups in concrete examples while also inventing teaching in response to what your children need.

This responsiveness includes an eye for the level at which each child is reading. Although any skill can be taught with texts at any level, there will be times when you want to reference touchstones that mirror the level of the books that a child is holding—so be sure your stack includes texts that represent various bands of reading difficulty.

> ## MID-WORKSHOP TEACHING POINT
>
> *continued from previous page*
>
> Scanning the room, I waited until most of the students seemed prepared to share with their partners before I said, "Turn and tell your partner about your character's motivations and struggles." I gave the students a few minutes before I stopped them. "Readers, I'm noticing that your discussions about your characters have taken on much more significance now that you are thinking about what motivates your characters, what their deepest desires are, and what seems to stand in their way. You are getting much deeper inside the hearts and minds of your characters as a result of this kind of thinking.
>
> "Before we go back to reading, I want us to think carefully about what helps our character along her journey to get what she wants. We know that characters draw upon their inner resources, like Lance Armstrong drew upon his competitive spirit and his incredible focus and Willy drew upon his determination and bravery. Characters also often draw upon external, or outside, resources, too, like their relationships with other people. Often in books, it is a relationship with another character that helps our main character get what he wants or come to understand something about himself or the world in a new way. It seems as though Willie May is that kind of character for both Rob and Sistine. Let's reread a brief part from *The Tiger Rising,* where Willie May meets Sistine and Rob in the parking lot outside the laundry room.
>
>

Using *Dancing in the Wings* as a Touchstone Text

Listening to Kobe retelling the plot of his book, I noted his tendency to confuse secondary characters. He'd refer to a character as "the first guy" or "the mom," often catching himself to amend what he'd just said, so that his retelling went something like "Then the first guy—no, no, the *neighbor*—decided to phone and ask the sheriff for himself, but the sheriff called and told his mom—I think maybe it was the mom's friend—that the guy was dead." I had a ready-made conference in my head for such occasions: teaching that readers keep track of and use characters' names while retelling. Calling characters by name allows readers to develop a greater connection with people and with the book. But I'd already had that conference with Kobe and knew that his plot and character amnesia were symptomatic of a larger pattern. He was plot-driven to the extent that for him, characters were hardly memorable in their individuality.

I whipped out a touchstone text I tend to carry as I confer: *Dancing in the Wings*. I was quite sure that the strong-voiced characters in this book would support my teaching point for Kobe. "Sometimes," I told him, "It takes more than a *visual* mental movie to imagine the characters in your book. You need to turn the volume way up so you can *hear* the way your characters sound when they talk. For instance, when I picked up *Dancing in the Wings* for the first time, I could *hear* Sassy and Hughie and their mom when they spoke." Mustering up the appropriate drama, I read aloud the following lines, careful to differentiate between the three characters by varying my voice for each—a higher pitch for Mama, a deeper voice for Hughie, and a defiant, rapid speaking style for Sassy.

> "You should join the swimming team, since you got those long toes and don't need any fins," my older brother, Hughie, teased.
>
> I shot right back, "At least I don't have that big forehead lookin' like a street lamp."
>
> Mama said, "Stop all that bad talk! You act so ugly sometimes. Hughie, your big head is a sign of intelligence. And Sassy, your big feet will make your legs look longer and prettier in your ballet shoes."

Turning to Kobe, I said, "You see how different Mama sounds from Hughie and Sassy? I feel like I know a character better once I try to hear his or her voice in my head. If you can hear a character in your head, with their own special voice and accent and style of speaking, you'll remember that character better, even after you put your book down. *In addition to* referring to characters by their names while retelling, try also to imagine the way a character sounds. This will help make the character more memorable to you." Silently to myself I added, "This will also help you have a livelier mental movie of your reading, and hopefully it'll help you continue your progress toward increased engagement in reading."

Dancing in the Wings proved useful through many conferences that same day. In a conference on decoding hard words, I'd pointed out words such as *tendu* and *adagio*, declaring, "Now, I'm no ballerina, never been to ballet class, and so I had no clue what these words meant when I first read this book. Guess what I did to figure them out?"

Having established that readers encounter tricky and unfamiliar words as we read, I'd then demonstrated the strategies I use to figure out the meanings of such words.

To a reader who is only making surface-level observations about her character, Sassy may serve as an exemplar of the fact that characters often act in one way and yet feel in a contrasting way. Sassy's actions, like those of many characters that readers encounter, mask hidden feelings. For instance, Sassy acts tough with her brother and makes quick remarks to her classmates and even to her dance teacher, but underneath that quick wit, she yearns to be special and fears that she is too tall or big-footed to be the kind of dancer she dreams about becoming. On more than one occasion Sassy holds back tears, and she secretly watches from backstage as the other dancers are in the spotlight. "Perhaps she *acts* sassy because she doesn't want to appear vulnerable, scared," I proposed to my reader. "Maybe she uses her quick wit to stand out and be special, even though she feels insecure about being taller than everyone else. Do you see how she can act one way on the outside, but be feeling a different way? Deep characters are sometimes like that, and it takes a deep reader to see it."

I let it sink in that Sassy has such depth before nudging my reader with, "What are you noticing about the way *your* main character acts? What might those actions be showing us about the character?" Or, "Where are some places where your main character acts one way but feels another?"

Sassy from *Dancing in the Wings* can help if you pull alongside a reader who needs support looking across a text to understand the way in which a character changes—or to understand how different parts of a story fit together. You might say, "Let's look at the way Sassy changes from the beginning of this story to the end," and count the stages across your fingers, one by one. "*In the beginning,* Sassy talks back to mask her hurt feelings, and she watches from the wings wishing she could dance in the spotlight." Counting across the next finger, add, "*When she tries out* for the special program, she wears a bright yellow leotard to stand out, and she shows off holding her leg up and leaping across the floor. *At the end,* she is chosen to attend the special dance program in DC and dances with a similarly tall male dancer at the final concert."

You could use these steps as props for thinking about character changes by then asking, "How do you imagine Sassy has changed from the beginning of this story? What do you think Sassy has learned?" Students might point out that Sassy learns to appreciate the way in which she is different, that she has become more confident because she says, "Mama was right—being tall wasn't so bad after all, and neither was having a big head." She may not need to wear the orange leotard or show off or sass people because Sassy has learned to appreciate her uniqueness, and the way in which being tall is indeed a gift. The important thing is that after helping students join you in this work within a mentor text, you channel them to try similar work in their own texts. You might prod them,

"How is your character changing from the beginning? And how do you know? How does the ending fit with the beginning in your book?"

You could also use this text to help children pay attention to the way in which secondary characters either get in the way of or help a character get what he or she wants. You could teach readers that it sometimes helps to ask oneself, "Who in this story helps the main character (in this instance, Sassy) get what she wants?" Readers might say it was Sassy's Mama, who makes her feel good about her big feet, or her Uncle Redd, who reminds her that being tall is a gift and who drives her to practice. They might also mention Mr. Debato, who lets her into the program in Washington DC. You might also show readers the way in which Mona and Molly, the girls who tease Sassy, indirectly help her get what she wants because they make her more determined. They light a fire within her to dance her best and stand out in the audition.

This is important work because you are showing readers that the plotline in a story is not comprised simply of a single protagonist who has motivations, who encounters trouble, and who finds a way to deal with the trouble. The forward progression in stories is often created as various subplots and elements of the story come together. In dense texts, there will often be seemingly minor characters who end up playing a more important role in the story than readers are apt to anticipate. Even in a brief picture book such as this one, the minor characters contribute to the main story line.

Of course, after using *Dancing in the Wings* to demonstrate the role of secondary characters, you might ask your reader, "What secondary characters in *your* book help your character get what she wants?" In addition, you might ask, "Is there anyone in your book who functions like the mean girls Mona and Molly—secondary characters in your book who help your main character in *unexpected* ways?"

Using *The Tiger Rising* as a Touchstone Text

You'll always want to carry your read-aloud books (the current one and earlier ones) with you in your short stack. *The Tiger Rising* will be an especially important mentor text for readers working at higher levels of text complexity, who need to follow multiple threads of significance woven through their plots. But of course, because all your readers will know this text well, you can use it to teach any reader, and frankly, you can use it to teach almost any skill. To use this book as a teaching text throughout your unit of study, you will already have spied on your own reading of the text, noticing the work the text seems to want you to do, and you will have thought, "Is the work I am doing with this text work that my students should be doing with their texts?" If the answer was yes, this or that particular sort of work is something all or most readers should be doing with their texts, then you may have used *The Tiger Rising* to teach readers to do that sort of work. If you decided that probably only readers working in texts that are as layered and crafted as *The Tiger Rising* in a minilesson would get a payoff from that sort of work, you may have decided to do that teaching during conferences or small groups. In any case, you'll want to look through this mentor text, like any mentor text, finding lots and lots of possible teaching points so that when you pull a chair alongside a reader and learn what he or she is trying to do, you are ready to say, "I've been trying to do similar work in this book," and then draw forth your well-marked Kate DiCamillo text.

If one of your readers has been envisioning the main plotline of a story but not bringing much detail into her mental pictures, you might recall any one of the moments in this book that is rich in powerful visual imagery to draw from. The freed tiger runs fast like the sun, rising and setting in time to Rob's heartbeat, its muscles moving like a river, for example. Or there is the visual image of Rob's father ripping a hole underneath the arm of his jacket as he slapped Rob to make him stop crying.

The same spots in the book may serve you *even* when you're teaching skills other than envisioning. The image of Rob's father busting the seams at the underside of his sleeve, for instance, may be referenced in more conferences than one. When Emma, with her plot-driven tendency to race through texts, read halfway through *Bridge to Terabithia* without batting an eyelid, I knew I had to intervene with a conference about empathy. "There are moments in our book that are especially poignant," I told her, deliberately adding this new word to her reading repertoire. "There is something heart-wrenching or oddly touching about a part that kind of makes us pause for a second to go, 'Oh!'" I clutched my heart and made a stricken face. "Like when Rob's dad tore his coat under the sleeve. He didn't just *hit* Rob. He hit him *hard*, so hard he lost control and looked foolish himself. So instead of feeling upset with the dad for hitting Rob, I wound up pitying the dad, too—the poor, out-of-control dad with the ripped jacket, who couldn't deal with his *own* emotions. Nowhere in the book does DiCamillo *tell* us all these details about the dad. She *shows* us instead, through poignant moments. Readers *pause* at such parts in our books and we let ourselves be affected. We let these moments move us into *feeling* more than the book is telling us. As you go through your book, try to find some of these poignant moments—moments that move you, that make you feel a little sad or a little shaken. Pause and let these parts sink in. Try to feel more than the author is saying and let yourself slip into the character's skin for a minute."

I walked away from Emma with the silent note to myself to teach her other ways of developing empathy for a character's problems.

The Tiger Rising can serve as a text from which we teach critical reading. For instance, while reading this book from an adult angle, we might note that Willie May rises above stereotypes of class. She is revered by the kids as a prophetess and a sage, despite her status as a vacuum-cleaner-toting, gum-chewing maid. Similarly, Sistine and Rob defy gender stereotypes, where *she* is the aggressive, risk-taking fighter-hunter (despite being presented to us initially in a pink frilly dress), and *he* is the shy recluse who'd rather whittle his life away in silent avoidance of confrontations. Such an awareness of class, gender, race, appearance, and so on comes easily to us as adults, but the question remains: Can we convert the observations that may be effortless for *us* into teaching points that helps our *kids* recognize a book's treatment of stereotypes? For example, "Sometimes, while looking at our books critically, readers ask ourselves, 'How does this book portray girls in relation to boys? Rich people in relation to poor people? One race in relation to another race?' Or we may look at a particular character as we read and ask ourselves, 'Is this character stereotypical of his or her gender (or class or race), or does this character *defy* stereotypes in the way that Sistine and Willie May do?'"

On the subject of interpretation, "What is this book really, really about?" is a question that helps push a reader's awareness out of the immediacy of the explicit story into the subliminal themes or issues that drive the plot. It is a question that we ask readers when we want to nudge them out of a surface-level retell into deeper interpretive analysis. "If a friend were to ask me what this book is really, really about," you could say as you hold up *The Tiger Rising*, "I wouldn't just start with Rob living without a mom at the Kentucky Star Motel and going to school (making your

voice drone out this list), and having a rash, and riding the bus, and meeting the principal. I wouldn't go into the details of what *happens* in the story. I'd tell her that this book is *about* friendship. About finding a friend in a person who seems very different from ourselves. I'd tell her it's about dealing with your pent-up feelings. Or facing your fears. Or accepting loss. Or healing your pain through friendship. Or about taking risks." (Of course you could write an entire interpretive essay on *The Tiger Rising*, but the point in this and any conference is to show kids how *they* may perform a task rather than showing off how well you do it.) "The way I figure out what my book is about is that I ask myself, 'What did the main character learn or how did the main character change? What was the big problem, and what were the lessons learned along the way to its resolution?'" This will be challenging work for young readers—to zoom out of the immediate sequence of events to look instead at the larger picture of what these cumulatively signify.

TEACHING SHARE

Readers Scrutinize Characters As They Encounter Trouble

Ask readers to think of themselves as characters to practice thinking about characters' motivations and struggles and resources.

"So, we've learned that one important way to get to know our characters more deeply is to have some questions in mind as we read: What do the characters want? What obstacles do the characters face, and how do they overcome them? What inner resources do the characters draw upon, and what does this reveal about them? You've done that work as you read. Listen to Emma's Post-it. *[Fig. XVI-3]*

> Jess and Leslie realize that they don't fit in so they imagine a world in which they have power. This brings them together and makes them feel accepted.

Figure XVI-3

"Right now, let's take a moment to practice training our minds to think about these things by imagining ourselves as characters. Take a moment to think about a goal or a dream you've had in your life. Imagine you're the character. What's motivated you? Turn and tell your partner about that." I listened as children talked to their partners.

When I've taught a particularly heady minilesson in which there are twists and turns and layers of work and understanding, I'll often use the teaching share to reinforce and provide more practice with the skills and ideas that I taught. This session certainly qualifies as complex, and it's worth the time to give readers another chance to use the strategies with my support.

I listen in as children share, and it's clear that this introspective stance or ability to reflect comes easier to some children than to others. I take notice of which partnerships are imbalanced, where one person is doing most of the talking. In the most imbalanced partnerships, all is not lost today, however, as long as one child is able to model the thinking.

Share an example of a child who has thoughtfully done this, and describe it in a way that helps others do this same work.

"So, Kobe talked to his partner about how he wanted so badly to make the travel basketball team. That was his dream. And Sarah shared how she wanted so much for her parents to get back together. And Tyrell revealed that his goal was to learn how to ride a skateboard down the railing outside of his apartment.

"Remember that expert readers know features that are worth attending to in texts. In stories, it is worth thinking about what characters want. It is also important to think about the obstacles that get in the way—so for a second, think of the challenges you faced along the way toward your goal. Talk about the hard stuff, and about what you did as you tried, tried, tried to get past that."

As I listened in, I sometimes offered quick prompts such as "So what did you do about that?" or "What stopped you?" or "Say more," or "What else?"

"Okay, partners, listen up. Kobe said his dream was to make the travel basketball team. That's what motivated him. But he faced obstacles, difficulties. He wasn't as tall as other kids, the hoops next to his building were missing so he couldn't practice, and so on. To deal with these obstacles, Kobe said that he changed his position. In his league, he could be center, but if he wanted to be on the traveling team, he knew he had to play point guard, so he retrained himself to do that. And although he couldn't practice shooting on the court next to his house, he could still practice other stuff, like dribbling and passing with friends.

"Now, it's time to get really deep. Think what your efforts suggest about you. What theory can you grow about yourself? Jot your theory down really, really fast, writing like lightning. Remember, to generate a strong theory, it often helps to say a bit more. Push yourself.

"Okay, let's get back together. Thinking about what a character draws upon from the inside when he is faced with difficulty can tell a lot about that character, even if that character is *you*. Kobe, do you mind if bring the whole class into our conversation?"

Kobe looked around at his classmates and shrugged. "Well, okay."

"When Kobe realized that he wasn't tall enough to play center on the travel team, he learned to change his position so he could make it. Kobe was trying to figure out what he is learning about himself by reflecting on this decision to change positions, but he is a little stuck. Can the rest of you help Kobe and me think about what theory this could give us?"

A few children threw out suggestions.

If I felt the kids could handle yet more information, I might point out that often there is a deeper, more internal goal that hides under the external, overt one. In Mem Fox's picture book, Koala Lou, the main character is dying to win the gum tree climbing event. But really, what she wants is affection from her mother, whose attention has been consumed lately by all the new koala babies. Koala Lou decides she'll earn that affection by making her mother proud. The goal then might seem to be winning the contest, but really it's winning her mother's love. She loses the contest, but on the final page, her mother finds her, desolate, and throws her arms around Koala Lou and says, "Koala Lou, I do love you. I always have and always will." And that is all Koala Lou wants.

I've chosen to thread Kobe's story through this share time because it's accessible, and because Kobe is a reader who could use some support in reading, and this is a way to celebrate his thinking and to help him feel more enfranchised during reading time.

"Kobe is such a good player that he can play different positions?"

"Kobe can do lots of different things?"

David, meanwhile, acted as if he would burst apart if I didn't give him the nod that allowed him to say, "Kobe is like Willy. He is so determined to play on the travel team so he will do anything?"

"You all are onto really great theories. The one I'd been thinking of was this. Kobe is not only a good basketball player. He is also flexible enough and determined enough that he makes things happen."

"Yeah, and when he couldn't practice shooting on the courts next to his house, he practiced other stuff," Malik added.

"Kobe, did you ever realize these things about yourself?"

"Not really, I guess," he said, and smiled, clearly pleased.

"And you know, the idea that we have grown about Kobe *does* go with the idea we have grown about Willy, and it is as if these two characters are teaching us a life lesson, aren't they? Do you know that saying, 'When life closes a door on you—open the window'? I think the lesson these two are teaching me is like that, and I'm pretty sure that Kobe and Willy are teaching each of you a somewhat different lesson. Cluster into small groups for a second and talk about what those lessons might be."

In this share time, I used real-life applications of the strategy to reinforce the teaching point from the minilesson, but some teachers chose to use The Tiger Rising *text during the share time to revisit the teaching point. They reread sections of the book where Rob faced a challenge, and the children turned and talked to name the challenge and to think about how he overcame it. Then they took the step of thinking about what Rob drew upon to overcome the challenge.*

IN THIS SESSION,
you will teach students
that readers can develop complex
ideas about characters by starting
simply and building on.

Authoring Ideas About Texts

hildren are natural theorists. Eavesdrop on children's conversations with each other and you might even hear some of these theories: theories about grownups, school, Santa Claus, or the best way to peel a candy, ride a bike, blow a bubble, whistle to one's dog, and so on. Yet in too many of our schools, there are often no theories—only wrong or right answers—and the consequent silencing of the babble that otherwise characterizes a child's discovery of the world around her. There comes a stage when kids actually look at a teacher with mild suspicion when we try to elicit an original thought or theory from them, wondering what it is that we teachers want to hear.

Reading provides a chance to undo some of that damage. The child whose eyes are riveted to text is inferring, predicting, synthesizing, all of which require developing mental models that subsequent reading will either confirm or challenge. That is to say, children are developing theories about plot and character as they read. "Junie B. Jones shouldn't be friends with Lucille," or "Fantastic Mr. Fox is just a thief," or "Wilbur the pig is sort of a cry-baby." And when you tell a child, "Jot down what you think," and later, "Let's make this thought bigger," you are in effect saying, "There is no right or wrong answer. There is only the process of you developing your own thinking."

GETTING READY

- Create and prepare to reveal the chart found in the Teaching section of the minilesson, "Conversational Prompts to Help Partner Talk Go Well." Consider any additions to this chart.

- Prepare to refer to parts of Chapter 25 of *The Tiger Rising* as you demonstrate how to push yourself to say more about your character theory.

- Ask children to bring their independent reading books and Post-it notes to the meeting area, where they will work in partnerships to expand upon their theories.

- On the last day of this unit you will read the last two or three chapters of *The Tiger Rising*. This means that you have three sessions (three days) to read Chapters 26 and 27. You may want to spend part of this time reading aloud from another text.

- To prepare for Session XVIII, gather passages with images that reoccur in *The Tiger Rising* as a way to teach children that authors thread things they want readers to pay attention to throughout a book.

This process of developing thinking, where a random thought is teased, turned, and built up, is far from simple. It requires contemplation and discussion, jotting and questioning. It involves taking one thought and looking at it from multiple angles. Such is the challenging, invigorating work that this session introduces. The process of starting with a casually scribbled Post-it and ending with a well-articulated theory will transform the way our readers approach their

> *Ultimately, when we teach children reading skills, we teach life skills.*

books—until they actively cocreate the characters of their story, in much the same way that adult readers theorize about Mitchell's Scarlett O'Hara or Brontë's Heathcliff, filling in the blanks that an author leaves with our *own* theories, until we own the characters we love.

The theories that our children come up with at first may be neither profound nor convincing, and we will need to remind children to ground such theories in evidence from the book itself. Even as we release their thinking and urge them to be creative, therefore, we are simultaneously delineating the boundaries that will anchor their thoughts back into their books, outlining that mild tug of war that researchers since Rosenblatt refer to as a transactional process between reader and text. We'll hope to have engaged readers, readers who haven't merely envisioned or empathized with a character, but who have actually thought deeply about what makes the character tick. How important it is to teach young people to read between the lines!

Taking a random scribble and blowing it up into a credible theory can become second nature to children. Such thinking requires alertness, the insertion of judgment and analysis, and the weighing of what the text states versus what the reader knows to be true from experience. Ultimately, when we teach children reading skills, we teach life skills. As they learn to develop informed theories about the characters they meet in books, understanding that these characters are not just one way, readers learn to search for and recognize complexities in their friends, their family members, themselves. We hope then that teaching reading involves teaching young people that there is more to a person than meets the eye. We trust that thinking and reading with nuance ultimately pays off in the form of reflective, thoughtful, social citizenship.

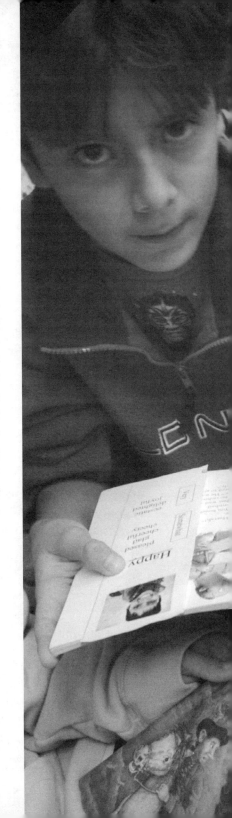

# MINILESSON

Authoring Ideas About Texts

CONNECTION

Remind readers of the work they've been doing in a way that helps them remember they can carry on with this work whenever they read.

"You've been growing such important ideas about characters—their motivations and struggles and lessons. And I've watched you pause when you reach the middles of your books, especially to sort your Post-it notes into piles that help you develop theories about not just the main character but also his or her relationships to others. You've been carrying those theories with you as you read and searching for evidence to support them. This morning as you were walking in, I heard Jasmine say that last night she found five parts of her book that all supported her idea.

If you think about the progression of minilessons, this session really extends Session XV. The previous session, about the way in which the narrative code can help a reader know aspects of a story that are worth attending to, felt like it balanced rather than extended Session XV. This connection, then, attempts to synthesize both Sessions XV and XVI, showing how they go together. The truth is, though, that probably each of those sessions will speak to different readers. One was more step-by-step and procedural and one more artistic.

"Carrying your theories with you as you read and finding support for them is spectacular work. It makes tons of sense, for example, if you are reading *Horrible Harry*, to reread, thinking, 'Yep. Here's more evidence that Harry is horrible.' And if you are reading *Flat Stanley*, it makes sense for you to read on in the book, thinking, 'There it is again—evidence that Stanley really, truly is flat!' So it *is* important to find evidence for ideas such as 'Horrible Harry *is* horrible' or 'Flat Stanley *is* flat.'

It's natural for readers to feel proud as they see their theory charts filling up with writing—just as they will when they see their count of pages read increase and as they are able to write more pages or complete more math problems. While we enjoy their enthusiasm, we know that it's time to steer them away from thinking in terms of quantity in favor of measuring the quality of their work.

"I want to tell you that the theories you create early on in a book—theories like 'Harry is horrible'—are likely to have a lot of truth in them. But they are also apt to be obvious, easy theories. Chances are that most people who read the book will have the same idea. So, the question I want us to think about today is this: How do we grow interesting, important, original theories about a character, a book?

"Here's a tip: When readers have a theory that feels obvious in our minds, we don't throw it away. We know these initial, obvious theories are important because they give us a place to start. They're like the first rungs on a ladder. They're useful, even necessary, if we want to get to the top of the ladder. *But*, we don't want to make those first rungs our stopping place.

I love this. Sometimes I happen upon an idea that seems pretty important—this is one of them.

"If someone met me, they could easily—and swiftly—develop a conclusion like this: 'Lucy is messy.' And it wouldn't be hard for someone who was looking for evidence to find it, and plenty of it. But that person would be missing out on other, more interesting parts of me, on the truth of who I am. Some of you are growing ideas about your characters that are like 'Lucy is messy.' You're developing a fairly simple, obvious theory about your character and then reading as if it's your job to find heaps of evidence to support it.

"Instead, I want us to challenge ourselves to see in our characters all the complexity that we find in real people. For now, let's ignore the task of finding evidence. We'll read as if it's our job to see our characters in new and interesting ways. We'll grow theories that are just as layered and complex as characters are themselves—and just as unique as we are, too. So that's what I'm going to teach you today. Today, we are going to move on from a sort of ho-hum, obvious theory—'Harry is horrible'—to one that is more complicated, more unique, and more true."

Name your teaching point. Specifically, tell children that a few ways we make our theories about a character deeper and more complex is to talk more, write longer, and think more deeply.

"Today I want to teach you that a simple, obvious idea about a character or a book is a great place to start, even if your goal is a complex idea. Readers sometimes find that to take that simple idea as a starting place and to climb to higher levels of thinking, it helps to use a few phrases as thought prompts, grasping those phrases like we grasp rungs on a ladder, using them to help us climb higher and higher."

TEACHING

Help readers expand upon some of their best ideas by introducing the use of key phrases or prompts. This will aid in the development and engagement of more complex character theories.

"Earlier, we talked about how using precise words helps us express what we really mean to say about a character. But the truth is that words can help us not only to express what we mean but also to *discover* what we mean. Remember when we pushed ourselves to use precise, true words to express our ideas about characters in *The Tiger Rising*? We started off by saying that Sistine was 'bossy,' but then realized that she is

I chose my example, "Lucy is messy," deliberately, because I knew that it was one the students would recognize straight off. When choosing your own example, choose something your students will recognize easily—something "obvious". Our students know us well after spending their days in our company—and they study us thoroughly. Choosing an example that they recognize easily will help them make the transfer to doing this work in the context of their characters.

As mentioned in the Guide, Steve Graham from Vanderbilt recently completed a major Carnegie-funded study, "Writing to Read: Evidence for How Writing Can Improve Reading." After an extensive search, the research team located ninety-three research studies documenting the effect of writing on reading, and they found that any writing done about reading has an extremely large effect on comprehension, outweighing even the effect of focused comprehension strategy instruction. Nine of the studies yielded positive results. Results were especially dramatic when students responded with personal reactions or interpretive ideas. They concluded, "We need to stop pussyfooting around about writing and make writing a central element of the reform movement." (April 12, 2010, Writing to Read panel discussion, Washington DC)

more complicated than that one-word description. All of us are. So we revised our idea, trying on different words, asking ourselves as we did, 'Is this true? How about this?' We found that to be as precise as we could, we usually had to use more than just one word; finding the exactly right words took a little time, a little experimenting. I'm going to show you how I grow a theory as I read that is complex and original. You'll see that I reach for more words, and it helps me a lot to use some phrases as thought prompts to help me climb up the ladder of my thinking.

"There are lots of phrases that we can use to push ourselves to say more about our thinking. The good news is that you already use many of these."

Conversational Prompts to Help Partner Talk Go Well

- Or it could be . . .

- But what about . . .

- This is really important because . . .

- A stronger word to describe that is . . .

- It's just like . . .

- Maybe it's because . . .

- Remember earlier in the story when . . .

"I'm going to reread a bit of *The Tiger Rising*. Watch me while I take an idea that I already had—a not-so-original idea—and use one of these phrases to discover some deeper thinking. This part is from Chapter 25, when Rob and Sistine are asking Willie May what they should do about the tiger."

"I can't wait until my father comes to get me," said Sistine. "He knows what's right. He'll set this tiger free."

Rob looked at Sistine. "Your daddy ain't coming for you," he said softly, shaking his head, amazed at what he suddenly knew to be the truth.

This lesson gets to the heart of why we teach children to talk and write about their ideas, instead of just thinking them. Teaching children writing and talking moves is actually teaching them how to develop an idea by following a journey of thinking. As children become more accustomed to how these journeys generally go, they will become more skillful at talking back to their own thinking and will be able to do this work internally, just by musing. But first many readers will profit from encouragement to use their pens, their partners, and some thought prompts.

Feel free to add other phrases to your own version of this chart. The idea is that you are reminding the children of phrases that you have already introduced at some point, maybe with one or two new additions. If you bring out a chart of conversational prompts that children have never seen before, it will be very difficult for them to use the prompts effectively today without lots of guidance from you.

* Conversational Prompts *
to Keep Partner Talk Going . . .

- Perhaps it's because . . .

- Or maybe it's . . .

- Another thing it could be . . .

- This connects to earlier in the story when . . .

- That reminds me of . . .

- A stronger word to describe that is . . .

- This seems significant because . . .

"My father is coming to get me," Sistine said through tight lips.

"Naw," said Rob sadly. "He ain't. He's a liar. Like your mama said."

"You're the liar," said Sistine in a dark cold voice. Her face was so white that it seemed to glow before him. "And I hate you," she said to him. "Everybody at school hates you, too. Even the teachers. You are a sissy. I hope I never ever see you again."

"Wow, that part is really hard to read because of all those mean things Sistine says to Rob. The first time I read this part, I put a Post-it there. It says, "Sistine is acting mean because she's mad." That's a pretty obvious idea, though. I bet a lot of you were thinking the same thing, so it's not an idea like my fingerprint, an idea that's unique to me.

"I'm going to use my first theory as a rung on the ladder of thinking, and then use these phrases to help me reach past it and move on to discover a more complex, more true idea."

Shifting into the role of dictating my thoughts, I said, "'Sistine is acting mean because she's mad.' I'm going to grab one of our phrases—any one—and see if it works. *Remember earlier in the story.* . . . Hmm. . . . Yeah, I remember earlier in the story." Then I paused, almost backing up to examine what I had just done with the use of a thought prompt, and I critiqued my work, saying, "That didn't really help me. I guess I have to go to the next phrase." I started to move to another phrase on the list, but then I caught myself.

Self-correcting, I said, "Wait. I'm supposed to use these phrases *to push myself, to squeeze my brain.* Let me try again. *Remember earlier in the story,* Sistine was always acting mean. Back then, I think she acted mean because she was nervous about being in a new school. I wonder why she's acting mean now." Then I gestured to a second thought prompt and used it to continue. "*Maybe it's because.* . . . Maybe it's because she's also scared now. I know if someone told me that my dad was never coming back, I might be scared to hear that. I'm beginning to think that Sistine is the kind of person who acts mean when she feels really frightened."

Shifting out of that role, I leaned close to the children and said, "Readers, I'm going to stop there even though I'm realizing that there's a lot more for me to say and think just in this one part of the book. Did you see how using these conversational prompts—and I had to use more than one—helped me push through the first idea I had, the obvious one, and grow some thinking that feels more unique? This is thinking that came from my brain and no one else's."

Of course, many children do simply say one thing about a character and then stop. In whole-class book talks, this creates a kind of tennis-match style of conversation: One person states an idea, then another takes a turn stating a different idea, and so on.

Here I am modeling what children are apt to actually do; many of them will recognize themselves in the demonstration. Feel free to exaggerate the way you do something in a totally cursory fashion and then shrug and begin to move on. Showing children an example of a mess-up that many of them are apt to make can be an effective way to teach them what to do instead.

Active Involvement

Ask readers to sort through their Post-it notes, searching for an idea that can be the starting point for some more complex thinking.

"Now it's your turn. Look through the jottings you made yesterday or the day before in your independent reading book and find your own version of a 'Horrible Harry is horrible' jotting—an obvious, 'any' idea. Just take a second, and if you have trouble, you can borrow this one, for practice," I said and stuck a Post-it on which I'd written "Sistine is bossy," onto the easel.

After about a minute, I said, "Give me a thumbs up if you've got an idea in mind." A flurry of thumbs went up.

Channel readers to use the thought prompts to push themselves to grow deeper ideas and then to meet with partners, with one sharing their ideas and the other using thought prompts to help the first one develop those ideas even further.

"Okay, now starting with that 'any' idea, use one of our thought prompts (I gestured to the chart) to push yourself to go deeper. Imagine you are using a key to unlock more unique thinking. After you've done this in your head for a couple of minutes, I'll give you time to turn and share with your partner."

After a few minutes, I said, "I know that some of you are just starting to push deeper, but I want you to share whatever you have. Partner 1, share your thinking with Partner 2. Partner 2, use the prompts on our chart or ones you come up with yourselves to help push Partner 1's thinking even more."

Link

Send readers off now and forever not only to collect more evidence of their theories but also to aim to grow more original, interesting ideas.

"Readers, this work is not easy, but it is very important. We want to be the kind of readers who let a text in so that it affects and touches us. Part of reading that way involves pushing to think past the obvious ideas that most anyone might have. Instead of having theory charts that are crammed with evidence, we'll spend more time pondering, mulling over our ideas. The more you practice, the more this type of reading will become a natural habit of thought from now on."

Notice the little ways in which you can provide scaffolds for children who need them, allowing your teaching to always be differentiated.

You will want to make sure to vary the active involvement so that sometimes children are thinking or jotting to themselves, sometimes talking to a partner, and sometimes dramatizing. And keep in mind that your minilesson should be as close to ten minutes as possible. So, on a day when you use an active involvement that might take longer, you'll want to compensate by slimming down the teaching part of the lesson. Some classes tend to take a little longer when writing, and others seem to take longer when having partner talks. [Figs. XVII-1 and XVII-2]

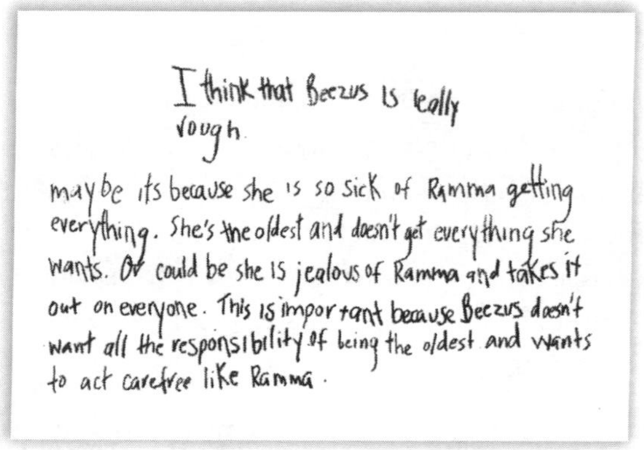

I think that Beezus is really rough.

maybe its because she is so sick of Ramona getting everything. She's the oldest and doesn't get everything she wants. Or could be she is jealous of Ramona and takes it out on everyone. This is important because Beezus doesn't want all the responsibility of being the oldest and wants to act carefree like Ramona.

Figure XVII-1

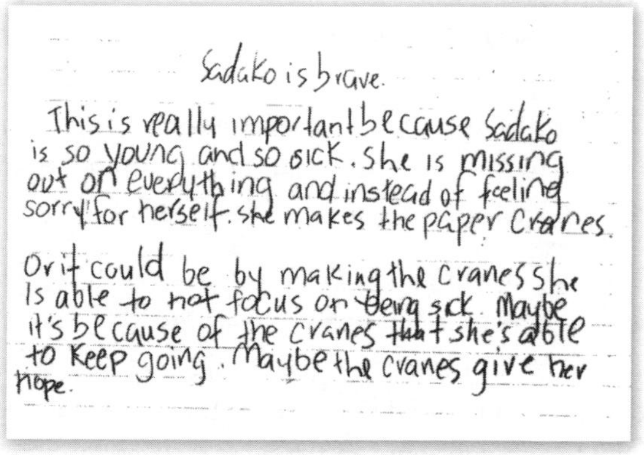

Sadako is brave.

This is really important because Sadako is so young and so sick. She is missing out on everything and instead of feeling sorry for herself she makes the paper cranes.

Or it could be by making the cranes she is able to not focus on being sick. Maybe it's because of the cranes that she's able to keep going. Maybe the cranes give her hope.

Figure XVII-2

CONFERRING AND SMALL-GROUP WORK

Support Readers Working in Complex Texts

On some days, we throw ourselves into the task of conferring as if we were sailboats. We open ourselves to the winds in our classrooms and travel wherever those winds take us that day. On other days, we chart a course beforehand. We may do so based on observations: These children struggle with stamina or start and drop books frequently or have a hard time settling into a book or seem ready to move from Post-its to longer notebook entries. Alternatively, we may chart a course for our conferring and small-group work by drawing on the fact that readers who are working within a shared band of reading difficulty will tend to need some similar coaching.

Preparing for Conferring by Studying the Challenges Posed by a Band of Text Levels

Prior to this particular day, colleagues across grades 3–6 and I had spent some time talking together about the fact that we had been spending more of our time supporting readers in the level K/L/M and the N/O/P/Q bands of text difficulty than we'd spent with readers in the R/S/T or the U/V bands of text difficulty. To address this, we devoted one of our study group sessions to looking again at books we knew well in the level R/S/T band, rec-

---

> ### MID-WORKSHOP TEACHING POINT
>
> #### Readers Grow More Complex Theories by Asking What Characters Learn
>
> "Readers, give me your attention so I can teach one more way that readers sometimes move past those first, obvious ideas as they read further in a book.
>
> "It often pays off when growing your theory to ask yourself what the character is learning through all of his trying. When Willy is trying and trying to save Grandfather's farm, he is learning something. When Rob tries to find a way to open his suitcase, he is learning something. Characters learn about themselves or their friends or the world. We can pay attention to the parts where they're trying, trying, and ask ourselves, 'What is my character learning right now?'
>
> "For example, I was just talking to Emma about her book *Because of Winn-Dixie*. She started off with an idea about the main character, Opal, and the fact that she doesn't have many friends. Then, as she read more about Opal's struggles, Emma began to think that perhaps Opal was learning about how to depend on people, to trust them and open her heart. Emma has the makings for a really interesting theory here.
>
> "Remember that as you read further and learn more about your character's struggles, often you will see that your character is learning something—about herself, about her friends, about the world. Asking yourself what the character is learning can help you discover a more complex and unique theory."
>
>

---

ollecting what we knew about the new challenges readers of those texts could expect to encounter. We kept that information in mind as we created pages of mailing labels full of suggestions we planned to draw upon as we conferred with these readers. Then we duplicated that mailing label page of suggestions to have on hand to use with readers working with texts in the level R/S/T band of difficulty. We transferred the appropriate sticker to each child's file as a record of our conference.

For example, because we know that readers of books in this band of difficulty must accumulate information about the setting as they read, learning about times and places such as Denmark during the Holocaust, Mississippi during the 1960s, or Terabithia, and because we know that often the setting plays a role in the plot, with different characters reacting to the changing setting in different ways, we made this note on one mailing label:

Readers might use one color of Post-it only to accumulate info on the setting. Later, readers could star important events and talk about how each character reacted to each one.

Because we know that in books at these levels, subordinate characters and seemingly small subplots often become more important than a reader might at first think, we jotted this note to ourselves to use while conferring:

> Reader might flag subordinate characters/plotlines that disappear—"might reoccur?" When predicting, reader could weigh whether flagged bit might influence upcoming story.

Then, too, because we know that texts at these levels might call on readers to deal with tricky chapters, we brainstormed these suggestions:

> If first chapter is confusing, think of it as a puzzle piece that doesn't fit. It is not a mistake! Reader could ask "Why might the author want me confused or up in the air?"

We know, too, that readers of these texts, in this band of difficulty, as we've come to call it, find that characters tend to be neither good nor bad, but both. The people, such as Rob's father in *The Tiger Rising*, are deeply flawed, but they often redeem themselves in surprising ways. We wondered if it would help to point out to readers that not only do characters have strengths and weaknesses, but their strengths are often flip sides of their weaknesses, and vice versa, and again, we made such a note on our record-keeping sheet. We did similar work for the level U/V band of text difficulty. Each of the teachers and I then vowed to devote a day or two to supporting stronger readers, using our notes about what these readers are apt to need to help us feel less empty-handed in our conferences.

Leading a Small Group that Ends Up Helping Readers Construct Meaning Out of the Many Pieces that Comprise a Book

I called over a group of readers. Emma, who was reading *Bridge to Terabithia*; Izzy, who was reading *Journey*; Sarah, who was reading *Baby*; and Lily, who was reading *Because of Winn-Dixie*, joined me on the rug with their books in hand. I started off, "Readers, thanks for joining me today. I've noticed the books you guys are reading, and they are so perfect for the work we are trying to do! The characters are complex and interesting; they speak right to your heart. You have probably already noticed that as you read more difficult books, the characters and stories become more complicated. I thought we'd talk about ways in which your books might seem a bit challenging to you. Look over your book right now and think a bit about ways in which reading your book really well can be hard."

The girls looked over their books, and after I signaled for them to do so, they talked among themselves and in no time had agreed that their books definitely had confusing parts.

I confirmed this. "And it is not confusing *words*, is it, so much as confusing *parts*—chapters even, or whole passages." I gestured to one of the italic interludes in *Baby* as an example. I didn't need to check my record-keeping sheet with the new mailing label full of tips. The act of making it seemed to have done the trick because I was ready to respond. "I'm glad you brought that up because I want to tell you a secret. Even if you were the smartest person in the world, those sections of your books would still be confusing—because they are meant to be! That's because books at these levels of text difficulty—books that are labeled R and beyond—are like black diamond ski trails—you know, the really hard trails with moguls and icy cliffs! You are reading books that *are meant* to make you do a lot of work! Earlier, when a book didn't make sense, you sometimes figured it must be too hard for you. But now you need to keep in mind that some parts of books are supposed to be confusing. Reading can be like puzzles with all these little pieces that you are supposed to put together, to click into place." I mimed picking up a piece, looking carefully at it, turning it, then fitting it into the growing puzzle. "Have you ever put together a grown-up puzzle, a really hard one?" I asked.

The children talked for a minute. Some had, some hadn't, but they all had an image of what constructing a puzzle entailed. "Sometimes I sit there for five minutes with one little piece thinking, 'Where does this go? Here? Here? Here?'" Lily said, as usual acting out what she was saying.

I agreed with Lily. "Same with me! And here is the thing: If I can't connect a puzzle piece, if it feels like it doesn't 'go' anywhere, I don't throw it away entirely. Do you?" Lily agreed that no, she kept it to the side. "That's what most puzzlers do. We keep the hard pieces in a special pile. And we keep picking those pieces back up and turning them around,

seeing if we can find where they fit as we complete more of the puzzle. Eventually, I've done enough of the puzzle that I can snap all the pieces into place." The girls all nodded at my puzzle analogy.

"I'm telling you this because your books will have confusing parts. You might read those parts and think you messed up because they don't make sense to you—but even adults know that sophisticated texts often leave a reader unclear about exactly what is happening or how the part they are reading connects with everything else. So my first tip to you is that it is the reader's job to know the difference between that feeling of "Oops, I must have missed something" and the kind of confusion that an author wants you to feel, a confusion that makes you think, 'The story is still unfolding. I should keep reading.'

And my second point is that if there is a confusing part, you will want to think of it as a puzzle piece. Think, 'How might this fit into the rest of the puzzle?' and try one possible way, in your mind, and then another. But then, if the confusing part is like a puzzle piece that just doesn't seem to click into place, put that puzzling part to the side like you'd put a puzzling piece of a puzzle to the side, and keep reading, thinking, 'Now does that piece fit? Now?" Often it will take many pages—even most of the book—before the puzzling pieces click into place. And sometimes, you need to get to the end of the book and reread to see how it all fits into a whole.

"Right now, I want you each to see if you can locate a confusing part of your book." I gave them time to do this. "What are the big questions you are still trying to fit into place? Find a bit that makes you ask, 'How does this fit into the whole of this story?' and for a few minutes, try thinking about possible answers."

As the readers bent their heads to work, I noticed that Izzy began jotting immediately. The others looked thoughtfully through their pages. Soon, they had all jotted and were sharing with partners. I sat next to Izzy and Emma so I could hear them. Izzy was sharing her thinking, saying, "So, Journey has these sort of memory dream things. See, the author puts them in a different font." She showed Emma the page she was on as an example. Then she continued, "I don't really know what they mean. I don't know why the author keeps going back to them. In the memory, Journey is on his mother's lap. It must be important, because it comes up again and again, but I don't really see why yet. Except for the fact that Journey is missing his mom."

"Izzy," I cut in, "it's great how you knew right away what your missing puzzle pieces were. I can tell by the way you say, 'I don't see what this means *yet*,' that you are holding on to your curiosity as you read on and that you are looking for information that will help you snap that puzzle piece into place."

After a few moments, I called for the small group's attention and shared what Izzy had said. "Remember, readers, as your books get more and more sophisticated, there will be parts in which the author intends for you to be confused and unclear about what's happening. Izzy found that for her, some of those parts seemed to be flashbacks that her main character has from time to time, and she is so wise to ask, 'Why does he keep

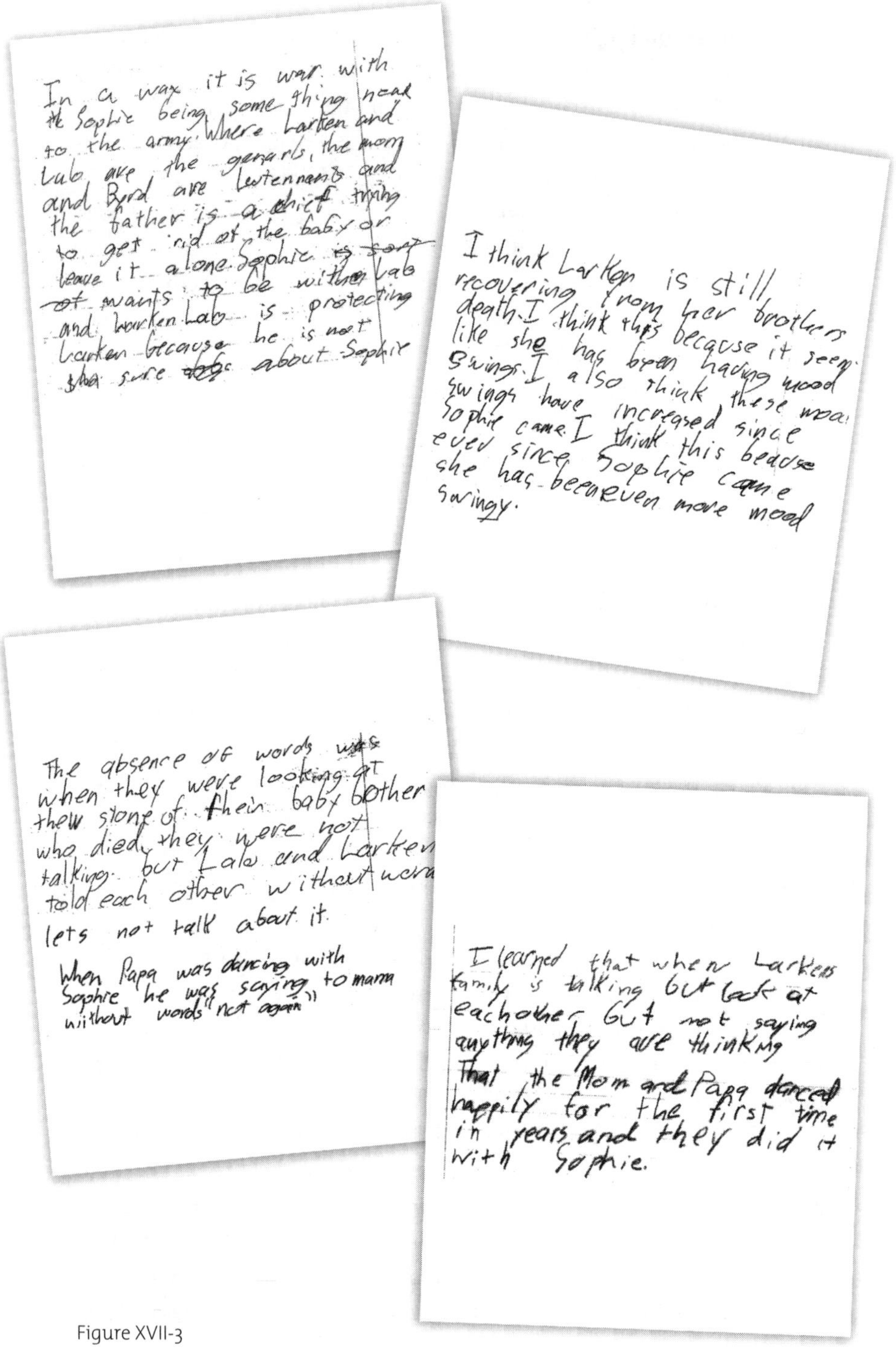

In a way it is war with
Sophie being some thing head
to the army. Where Larken and
Lalo are the generals, the mom
and Byrd are leutennants and
the father is a chief trying
to get rid of the baby or
leave it alone. Sophie ~~to~~
~~of~~ wants to be with Lalo
and Larken. Lalo is protecting
Larken because he is not
~~to~~ sure ~~that~~ about Sophie.

I think Larken is still
recovering from her brothers
death. I think this because it seem
like she has been having mood
swings. I also think these mood
swings have increased since
Sophie came. I think this because
ever since Sophie came
she has become even more mood
swingy.

The absence of words was
when they were looking at
their stone of their baby brother
who died they were not
talking but Lalo and Larken
told each other without words
lets not talk about it.

When Papa was dancing with
Sophie he was saying to mamm
without words "not again."

I learned that when Larkens
family is talking but look at
eachother but not saying
anything they are thinking.
That the Mom and Papa danced
happily for the first time
in years and they did it
with Sophie.

Figure XVII-3

remembering those things?' Read the puzzling parts very carefully, like you are turning them this way and that in your mind and trying to fit them into the bigger picture. But remember, the answer might not be in the puzzling piece. It might be in the rest of the book, so ask, 'What might this have to do with the whole message the author is trying to say?'"

Writing Can Be a Way for Readers to Synthesize and Extend Their Thoughts

Later that evening, I looked over a page of entries that Sarah had written as she mused over puzzling bits in MacLachlan's *Baby*. I was eager to read her thoughts about the book because it's one of my favorites. For those of you who do not know the book, it tells the story of an abandoned baby arriving at the doorstep of a family that had already been dealing with the recent death of an infant. The presence of the new baby jostles the family to deal with the submerged grief. The entries Sarah had written are shown in Figure XVII-3.

The next day, I pulled my chair alongside Sarah again and told her I'd been interested in her thoughts about Baby. "It is one of my all-time favorites," I said. "It is so deep, isn't it?"

She agreed, and added, "I read *Journey* before, but I like this even better. It's so sad though!"

"It's a special kind of sad feeling, isn't it?" I said, "when a book gets you right in the heart. It is both a hard feeling and a good one because it means you really care about the characters. You're really in the story." Because I'd already read Sarah's entries and had some vague sense of a direction in mind for the conference, I cut the research component of the conference short.

"There are so many things I notice about these ideas you've recorded about *Baby*," I said.

Looking unsure, Sarah glanced at the page I'd opened between us and said, "Are they too short?"

I knew that Sarah was not always confident and that she was looking at her work through the "What's wrong with this?" lens.

"That's not the main thing I noticed," I said. "The main thing I noticed is that reading your notebook is like opening a treasure chest because it is full of all these jewels of thoughts."

Sarah glowed.

"I also noticed that in most of your ideas, you really are doing the work of putting the pieces of this beautiful story together. Other people might take a bit on a particular page and write just about that bit, but you are always thinking about how that bit fits in with everything else. Like this last point. You notice a pattern across the family (they are not talking to each other, looking at each other), but then you notice a break from that—the parents dancing with each other—and you notice how the new baby fits into that, too. It's like your one idea is your effort to put pieces together, and that is just the hugest thing in the world. I really want to congratulate you on that."

Sarah climbed up on her knees, leaning toward me, her energy palpably rising. I knew I could raise the bar for her now, and was reminded of Don Murray, the founder of the writing process approach, who once said, "In a good writing conference, the writer leaves, wanting to write. The writer's energy should go up, not down."

"Sarah, because these are so thoughtful, they really got me thinking. All last night I was mulling over in my mind what the next steps might be for you as a reader, and I've come to one suggestion that I think is a really powerful one. I've never made it to a kid your age before, and it might just be too sophisticated, but do you mind if I tell you this suggestion and then we think together about whether maybe we should wait so you work on this when you are in high school instead of now?"

Sarah giggled, and I continued. "What I am thinking is that even though each of your thoughts brings together different bits of the book, the way to make your thoughts even more powerful is for you to reread them, and to think of them as puzzle pieces of their own, and for you to think, 'Is there a way that these separate ideas that I have somehow could be fit together, like pieces of a puzzle?'"

Sarah's eyes flicked to the page as she weighed what I was suggesting. I figured I needed to be more specific. "What I'm wondering is if, when you look back at all of these entries, you see any through lines, any themes, any larger ideas about the characters or the whole book that you might want to think more about. What you've done is wonderful. I'm thinking you're ready to do some even deeper thinking, and that you can use what you've already noticed and written to help you. Do you notice any ideas or thoughts or even images that keep coming up in what you wrote?"

"Does it have to fit with every entry?" she asked, looking a little nervous again.

"Not necessarily," I said. "This would mean today, and often after you've jotted a bunch of thoughts in your notebook, you'd scan over your entries and ask, 'Are there bigger ideas that act like the threads in a book that keep resurfacing—bigger ideas that resurface in my ideas?'" Then I suggested she reread her thoughts to see what she could find.

"Well I was thinking that Patricia MacLachlan keeps writing about words, and talking or being quiet. That keeps coming around."

"Huh!" I said, enthralled by this brand-new idea (which actually is not so very new to a good reader of the book). "You are right! That is like a refrain in the book, and in your jottings," I said, beckoning to her second and last points, both of which addressed this. What other things keep coming around?"

"Oh, the dancing. That keeps coming around, too." Building steam, Sarah said, "Look, in this last entry, there's stuff about both things—the mama and papa not talking and the dancing. But what the things mean is different as the book goes on. Like sometimes the not talking is sad not

talking. And sometimes it's happy. It's like things keep going in circles but changing as they go."

"Wow, you're right!" I had a feeling Sarah was onto something bigger, but I didn't want to push her into writing *my* interpretation if what she'd noticed was different. I wanted to help her to clarify what she was noticing on her own. "I think you're onto something important. You're beginning to build a bigger idea out of what you're noticing in these entries. One way to make an idea even bigger is to think about whether there is a message here that connects to your own life or to life in general."

"Well, I guess that in everyone's life there are things that keep coming around. Like my mom used to bake this special bread with my grandma, and now she's teaching me how to do it. Life is full of circles," she said thoughtfully, "and there are lots of them in *Baby*, not just what I wrote."

"Sarah, you are putting pieces together that are here, in your writing about the book, and in your thinking about the book. And there are pieces that click into this puzzle picture that come from your life, not from the book at all. You've got to take some time and write your thoughts down, and this time will you aim to make your writing be one big put-together puzzle rather than a collection of pieces? And after this, you can always remember to do as you have done and collect jewels of thought, and then, remember, you can reread your thoughts and think about whether they can be pieced together into something bigger."

As I left, Sarah wrote a sentence that reflected her understanding at the top of a blank page. *[Fig XVII-4]*

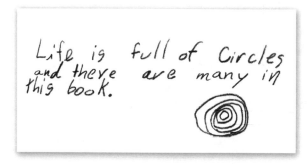

Figure XVII-4

TEACHING SHARE

Readers Use Talking Prompts to Grow Thinking

Celebrate the work of a partnership by telling the story of what happened in a way that encourages others to try the same work.

"I want to give you all the chance to hear about some of the excellent reading work that is happening all around you. During this workshop time, this is some of what I saw and heard: Gabe flipped through the pages of his book, *The Comeback Dog*. He read over several of his Post-its before choosing one from early on in the book. It said, 'Daniel is acting so mad and breaking stuff because Captain died.' Gabe shared his Post-it with his partner and then sat for a moment, staring up at our chart of prompts. He continued, '*That all makes me think* that Daniel is so upset that Captain died, he wants to take it out on something. Like how he yells at his parents. *Another possibility is* he is trying not to be sad so he's being mad instead. Like if he smashes stuff and is really angry, he won't have to feel how much he misses Captain.' His partner Rosa responded, also using a prompt, "Yeah, *I agree and I wonder if* breaking the ice fits with that, too. It makes him feel better to break it, the author says.' That is the kind of work you all are doing together here. You are helping each other grow a very small idea into something so much more impressive. Turn to your partner now and name some of the great work you did today with each other."

After letting the partners talk for a few minutes, I asked for their attention. "Don't forget that these phrases can help grow thinking whether you are the one having the idea, like Gabe, or the partner. Did you notice how Rosa also used a prompt to help Gabe make his idea bigger? Listening partners can use these phrases and many others—phrases like 'What do you mean by that?' and 'Have you thought that perhaps . . .?' You can use these sorts of prompts on yourself or to help others when you are having a conversation or when you are writing about an idea or at other times throughout your life when you want to grow an idea."

While it can be particularly powerful to have students describe their work in their own words, I decided that in this case, I would be the storyteller. I already knew that the students would be talking with their partners, so time was of the essence. I wanted to make my point very clear, very quickly, and hadn't had time to "rehearse" with Gabe and Rosa. It is important to choose the method of delivery that best fits each situation.

SESSION XVIII

Tracing Ideas Through Texts

IN THIS SESSION,
you'll teach children that paying attention to recurring themes and details helps readers develop complex ideas about our characters and stories.

eachers, when you look over the minilessons in this book, you may think, "Where do you get ideas for minilessons?" The truth is that the books themselves give us many of the ideas. The idea for this minilesson comes from *The Tiger Rising*. I'm sure that as you read *The Tiger Rising*, you found yourself noticing images that reoccur. You probably thought to yourself, "There's that tiger again," or "There's that image of a suitcase." One way to author ideas for teaching is to spy on yourself as you read, noticing what you do, and then to think, "Is this something *most* good readers would probably be doing?" I'm pretty sure that most good readers would notice the reoccurring images and references in *The Tiger Rising*.

The next thing I do, when thinking about teaching reading, is pause and say to myself, "So what skill am I using as

I do this work?" Usually, the work that we do as we read does not fit neatly into any one reading skill. For example, when I notice that references to Rob's suitcase reoccur in *The Tiger Rising*, part of what I am doing is asking, "*Why does this repeat?*" You could refer to what I am doing as asking questions. Then again, I'm also thinking about how the author has crafted the story, wondering why the author made the decision to revisit this one particular image. You could refer to that as thinking about the author's craftsmanship. Then again, I'm also thinking between a part of the story (the tiger, the suitcase) and the whole, asking, "What does this one part have to do with the larger meaning in this story?" That's synthesis and it is also interpretation. And I could continue. Skills overlap. It isn't easy, therefore, to go from spying on one's work as a reader to homing in on a reading skill or two. We're left asking our-

GETTING READY

- Photocopy some pages from *The Tiger Rising* that reference reoccurring things in the book. Distribute these to partners during the active involvement as they will determine what reoccurring things may reveal about a character. If you are using another read-aloud text, be sure to photocopy passages from the book that contain ideas or images that reoccur throughout. Be prepared to have children work in small discussion groups of four.

- See the *Resources for Teaching Reading* CD-ROM for additional resources, including suggestions of things that repeat in *The Tiger Rising* and passages (or pages) which features those things.

- Be prepared to share Post-its from *The Tiger Rising* that reveal the kind of reader you are to show children how to learn about yourself as a reader.

selves, "Out of all the skills that play a part in the mind work I'm doing, and in the mind work that I think readers of books like this one will need to do, which skills seem especially important to teach at this point?"

> *To interpret a text, a person needs to shift between looking at a specific passage and thinking more globally about the whole of this book, or even more globally about lessons that matter to all of life.*

In this instance, I've decided that to help readers think about the significance of reoccurring images and references, I'll teach them the higher-level reading skills of noticing the author's craft and of interpretation.

Once I have decided to use *The Tiger Rising* to teach a lesson that brings together interpretation and the importance of noticing the author's craft, the next thing I do is recall what I know about the skills I'll be teaching and do some research so that I extend my knowledge of those skills. Before writing this minilesson, for example, I recalled that to interpret a text, a person needs to shift between looking at a specific passage and thinking more globally about the whole of this book, or even *more* globally about lessons that matter to all of life. I reminded myself that objects often take on symbolic weight, helping to represent larger meanings. I made note of the fact that I'd probably want to channel children to grow ideas that are tentative, using phrases such as "Could it be that . . ." and "Another possibility is . . ." and that I'd want them to read with their ideas as a lens, looking to see if their tentative theories actually work. I also thought about the fact that there are big interpretive ideas that already exist in the world, and that part of what a person does to read interpretively is link a text to one of those big ideas. That is, I know that some texts teach, "There is no place like home," and I can read *The Wizard of Oz*, for example, and say, "Baum has written this story to remind readers that there's no place like home."

Finally, before I write the minilesson, I need to think about the method of instruction I want to use. Usually in minilessons that aim to teach skills, I demonstrate a skill or strategy and then scaffold children as they give that same work a try. In this minilesson, I decided to use the skill of inquiry instead, inviting kids in on the thrill of discovery. The architecture of the minilesson is a bit different because of this decision. Use this as a template for other inquiry minilessons if it works for you.

# MINILESSON

Tracing Ideas Through Texts

CONNECTION

Ask children if they've ever noticed that a song's refrain usually conveys the song's most important message. Cite examples to show that big lessons can be carried in small refrains.

"Readers, have you ever noticed that a song's refrain—that's the part that repeats over and over—is the most important part of the song? When a songwriter wants you to pay close attention to a certain part of the song, he or she will use a refrain to make that part more important. So, for example, in the song 'Twinkle, Twinkle, Little Star,' the repeated line, 'Twinkle, Twinkle, Little Star/How I wonder what you are!' is the songwriter's way of celebrating the mystery of those magnificent sparkling things in the sky. In the song 'It's a Small World After All,' those same words repeat again and again to let us know that despite all of our differences, we humans are really very much alike. The world is small because it's full of people sharing the same hopes and fears, struggles, and celebrations. These are big lessons in small songs, and by singing the refrain again and again, we learn both the lesson and the song.

"'Twinkle, Twinkle, Little Star' popped into my head the other night as I was looking out my window at an unusually clear sky. I'd been trying to figure out some really important lesson to teach all of you. And then, as that catchy refrain played again and again in my head, it occurred to me that the authors of the books we've been reading this year *also* repeat things. The repeated parts of books don't jump out at us in quite the same way as refrains do in songs. And in books, instead of repeated refrains, authors repeat images, objects, situations, bits of dialogue, metaphors, and actions. The repeated parts run like threads through the text, weaving in and out of the fabric of the story. These repeated parts are the author's way of saying, 'Reader, this means something! This matters!'"

I'm hoping that the minilessons in these books function as mentor texts for you and that from time to time you pause and think, "What can I learn about minilessons in general from studying this particular example?" I believe this particular minilesson can help you remember that the job is to rally children to invest themselves heart and soul in the big and important work of becoming strong readers. It can be tempting to use minilessons as a time to load kids up with a trillion little assignments and strategies, but do kids profit from feeling as if reading involves juggling a whole bunch of little strategies? I'm not convinced. This minilesson aims to recruit kids to invest in the big work of interpretation. I hope you think about whether it succeeds, and if it does, about the transferable strategies you can take from it that can help you write other minilessons. I, for one, think that often it helps to describe reading by going away from reading. I also think that in this minilesson, referencing those magnificent sparkling stars helps. You'll recall that earlier, I was uneasy when I suggested that reading is a bit like walking a dog. This minilesson reminds me of why that earlier metaphor made me uneasy. It didn't bring a special sparkle to the minilesson. You may disagree. That's the whole point; by pausing, we can think about teaching, talk it over among colleagues, and ask, "What works that I want to do again? What doesn't work that I want to revise?"

Name your teaching point. Specifically, tell children that readers notice the reoccurring parts of our books, and we grow ideas from them.

"Today what I want to teach you (listen really closely) is this." Then, speaking almost in a whisper, I said, "The stuff that keeps reoccurring, that resurfaces often, that is threaded in and out of the fabric of a narrative, is the biggest stuff. That's often true in life. That's often true in books. In books, the things that the author mentions again and again are the ones that she really wants you to notice, the ones that are critical to understanding the essence of the character and the story."

Teaching/Active Involvement

Find another way to convey your premise—that authors repeat images, objects, and dialogue as a way to accentuate ideas that are important.

"Readers, when an idea is important in life, when there is something that we desperately want someone else to know, we don't just say it one time. In this class, when I want to make sure that you all learn something especially important, I don't just say it once, right? And, at home, when you want to talk to your parent about something that's critically important to you, like your birthday party, I bet you don't just mention it one time and then never again. You probably talk about it at dinner, and then again at bedtime, and then on the way to the grocery store. Authors are the same way. If an idea is important—an idea about a character, or about a story, or even a big idea about life—an author will bring it up every chance she gets.

"Only—and here is the important thing—an author might not come right out and say the idea over and over. The author will often use gestures or phrases or symbols that contain the idea. By bringing those up over and over, she hopes readers will think about the important idea over and over. It would be as if I kept making a sign like this to you," and I made a peace sign with my fingers.

Channel partners to revisit selected passages from the read-aloud text to notice reoccurring things and to speculate on their significance.

"Let's pretend we have just been reading *The Tiger Rising,* and we put the book down for a moment to think about what the author is really, really trying to say. We could just think, 'What are the big messages in this book?' or we could get to that question by first thinking about the bits that reoccur and then asking ourselves, 'Why might the

It sometimes feels that what we consider as the most crucial content in our teaching should be dramatically shouted from the rooftops. Sometimes, though, it's even more engaging to whisper, to lean in and teach your kids like you're telling the best secret ever.

You know your class best—so if the peace sign doesn't make sense to use with your students, choose a familiar gesture that will convey meaning to them—maybe a thumbs up, maybe a salute; whatever you choose, keep it simple and clear.

author have decided to make this reoccur? What bigger meaning could it perhaps represent?'

"Can I recruit you to help me think about things that keep reoccurring in *The Tiger Rising*? We'll mark places where something resurfaces again and again, and then say, 'What deep, significant, true idea might the author be trying to reveal about Rob, or about his dad, or about Sistine, or about life?"

I continued. "I'm going to give you and your partner each some pages from *The Tiger Rising*—these will be one or two pages from each of two different chapters—and I want you to scan the pages I give you and try to see if you notice little things that seem to reoccur. These could be small things. Then, you and your partner think, 'How could this represent something really big in the whole story, to this whole character?' In five minutes, we'll reconvene to see what you've found in your treasure hunt."

For this to be successful, you will want to make sure that the selections you distribute from The Tiger Rising *have some reoccurring images for children to sift through. You might even pick out a couple of pages in which the reoccurring image's significance is a bit more obvious (Rob's suitcase, for instance) to distribute to a partnership of struggling readers. Although you'll select pages that contain reoccurring images, you needn't plan in advance what children will find or what they'll make of what they find, and they'll probably surprise you. That is the electrifying piece of this lesson—both for you and for your readers.*

I passed each partnership a handful of pages, some chosen to spotlight Rob's rash, others, the caged tiger, the suitcase, and Sistine's dress. I didn't tell children that I'd preselected pages in which things reoccurred and that also conveyed some of the meaning behind the reoccurring object.

There are many ways this active involvement could go. Depending on the sophistication of your readers, you might not feel as if you need to scaffold children's work by providing them with a small selection of carefully chosen pages. You might, instead, simply suggest that partners look at the whole of the text together, skimming through it for reoccurring things. If you have a class full of strugglers, you may need to offer more scaffolding. You might even read aloud two passages, each of which contains another reference to a reoccurring image, and you might point out those repetitions as you read aloud and set children up to surmise why the author might have made that image reoccur, why that image relates to the whole of the story. You could then help children grow big thoughts about these.

Some children read silently, and others, aloud to each other. Some partners read all the way through and only then stopped for discussion, while others stopped frequently to discuss their ideas, underlining and jotting in the margins. I called out little tips: "Readers, even though you're looking at particular pages, remember, the idea is to think about the bigger meaning that might relate to the message of the whole character, the whole text, or to life even."

One teacher who spotlighted this work decided to disrupt the usual schedule of her reading workshop. After children called out images they believed reoccurred, she wrote each image on a big piece of chart paper and placed each piece of paper on a different table, and then her children essentially floated from one piece of paper to the next, writing their ideas about what makes that reoccurring thing meaningful to the text onto the chart paper. To increase intensity, this teacher suggested that the work needed to be done in utter silence, but that children could use arrows and notes to communicate with each other. The class vibrated with energy after doing this for even just twenty minutes—and these were third graders!

Ask partnerships to double up so that children grow even larger ideas about the meaning revealed through reoccurring images in the read-aloud book.

Before the five minutes had passed by, I suggested that partnerships team up with the partnership next to them to see if doing so helped them grow even bigger ideas. "Help each other wrestle with the question 'What might this repeating thing have to do with the big meaning of the whole story?' Turn and talk!"

Ask a few children from several groups to tell the class the reoccurring things they noticed in their pages of *The Tiger Rising* and to also share the bigger meaning they found behind each repeated thing.

After a few minutes, I reconvened the class. "Eyes and ears up here." I waited until I had everyone's attention, and then I said, "I'm so excited to hear what you all came up with! Could we hear from some of the groups? Decide quickly who your group's spokesperson will be. If you can't make that decision easily, I'll choose." I gave children five seconds to figure this out, then called out, "Raise your hand if you're the spokesperson for your group." Six eager hands shot up.

"Sam, you go first. Tell us just one reoccurring thing you and your group discovered in these pages and also what that repeated thing reveals about the essence of a character or the story."

Sam said, "We noticed that Rob's rash keeps coming back in the book. Kate DiCamillo mentions Rob scratching his rash a lot, and we decided that this must be important, but at first we weren't really sure why. So we asked, like how you said it, 'What is the big deal?' We came up with a few ideas. Like, first we thought that maybe Rob's rash is the author's way of showing that he feels not right or something. Uncomfortable. Even though we agreed on that idea, we thought there might be something else, too. So then we decided that maybe Rob's rash has to do with how other kids stay away from him. No one wants to go near him because the rash makes him different." *[Figs. XVIII-1 and XVIII-2]*

When Sam was done speaking, I jumped in, wanting to bring out something I'd heard his group say that he hadn't mentioned. "Sam, when I was listening to your group, one of you said that it was sort of like the rash was the bad stuff inside of Rob coming out, like his sadness coming out. Am I right that you also thought that?"

Sam nodded. "We talked about how sadness is invisible and the rash isn't." *[Figs. XVIII-3 and XVIII-4]*

You will notice that this minilesson is longer than usual. The teaching and active involvement are merged, and the minilesson is also longer than usual. You'll make the decision to alter the format of minilessons when this seems the right thing to do.

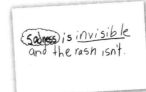

Rob's rash keeps others away.

Figure XVIII-1

He got the Rash from stuffing his feelings.

Figure XVIII-2

Sadness is *invisible* and the rash isn't.

Figure XVIII-3

It's his anger!

Figure XVIII-4

I repeated the idea. "Can you all hear how huge these ideas are? It is as if Rob's sadness on the inside comes out through his rash. The sadness is invisible. The rash isn't." I left a pool of silence in the room.

Then I said, "Grace, tell us about one of the reoccurring things your group found."

"We noticed a few things, but especially the suitcase," Grace said. She gestured to the chart she and others had made:

"Rob always thinks about shutting his suitcase tight, but it's not a real suitcase. It's an imaginary one. It's Rob's way of keeping his feelings from showing. Later, when he meets Sistine, it's like he can't keep the suitcase closed so tight. He starts to let his feelings show more."

Lily tugged on Grace's shirt sleeve and motioned to something on the paper in Grace's hands. Grace looked at Lily and mouthed the word, "What???" Lily mumbled, "Tell the rest," and pointed.

"Oh yeah," Grace said after glancing at the paper for a moment. "We decided that Rob's suitcase is kind of like the tiger's cage. It's like his feelings are locked in that suitcase just like the tiger is locked in the cage." Grace looked at Lily for confirmation, who gave it.

"Wow. I love how you made a connection between *two* reoccurring things in the book," I said. "That's the other neat thing that authors do sometimes. They weave threads—images, objects, and other repeating things—throughout the book so those reoccurring bits connect, creating an even bigger statement. Let's hear from a couple more groups."

The final spokesperson was part of the caged tiger group, and she reiterated the thinking that the tiger is caged just like Rob is—that Rob feels trapped, too. Again, I pointed out that the children, like the author, were making connections between reoccurring images.

"You have done such sophisticated work today, and the really exciting thing is that you can continue this thinking and grow it even bigger! That's the beauty of threads in books; they can mean so many different things, and often you see one thing and later another and later yet another thing. So what I'm thinking we can do as a class is to hang up pieces of paper with our reoccurring things in *The Tiger Rising* and then, whenever you have a new thought about the significant, true, deep meaning or statement behind one reoccurring thing or another, you can add it to our piece of paper."

LINK

Recall for children that just as we share important events from our lives over and over again, so, too, authors write about important things that reoccur in their stories.

"Readers, today you learned that when an idea is important in life, when there is something that we desperately want someone else to know, we don't just say it one time. We repeat it. Just like you do when you want your parent to know something about your birthday. From this day on, I hope you always remember that authors, too, repeat ideas that they think are true and deep, ideas that they hope the story conveys. And often authors don't come right out and repeat the idea itself. They repeat the image, the object, the rash, the suitcase. For example, if Sam, Aly, Josh, and Fallon had been reading in a lazy way, they might have breezed right past all the mentions of Rob's rash and never stopped to ask themselves, 'What's the big deal about this?' But they read in a really alert way. And all of you have done that same work. That's the job of a reader, every single day."

The children who made these connections between images are a particularly sophisticated bunch. Do not despair if your students don't land on such realizations. You can always paraphrase what they do say as if they have made the connection on their own. Of course, you'll want to keep the spirit and sense of what the children said, if not all their exact language. You might also say something like, "Readers, may I share some of what I heard you say? Make sure you tell me if I get your idea wrong." Then, check in with them: "Am I getting this right?" It's true that it's often more expedient for the teacher to do the talking, but you don't want to rob these readers of the satisfaction that comes with their ideas being showcased.

CONFERRING AND SMALL-GROUP WORK

Support Readers in Writing About Reading

Writing provides readers with an important way to respond to texts. Because writing allows us to slow our thoughts down, it gives thoughts the space in which to grow. This is one of the reasons people keep journals. The act of writing allows a person to put racing thoughts and emotions onto the page. In the process of writing, new thoughts surface. The physical act of pencil on paper (or fingers on keyboard), organizing a head full of flying images and unformed emotional reactions into words and sentences, can spur flashes of insight that we might miss out on otherwise—about life and about the lives we encounter in books we read.

But writing about reading is not just helpful for those whose minds are full and zooming. For those who struggle to isolate their own thoughts, ideas, and reactions, writing can be a physical way to oil the machinery of the mind, to unlock what might be shimmering just under the surface. And for those readers who don't yet have many reactions to what they read, writing that begins as a catalog of what a person knows can end up stimulating ideas, word by word by word. When we write about what we read, then, we are not simply recording what we think. We are not simply taking dictation from our brains and capturing fully formed ideas onto the page. We

actually *make* meaning as we put the words down, embarking on a journey that leads us to unexpected insights.

Of course, writing about reading becomes an especially intense process of making meaning when the reader not only writes his or her thoughts about a text but also rereads the jottings, searching them for patterns and contradictions and loose ends that deserve to be tied up.

In writers' notebooks, young people capture the stories and ideas of their lives onto the page, letting these become invitations to reflect. You may want your youngsters to partition their writers' notebooks so there is one section for reading, or to become accustomed to living with a reading notebook as well as a writing notebook. One way or another, as this year unfurls you'll want to help your students see that writing about reading is something they can do for themselves. You'll help children who are stymied over how to write and think in response to reading by providing them with possible "on-ramps" into written reactions, but ideally, your on-ramp will be transferable to other days and other texts so that all children learn that they can jot quick notes, charts, and questions as they read, and they can do so without requiring teacher assignments.

MID-WORKSHOP TEACHING POINT

Readers Can Grow Big Ideas from Seemingly Small Events in Stories

"Listen closely because the work you are doing is really sophisticated, and I want us to make it even more so," I said, and waited until I had the class's full attention.

"Earlier we talked about how something seemingly small—the rash on Rob's legs, Sistine's dress—can end up taking on symbolic meaning in a story and be more important than you at first realize. In stories, little actions as well as objects often take on importance—either because a character reads meaning into the little action or because *you*, the reader, read into the action. Or both. For example, let's say your character is walking down a hall and the door ahead slams loudly in her face. That's not a big event—the wind blew, the door slammed. *But* the character could think about that door in a really deep way; she could say to herself, 'That's what my life is like these days. Doors keep slamming in my face.' To the character, that slamming door becomes a symbol for things not going right, for missed opportunities, for people shutting her out, and so on. She doesn't mean literal doors, but when this one door does literally slam in her face, she thinks, 'That's just like all the other figurative "door" slamming in my face.'

"Notice that in that instance, the event itself was a small one, but the character's thinking made it big. And that one slammed door could end up changing that character's life. She might

continued on next page

Hopefully they all learn, too, that they can also move beyond jottings (which may be on Post-its) to occasionally writing at length, giving themselves the time and space to think deeply.

Making a Thought More Complex

Most of us want students to learn to produce thesis-driven essays in which they state an idea about a book (perhaps the theme of the book) and develop that idea with references to the text. I write about the process of teaching this to students in "Breathing Life into Essays" from *Units of Study for Teaching Writing*. But for now, the important thing is that writing must also be a tool to support the richest, most intellectually alive sort of reading possible. The goal in writing about reading can't be for each child to reduce a book to a cliché that could be fit inside a fortune cookie: "Life is like the seasons." Or "Friends need to help each other." Or "Communities are like a family." Even when we want children to be able to write essays that advance thesis statements that are a bit like that, we hope these ideas come after a reader's mind has buzzed with lots of thoughts.

I called Grace, Izzy, and Isaac together and asked them to bring their books and readers' notebooks. I'd noticed that all of them were responding insightfully in class discussions and after read-alouds, but when they were reading independently, their thinking tended to stop with platitudes. I suspected that writing could be

---

continued from previous page

> ## MID-WORKSHOP TEACHING POINT
>
> decide, 'That's it. I'm going to . . . .'" I let my voice trail off and then asked children to throw out suggestions for how the character could respond to the slammed door.
>
> Children called out, melodramatically, "Jump out the window!" and I said, "Or stop putting ointment on my rash, or . . . ," and this time, their suggestions were smaller and grounded in the text: "Stop hoping his dad will listen to him talk about being sad." "Stop trying to be friends with Sistine."
>
> "Sometimes in a book and in life, the events that have the biggest impact aren't the ones everyone would think of as 'big events.' They are, instead, events that for one reason or another, take on a big meaning for a character, and perhaps lead a character to act differently in ways that are consequential.
>
> "As you read, watching for things that repeat, you may discover that those things that seem to you to be extra meaningful don't necessarily register for your character as important. Maybe *you, the reader*, notice something that the character just breezes past. That happens sometimes in books! It can take a character some time before he realizes that little things in his life—objects or actions—are reoccurring for a reason. That they are significant. Here's a tip: Whether or not the character herself finds significance in a repeated action, you, as the watcher looking into her life, can draw on all that you know about the character as a person to consider the layers of meaning behind a seemingly simple object or action. Right now, pause and look over the pages you've just read, and say, 'Have I breezed by something seemingly small—an action, an object—that actually might be more meaningful than I realized at first?' If you find something, note it, jot your thoughts, and keep reading."

---

a way to help Grace, Izzy, and Isaac understand how to travel on a journey of thought.

I'd spent some time with the kids' notebooks the previous evening. Izzy, who was reading *Boys Against Girls* by Phyllis Reynolds Naylor, had written, "Caroline didn't always say what she was thinking if she was thinking deeply. I wonder if Wally now knows if Caroline would go to Odket's Bookstore to find the bones."

Isaac, reading one of Gary Paulsen's *Dunc and Amos* books and had written, "I think that Amos will want to be a prince because of use of the food that the real prince gets and affords on a regular basis."

Grace, reading Beverly Cleary's *Ramona and Her Father,* had written, "Oh my goodness! Ramona's father is upset that Mother decided to try making her (Ramona) a costume and then Father called Ramona a spoiled brat!"

These were all interesting thoughts and reactions. There was no problem with them. But I wondered if it might help to show these readers that their thoughts didn't need to stop there. I asked the children to open their notebooks to those entries and to reread them quickly.

"So," I said, when they had finished. "I gathered you together because I think you have similar strengths. You come up with theories about your characters, like Izzy's thought that Caroline doesn't always say what she's thinking and Isaac's idea that Amos will want to be a prince. But you have so much to offer during read-alouds, it makes me realize that I need to help you do that kind of deep thinking in the context of your independent books as well. You all have these great ideas, but then you stop. You don't stop reading or even writing about reading, but you move on to another page, another idea, without following the first idea very far. One thing that researchers have learned is that it helps for people to train ourselves to think longer about one idea. Writing in your readers' notebooks can give you a chance to think deeply about your independent books just as our book talks give you a way to think deeply about the read-aloud book."

Looking slightly put out, Izzy said, "I write in my notebook a lot, though!"

"Me, too," said Grace, shyly.

"I know you do—and that's great! What we're going to work on today is staying with one of the great ideas." I took a deep breath, thinking, 'How am I going to explain this?' and just at that moment I caught a glimpse of one of those paper fortune tellers sticking out of Grace's notebook. Many of the children in the class had been obsessed with folding paper in complicated ways to make those fortune tellers. Here was my metaphor! Aha!

"Grace, can you take your fortune teller out for a minute?" I asked. She did. All three kids looked totally puzzled. "Thanks. So just like you unfold the different parts of a fortune teller to read different things, you can use writing to unfold your ideas so they say different things. A complex idea has lots of different flaps and folds to it, like your fortune tellers. Just like you can lift a flap here, unfold a piece here, you can do that with your writing."

I could tell that Grace didn't particularly want me to actually read what was written in her fortune teller, so I handed it back and she tucked it back into her notebook with a grateful grin. Continuing, I said, "So sometimes, you three just need to keep writing longer about your ideas. One way to do this is to ask questions and try to answer your own questions. You can also think, 'Maybe . . . ,' and put an idea down, and then think 'Or maybe . . . ,' and see if you can look at your idea from another angle!"

Taking out *Dancing in the Wings*, I said, "Let's try doing this a little bit with Sassy from this book that you all know really well. We were talking earlier about that line that keeps coming up about Sassy, 'All you have to do is walk into the room. . . .' We didn't get to keep talking about it

because we had to go to lunch, so let's do it now. Let's write in the air, unfolding different parts of your ideas to make them more rich and complex. Anyone want to start? Pretend you are writing, only talk, and say what you think the author means when she wrote that about Sassy."

Isaac said, "She gets noticed really easily, I think."

Gesturing to the class's chart listing ways to get readers to say more, I made a gesture that signified, "Add on."

"She gets noticed because she is so much taller than the other kids, and she has those big feet," he added.

I looked at Izzy, who could tell I was expecting her to contribute. She pushed up her glasses, as she often did before speaking, and said, "Well, she didn't need to wear that loud yellow leotard. I think that is related to this. I wonder why she wore it, when the instructions said not to wear anything but black."

"Hmm, interesting," I said. "It is wise to wonder, like you just did, Izzy, and especially wise to try answering your own wonderings. Let's try. "Maybe. . . ." I trailed off, hoping one of them would finish the sentence.

"Maybe she thinks she needs to do something to stand out, and yellow is so bright," said Grace.

"And maybe she doesn't need it, because her big feet would get her noticed anyway," Isaac snickered a little bit.

"Do you think the author is saying it's her feet that get her noticed?" I asked.

"Well it's not just her feet," said Izzy, jumping in. "I mean, she probably does stand out because of how she looks. But maybe . . . (I gave her a thumbs up as she used the word) *maybe* it's also about her personality, how she is inside. Maybe her sassiness makes her stand out, too."

"I wouldn't be so rude like that," said quiet Grace. "That is so embarrassing!"

"For you, maybe," said Izzy. "But I like her. She's tough."

The kids probably could have continued talking about Sassy, but I wanted them to actually get some writing done in their notebooks and to do similar thinking about the characters in their independent books. The brief conversation was mostly meant to show them that as you grow an idea, it helps to turn the idea over and over, unfolding it as you go.

"I'm going to interrupt you. Great thoughts. And did you notice that as you kept talking, you kept putting different thoughts out there—maybe this, maybe that—and your ideas became richer and more complex? Can you try doing that on your own now? Take the ideas you started out with and see if you can unfold them by asking yourself questions and trying to answer them. Give yourself the space in your notebooks to explore lots of possibilities—because your characters (and the world) are not just one way. Let your thoughts get complicated. This is one situation where complicated is good!"

Waiting until they had all started writing, I went off and had another quick conference, and refocused a couple of other students, and then dropped back in on my group.

They had each added on. Izzy was writing so furiously her handwriting was starting to get illegible! Instead of stopping them all together, I checked in with each of them separately.

After a few not totally related sentences (sometimes this happens), Izzy had written a paragraph about making a thought more complex. *[Fig. XVIII-5]*

Both Grace and Isaac wrote their thoughts down, too. *[Figs. XVIII-6 and XVIII-7]*

The children's thoughts were not necessarily earth-shattering, but they were much more thoughtful that those they'd recorded earlier. More importantly, the readers had incorporated some of the language prompts I'd introduced earlier in the unit, using phrases like "on the other hand" and "this makes me realize," and I knew that over time, using those thought prompts would pay off for them. I made sure to emphasize the fact that the work they'd done today was transferable to other days and other books and sent them back to continue reading.

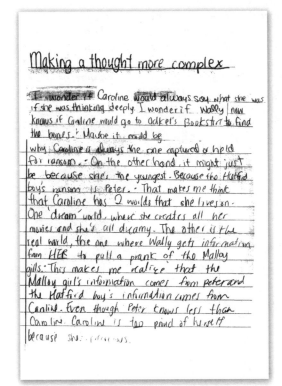

Figure XVIII-5

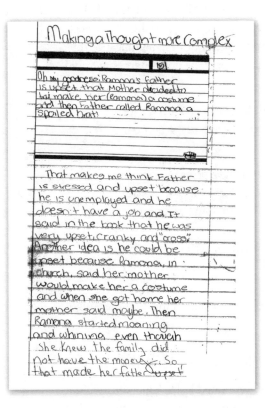

Figure XVIII-6

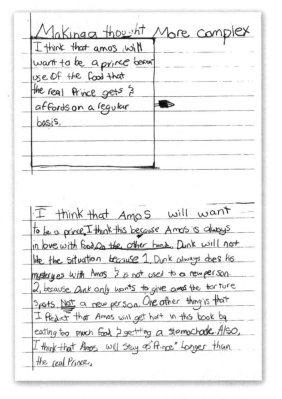

Figure XVIII-7

TEACHING SHARE

Readers Notice that Little Objects and Actions May Have Big Meaning for Characters

As you reread aloud a portion of the read-aloud book, ask children to pay attention to the little objects or actions that resurface in this story, and ask children to think about what significance the little objects or actions might hold for the character.

"Readers, the stuff we have been talking about today is really huge, and I think we need to talk about it as a group, so will you all gather in the meeting area?" I waited until the children had settled on the carpet. "I know we usually talk about your reading right now, but for a minute let's return to *The Tiger Rising*."

The children were thrilled, hoping for a continued read-aloud. "Listen while I reread the beginning of Chapter 16 in *The Tiger Rising*, and as I read, pay attention to the little objects or actions that seem to resurface a lot in this story, and think about what significance they might hold now, at this moment, for Rob." I'd copied this passage onto chart paper, and now read it aloud.

> Rob sat out on the curb in front of the motel room and waited for Sistine to come back from using the phone. He had her green bag wrapped up in a grocery bag.
>
> He had tried to fold the dress up neatly, but folding a dress turned out to be an impossible task and he finally gave up. Now he held the bag out and away from him, so that the grease from the medicine on his legs would not stain it.
>
> He was relieved when Sistine finally walked toward him out of the darkness.

"Quickly turn and tell your partner if there's an object or action in this part that might be important."

Ask some children to share their thinking and coach them to take it further.

"I heard a lot of you say 'Sistine's dress.' Some of you mentioned Rob's leg medicine. You are right that both of these things have popped up over and over throughout this book. I

I could have, of course, decided to teach this idea in a conference and then to highlight the work done with that child in the context of his or her book. I wanted each child to have the opportunity to practice this new thinking, however, in the context of the book they all knew well. I suspected that I'd be continuing to support this work in conferences coming up and knew that the idea of finding significance in small objects and actions would only become more powerful when resting on the shared base of understanding I was hoping to begin building during this teaching share.

wonder what importance they might hold here. Let's look closer. What is Rob *doing* with Sistine's dress? With his medicine? He's tried to fold that dress up carefully and now it's wrapped in a bag that he's holding at a safe distance from the grease on his leg. That seems important." I let my voice trail off.

In a voiceover, as children continued rereading the passage and thinking, I said, "To think what these objects—actions—might mean to the character—to Rob—you need to go back (I threw my arm over my shoulder in an action reminiscent of earlier work on synthesis retellings) and recall what you know about Rob. Why might Rob be treating this dress with such care? Why is he treating this prissy thing in such a special way? Sistine doesn't like the dress at all!" I stared at the ceiling as if deep in thought over these questions, hoping children were also mulling them over.

Then I said, "I'm just thinking, 'What do we know about Rob?' One thing for sure is that he takes care of the things that matter to him. Think about all those delicate, intricate carvings he's spent hours whittling. Then there's the tiger he guards so closely and the secret that the tiger exists. Oh! Rob doesn't have a lot, but what he does have he seems to guard. So what about this dress? What might it mean? Turn and talk to your partner."

After a few minutes, I said, "Readers, listening to you just now, I heard things like, 'Sistine's dress is like a symbol for Sistine. She means a lot to Rob, so when he treats the dress delicately and protects it, it's like he's protecting her.' That is so wise!"

Ask children to try the same work of the day in their independent reading, with a partner.

Then I said, "Readers, I know you have been finding actions and objects that carry huge meanings in the books you are reading independently. Get with your partner now and show each other what you are finding in those books."

You'll realize that I'm doing the heavy lifting here. I've preselected the passage that contains mention of the reoccurring objects, and I'm prompting the children to create significance around these. I'm scaffolding this process in the share but hoping that children will be able to find reoccurring objects in their own books and feel confident that they can use these to unearth significance.

Intensifying Interpretations by Finding Motifs

In word-association psychology tests, the tester rattles off a list of trigger words while the person being tested is instructed to respond with the first word that comes to mind. The trigger word *knife*, for example, elicits a response such as *fork* or *cake* or *blood*. There is no doubt what a knife is. Probably all the respondents recognize the reference to a sharp cutting utensil. The difference, however, lies in the *association* that is triggered in each respondent's mind upon picturing a knife. One imagines a knife cutting a cake, another pairs it with a fork, while a third imagines a cut finger. If a word elicited identical associations from everyone who heard it, the test simply wouldn't work. It follows that the process of reading, which entails the processing of word upon word, will stir up unique and personal associations in each reader. If texts contain gaps that the reader's imagination must fill, then the reader essentially *creates* aspects that aren't actually in the text but are incited by the text.

Of all the reading skills that we teach to children, interpretation is perhaps the most challenging. On the one hand,

there is the danger of being too prescriptive and taking away that crucial freedom that is the inalienable right of every reader: the right to create meaning for himself or herself. On the other hand is the worry of being too open-ended. After all, the interpretation, no matter how unique and unconventional, needs to ring true to the text, needs to be accountable to whatever is explicit in the text.

In this bend, as we teach kids to construct deeper meanings from their stories, it is tempting to cut to the chase and *tell* them why the book is named *The Tiger Rising*, why Sistine decides to befriend the unlikely Rob, why Rob whittles a bird, and why Willie May places this bird in the tiger's grave. After all, *we* should know; we're the teachers with years of experience in literature and in reading. Instead, we provide small prompts and keep our profundity to ourselves, watching kids painstakingly work at constructing bigger meanings, beating about the bush until they come to some sense of revelation. The process isn't unlike a long-legged parent slowing his pace to accommodate—and validate— the faltering first steps of his toddler, resisting the urge to

GETTING READY

- In this session, you will read aloud the final chapters of *The Tiger Rising*.
- You'll want to have on hand *Dancing in the Wings* and other picture books with which children are familiar.
- Be prepared to extend the read-aloud to fill the workshop time.

scoop the toddler up so that they reach their destination faster. Our teaching, after all, focuses on the journey more than the destination, the process more than the product, and we teach the *reader*, rather than the *reading*.

One way to do this is to return to a teaching point and deepen it. In the previous session, we taught kids to notice reoccurring images, reoccurring words, and reoccurring objects in their books, suggesting that whatever is worthy of repetition is certainly laden with significance. In this ses-sion we go further and teach kids that motifs are deliberate literary devices, that in crafting a text an author cleverly inserts motifs into a story, but that when we find these motifs, there really is no one answer and no right answer to the question "What does that represent?" Our aim, again, is to help kids experience books, to help them feel that there is so much more inside a great book than simply what happens.

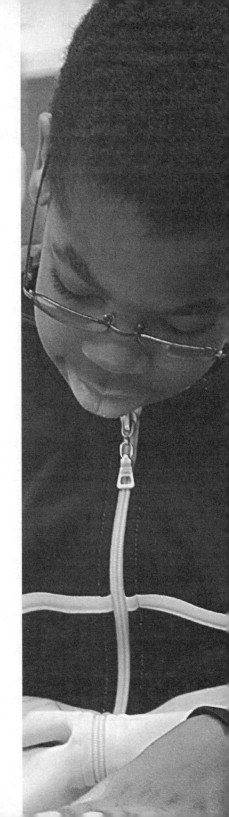

MINILESSON

Intensifying Interpretations by Finding Motifs

CONNECTION

Tell children a story that helps them understand that objects can carry symbolic meaning and that recognizing those symbolic objects can help them understand and make sense of texts.

"When I was a young girl, every summer at my camp would end in the same way. The evening of the last night, as it was just getting dark, our counselors would gather us together at the end of the dock over Lake Wannabee. They'd hand each of us a small candle fitted onto a little paper boat. Once we all held our candles, we'd sit in a tight circle and listen as our counselors spoke with reverence about being our true selves and following our hearts and consciences through thick and thin, just as we had all through our days at camp. The candle, they told us, was a reminder to us of the little light inside each of us. Then, one by one, each of us would light our small candle and set it afloat in the water, to drift off into the darkness, a spindly line of wavering pinpricks, heading off into the dark corners of the lake. As they floated off, we'd all sing, 'This little light of mine . . . I'm going to let it shine. . . .' And we'd promise ourselves we would.

"At camp, our counselors would end our experience for us just right. They decided what mattered most of all we did together, what symbolized the spirit they were hoping we'd take with us, and they gave us an image to help us carry that spirit once we all left that place forever. The job of ending something just right is not so different when we read a book, is it? We have to sift through all that has happened and catch hold of the essential spirit of it all, the part we want to take with us forever from this reading experience.

"At the end of summer camp, the counselors helped us find the right way to end our camp experience, to think about the whole summer. At the end of a book, the author, helps us catch hold of some of the lasting parts. Many authors will offer us up an image, an object, or some other small thing that has been part of the story again and again. We've talked about this before, remember? When the author repeats something—an

We have all had experiences that ended "just right," with the perfect blend of reflection, inspiration, and lasting image. If you can make the time to think through your own experiences and come up with a resonant one to share with your students, the payoff will be great. Maybe it was a beautiful graduation ceremony, a grandparent's birthday celebration, a jubilant "flying up" from Brownies to Girl Scouts. Of course, feel free to borrow this example, but it will mean more to your kids—and to you—to share something from your own life.

image or an object or a phrase—we know that thing is important, and it's worth asking ourselves why it's there. We figured out some lasting thoughts about *The Tiger Rising* from looking at some of the reoccurring objects and images. In stories, these important things are called 'motifs.'

"Since we're near the end of our read-aloud book, this is one of our last chances to let *The Tiger Rising* really mean something to us. It will be our job to figure out how to end this book, just like it was the camp counselors' job to help us end those summers alongside Lake Wannabee. And one of the ways I know readers take in the deepest and most intense parts of a story is by caring about the motifs, letting those motifs carry the spirit of the story."

Name your teaching point. In this case, tell children that readers can see more meaning in motifs, can go deeper into interpretive thinking, by thinking like writers as we read.

"Today I want to teach you a way that readers can intensify our reading, a way readers can catch some of the spirit of the book to hold onto for ourselves even when we are finished reading. Specifically, we can look for and hold onto the motifs of the story."

TEACHING

Explain and give an example of a person creating meaning for an object or image.

"I know you all have created motifs, even if you've never used that word. You know how to take something small, something that may appear insignificant, and imbue it with meaning, in a story or in your writing or in your life.

"Here's an example of what I mean. I knew a little boy who saved a crushed Coke can under his bed, and he brought it to show-and-tell. When he told about it to all of us, it went like this: 'This can is from the time my dad came to see me,' he said. 'He bought me soda that I'm usually not allowed to have. I smiled and smiled that day!' He didn't look so happy when he was telling us about it, even though his words were happy. The kids in the class asked him how come the can was crushed. 'My dad didn't visit again when he said,' he told us. 'So I smashed the can.' He didn't have to say a word more; we all understood him very, very well, just looking at that smashed-up thing he was holding so carefully. That smashed up soda can had so much meaning wrapped around it. It had the whole story of his wonderful, happy day with his father, and it had his anger and disappointment at his father's broken promises. And he kept it under his bed to hold onto, to keep the spirit of both of those stories. That can was a symbol for him, a motif in that story of his life. We didn't have to search very hard for it. It was right there in the center of his story."

ACTIVE INVOLVEMENT

Ask children to find, in their partnerships, key symbols or motifs in another story they've read.

"To get ready to read the last parts of *The Tiger Rising* with as much intensity as we can, let's practice, for a moment, finding important symbols, motifs, in another book we know well, *Dancing in the Wings*. This work is not so different from the work we have done other days, right? You think about an object or something else in the story that holds associations in it, holds bigger meanings, holds more about the story. Since you all already know the story *Dancing in the Wings*, think that one over for a moment and then turn and talk with your partner about what you are thinking. I think you'll find that looking for motifs will change the way you think and feel about this story and any other story you think about in these ways. Okay, take a few minutes to do that. I'll be holding up that book here and slowly turning the pages to remind you of the story." I let them spend a chunk of time reading and talking together about motifs and then called for their attention again.

I decided to have the children practice in Dancing in the Wings *because I wanted them to be able to sink into* The Tiger Rising *when I began reading, without having to break the flow to stop and practice.*

Let students know that today's workshop will be an extended read-aloud and discussion. Tell students that together you will all do what readers do when they read books that matter to them: bring intensity and resonance to their reading of the final chapters.

"Readers, do you see and feel how pulling together all your thoughts about a story into one object can add to how we are thinking about it? Doing that is one way to help ourselves get the most out of endings, especially endings of books that mean as much to us as *The Tiger Rising*.

"So here we are at the end of *The Tiger Rising*. Endings are a time when all that we've been thinking and wondering about comes together. Aren't you dying to find out what happened with the tiger? And how will Rob and his dad solve things? Does Sistine play a role in this? So let's end today's workshop in a special way. I will read to you the last three chapters of the book. We won't stop for independent reading, we won't have conferences, and when we share, it will be about this book and what we're thinking about it when we feel it as much as we can, pulling the whole book and its meaning into this ending in any way we can. As I am reading I want you to be figuring out what's most important. Readers, to do this you're going to think about not just the chapters I am reading but about the whole of the text. And not just what we've read but also all that we've talked about. I will stop a few times for you to write long in your notebooks."

I read to the end of the chapter, letting the power of the text affect my voice and pace. As I came to the book's final words, I carefully closed the cover and gently and gravely put the book in my lap. I let the silence fill the room.

After this pause I said, "Readers, pick up your pens and let some of the thoughts that are flowing through you fill your page. We'll talk in a moment!"

After a minute I asked a few readers to share what they were thinking. "The death of the tiger has opened up everything that Rob was trying to keep down for so long," said Emma.

"Yeah, he screamed at his dad and he never did that before. I think telling his dad he hated him and he wished he'd died instead is the bravest thing he's done. It's like the tiger is coming out of him," said Malik.

Since I didn't want a conversation to get going just yet, I asked if anyone else had paid attention to other parts. A few voices started to talk at once. Sam and Fallon stopped talking and let Jasmine go.

"His dad saying his mother's name is important. I got chills at that part because his dad hadn't wanted to talk about her at all," said Jasmine.

"I got chills when they both said they needed her," added Fallon.

"Okay, so as we read Chapter 29, carry all of this important thinking and see if we can grow bigger ideas."

At the end of Chapter 29, I gave the students another chance to write. I coached them by reminding them to connect what they were thinking and noticing to their ideas from Chapter 28 and to other ideas we've had in previous conversations and to earlier parts of the story.

Then I read Chapter 30. When I got to the last paragraph, I paused and then read.

> He lay in bed and considered the future, and outside his window, the tiny neon Kentucky Star rose and fell and rose and fell, competing bravely with the light of the morning.

I paused again and then said, "This is how the story started." I flipped to the beginning and read.

> That morning, after he discovered the tiger, Rob went and stood under the Kentucky Star Motel sign and waited for the school bus just like it was

If you think your readers need more prompting, though they probably do not, you might add some suggestions for their writing, like this: "You may have paid attention to Rob's interaction with his father and want to explore that significance. You might have noticed that the suitcase is referred to again and compare now to when it has been talked about before and think about the change and what's the significance. You may have noticed other changes and want to think about what they are showing."

At the end of a riveting book I often find myself flipping immediately back to the first page to read again how it all began. It can be moving to read those initial lines with eyes that have made the story's journey. What was just a sign the first time around is now so much more.

any other day. The Kentucky Star sign was composed of a yellow neon star that rose and fell over a piece of blue neon in the shape of the state of Kentucky. Rob liked the sign; he harbored a dim but abiding notion that it would bring him good luck.

"It's like we've come full circle, and yet so much has happened, so we want to think back on the whole experience of the book to figure out what's the message we'll take from this book. Take a second to think."

Give children a moment to think, and meanwhile, do so yourself. Wait for a child to signal he or she has something to share.

Grace began, "At the end Rob was lying in his bed, and he was thinking about the future. He didn't used to do that 'cause it said that Rob had a talent for not thinking about things. I think he couldn't because he wasn't able to talk about his mother's dying. Once he yelled at his dad, it was like he started to heal and he could think of other stuff."

"Who can add on to that?" I asked.

"I know we've said this before, but the suitcase represents that. Rob was stuffing all of his feelings and emotions into that suitcase because he couldn't deal with them and neither could his father. And once the dad shot the tiger, it's like everything poured out of him," said Sam.

"Does that connect to another image or object in the book?" I asked. There was a pause in the conversation, so I had the children turn and talk to get more voices out.

Notice when, in the middle of a whole-class conversation, there is a lull and ask children to talk with partners. This gives them a way to prime their thinking and allows me to be strategic about who speaks next.

"I think it connects with the tiger being in a cage," said Aly. "Rob is like the caged tiger. The tiger wants to get out and be in the wild but can't, and Rob's real feelings are locked up inside of him and can't get out. He won't allow them to. He is too afraid, but once Sistine convinces Rob to let the tiger out of the cage, then Rob's feelings and emotions get free, too."

"It's like he found his voice," piped up Lily.

I prompted, "Say more about that."

"Rob talks but doesn't really say what he wants or maybe needs to say. Like . . . like he has lost his voice. He is voiceless. So is his dad. And that creates a big hole between them, and I don't think either one of them knows what to do, so they avoid talking about anything that means anything to them. If they did, it might bring up the mom, and that would be too painful."

"But don't you think it was also painful to keep everything inside?" asked Gabe.

"Yeah, but I think it takes a lot of courage to go up to your dad who told you at your mom's funeral not to cry and not to talk about it, so he wasn't able to have that conversation. But when the dad killed the tiger, it was like Rob wasn't thinking," added Lily.

"I think he avoided thinking and speaking about it with his dad, and his anger grew and grew inside him until he exploded," said Kobe.

"He needed the tiger to die to set his feelings free and to break the silence," replied Lily.

"Wow, that seems to be an important idea. Turn and talk about breaking the silence."

I listened to one partnership. "I think this book is really about breaking the silence because Rob and his dad had lost each other by not really talking, and it's like their relationship was disappearing," added Izzy.

I prompted, "I'm taking away from this book. . . ."

"I'm taking away from this book the idea that when a really bad thing happens to you and you don't want to face it so you don't talk about it, you can be silenced by it. And if you're lucky something will happen that gets you to open up, but if you aren't lucky like Rob and his dad, you could slowly become invisible."

"Maybe Rob is right the sign was lucky," said Jasmine. The children discussed their ideas for several more moments, and then I called them together to end this unusual workshop day.

Be on the lookout for important, resonant ideas coming from your students so that you can pull them out like I did here and continue to guide the conversation into deeper thinking territory.

LINK

Let children know that books can matter to us in more intense ways if we let the endings take on more meaning, pull in more associations, and layer on more complexity.

"Today I think you felt how much the ending of a book can mean if we take time to care about the motifs in the book. I think we'll carry the images we have found at this story's end with us. I heard in our discussion that the same thing has happened to you. You will hold onto a few of the images in this book, probably forever, don't you think? Readers do that. You can do that from now on, too, not just with this book, but with any book that is important to you.

"Readers, our reading time is over now. It's not been a usual day. We have no time for independent reading—but do that at home tonight and remember to use what we did together today to help you read your independent books differently."

Spying on Ourselves as Readers

here is something wondrous about watching an infant stare intently for the very first time at his own hands, witnessing the dawning awareness of control. "I can flex these. I can put them in my mouth. They're mine." Doctors and parents celebrate the developmental milestones that suggest a child is growing more and more aware of himself. It is a big deal when the infant realizes that he is separate from his mother's body and when the baby recognizes himself in a mirror or a photograph. It is a big deal also when the child ascribes behavioral attributes to himself. "I hate broccoli!" or "I am sad." In our classrooms, before our noses, kids continue this lifelong process of becoming aware of themselves as individuals. They define themselves and assume roles accordingly. "I am the class clown." "I am good at math." "I am different."

How crucial it is that the reading workshop allows children to take a proactive role in understanding and controlling their identities, their sense of self. When you and I say to the youngsters in our classrooms, "You are the authors of your lives," we are inviting these young people to take active control of their lives. We are inviting them to direct their own lives, to adopt and strive toward self-imposed goals.

With empowerment comes responsibility. When we urge children to author their own reading lives, we also help children step up to that job, and there is no better way to do this than by helping children look at themselves objec-

GETTING READY

- Make the chart, "Readers Read Differently. Some Tend to . . ." to refer to during the minilesson.

- Jot Post-its from a previous read aloud so you can study the kind of thinking you tend to do as you read and place them in the book so that you can leaf through the book to demonstrate the work the children will be doing. You may want to make a second set of jottings on larger Post-it notes so that children can see your jottings when you analyze them. If you are using *The Tiger Rising*, some examples are found in the teach section of this minilesson.

- Ask readers to bring their books with jottings to the meeting area because they'll be studying them during the active involvement.

- Have the reading notebooks available for the children before independent reading time so they have the opportunity to record their new reading goals.

- Prepare blank bookmarks for distributing during the celebration.

tively—noticing what they tend to do as readers in school, at home, when reading silently, and when talking about books. In this minilesson, you'll suggest that your young readers can take the evidence they've left in the form of Post-its along the way and study those to self-analyze, to aspire, and to grow.

The message you give children today is powerful. You're inviting more than self-reflection. You're inviting self-

> *How crucial it is that the reading workshop allows children to take a proactive role in understanding and controlling their identities, their sense of self.*

initiated goals and change. And you're heightening readers' metacognition as you do this, setting them up to look at the process of their reading itself as an abstraction, one over which they have control. Even our best and most motivated readers, the ones who immerse themselves deep in the worlds of their books, do not necessarily think of their reading as a process that they can study, control, and develop.

"Everyone reads differently," you're suggesting. "You can choose how you want to read, what you want to do differently as a reader."

What was once invisible thinking will now be far more clearly articulated in your classroom. Since you'll be pushing all your readers into analyzing and evaluating what they do as readers, you'll be prepared to hear statements such as, "I guess I'm always Post-iting what I think will happen next. Maybe I should also Post-it what I'm feeling as I read exciting parts like the quidditch match." If you hear that, pat yourself on the back because your plot-driven reader will have just vowed to empathize more actively. Perhaps you'll also hear, "My Post-its kind of retell what happens. I'll try to Post-it what I think will happen next." Again, you'll have heard your great-at-literal-retelling reader set a goal to predict more actively.

How important it is that you advance the cause of self-consciousness. Your children will continue to find books they like and to start reading. The question is whether this child pauses in the midst of doing this to wonder why it is always a mystery that he winds up picking, and whether that child takes a second to recall that when he read the last book, he took the time to read the back cover of the book before diving in. Should he do the same again?

You're setting up a community where children make conscious choices, not just about *what* they'll read but *how* they'll read. As a result, your children won't just be reading the books in their hands; they'll be reading their thinking, reading themselves.

MINILESSON

Spying on Ourselves as Readers

CONNECTION

Tell children that they can look back at their jottings to research themselves as readers.

"Watching you read yesterday and listening to you talk, it is really clear you've learned that small bits of a story can take on enormous meaning to characters and to you, as a reader. Knowing this is helping you 'read characters,' and learning to read characters in books is important because this allows you to read your friends as well.

I never forget that I'm not only raising readers; I'm raising citizens. I often remind children that this thing called reading is really, truly, a life thing. We are trying to affect how children read when they are home alone on their couches. We are also trying to affect how they walk through the world, day in and day out.

"Readers, earlier this year, we talked about how each of you needs to not only be the author of your own reading life. You also need to be a researcher, studying what works for you as a reader and what doesn't work. From time to time we have looked back on our logs to learn about ourselves as readers, and today I want to tell you that we can also look back at our jottings, our Post-it notes, and we can think about the thoughts we tend to have as readers (and those we do not have very often). We can do this to learn about ourselves as readers."

Books often end by circling back to the beginning, and this unit is doing so as well. The unit is referencing the main idea from the first unit of study: You are the author of your reading life.

Name your teaching point. Specifically, tell readers that we can research our thinking about reading and give ourselves new goals.

"Today I want to remind you that we can look back on the jotted notes we make as we read and research our thinking, asking, 'What sort of thinking do I tend to do as I read?' After we spy on our own thinking, we can put together all the clues that we see, and together, these can help us construct a sense of ourselves as readers. We can come away from this saying, 'I'm the sort of reader who does a lot of this kind of thinking and who *doesn't* do a lot of that kind of thinking.' We can then give ourselves goals so we deliberately outgrow our current habits as readers and thinkers."

Notice that when I detail a procedure, I lay out the procedure in a very sequenced, step-by-step way.

I'm aware that children tend to construct reading identities based on text level alone. "I'm an R reader; what are you?" I try to enrich children's understanding of themselves, and their readerly identities.

TEACHING

Summarize and list the kinds of thinking readers do often. Demonstrate that readers can reread Post-its to notice patterns in our thinking.

"Readers, earlier we noticed there are differences among us in the number of pages (and minutes) we tend to read in a day or a week. But today I want to emphasize that there are also differences in the kinds of thinking we tend to do as we read. Some of us tend to wonder why characters do what they do, questioning their real motivations and trying to find reasons for surprising actions. Others do a lot of predicting, thinking about what will happen next, saying, 'I bet such and such will happen.' Some of us notice the way an author has written the book, appreciating or criticizing the writing style or thinking about ways that an author's choices shape the message of the book. Some of us constantly identify with characters, saying, 'I'm just the same as she is,' or 'I'd be so mad.' Some of us read with our eyes, saying, 'I can picture it,' and others read more with our ears, turning any page of print into a score that we hear as we read." I displayed a small chart.

"I am going to look through some of the Post-it notes I made earlier during this unit about *The Tiger Rising* and notice the sort of thinking I tend to do as I read. Watch me as I do this." Picking up my book, I leafed through the pages I'd marked with Post-it notes and paused to read one aloud.

"Let's see. On this note I wrote, 'Beauchamp seems like he has a lot of power even though he's a minor character.' That one Post-it note makes me wonder whether I

You can decide how complex or how simple you want to make this work and write your Post-its accordingly. If you want to do so, you could write four Post-its in which you notice an author's craft, three in which you do one other thing—say, envision—and then, during the teaching part of the minilesson, you can "notice" one thing you envision, for instance, and instead of asking kids to reread their own Post-its and name what they are doing during the active involvement (as suggested in the minilesson as it is presently written), you could instead ask children to research your Post-its and to name another way you tend to think about reading. Because your Post-its would illustrate a kind of thinking, say, noticing author's craft with crystal clarity, this would be a way to scaffold children's work.

You may want to write your thinking on large Post-it notes in advance of the lesson and to stick them on a piece of chart paper on your easel. That way, children can see what you've jotted and focus their attention not on recalling what you jotted but instead on categorizing the sort of thinking the Post-it suggests you've been doing and on analyzing patterns.

might be the kind of reader who pays attention to secondary characters. I'll have to see if I have more jottings about secondary characters. Oh, look! Here's one that says, 'Willie May is like the voice of truth when she tells Rob he's keeping all his sadness down in his legs and that he should let it rise. I think he should spend more time with her.' I'm noticing a secondary character again!"

Name what you have done in a way that helps others do similar work.

"Readers, do you see that I looked between my Post-it notes and noticed the kind of thinking I did when I wrote one Post-it (I gestured to the chart to suggest this list reflected kinds of thinking I might have seen myself doing, although there are certainly other choices) and then I looked to see if I tended to do that same kind of thinking again?

"I'm now going to notice the sorts of thinking I rarely do." I glanced at the chart I'd displayed earlier and then across my Post-it notes. "Hmm . . . ," I said, letting time go by.

"You know what I'm noticing? I don't seem to predict all that often. I'm not sure why," I said, as if this was just dawning on me, although of course I have designed the Post-its to illustrate this.

SOME READERS TEND TO . . .
* Predict what will happen next
* Ask questions
* Think about the main character
* Compare a book to her/his life — or another book

Two things: First, notice that this is an expendable section of the minilesson. You could decide to not do this and to relegate it to the mid-workshop teaching point. Second, notice that there is a thin line between demonstration and guided practice. In this instance, I name the mental work I am doing next—noticing the sorts of thinking I do not tend to do—and then I deliberately proceed in the step-by-step way that I hope children will rely upon later when they are asked to do this on their own. I'll do this often—setting children up to participate in the demonstrations that are embedded into the teaching component of my minilessons. It will, of course, be important to have a way to silence children who call out the answers. I tend to hold up a hand, as if blocking off their contributions, saying, "Wait, wait, let me do my own thinking."

"So, readers, I'm noticing a kind of thinking that I do a lot, something we haven't talked much about. I notice the author's craft. And I also notice that although I ask you to predict, I don't seem to do much of this myself. So my self-study gives me direction. I know that I'll want to continue to do the sort of thinking that is so essential to me—noticing the author's craft—and I'm going to want to share it with others, too. But I also want to nudge myself to predict more often."

Sometimes our tendency is to notice what readers tend to do and then promptly tell them to start doing whatever it is they don't do! Avoid this. There are ways of seeing the world that are bone of our bone, flesh of our flesh, and it is critically important for all of us to embrace and use and share our gifts, not just to deny them so we become well-rounded!

ACTIVE INVOLVEMENT

Channel readers to reread their Post-its, noticing the kinds of thinking they tend to do, and not to do, and then to share with partners.

"Now it is your turn to study yourself as a reader. Look across the jottings (or entries) you've made over the past few days and ask, 'What is the thinking work that I tend to do as a reader?' Take a minute to reread and research this question. You might find that you tend to do a kind of thinking that isn't on our list, and we'll have to add it to our chart."

After a few minutes, I said, "Thumbs up if you have a theory about the sort of thinking work you tend to do as a reader." Then I said, "Turn and tell your partner what you are noticing about your own thinking. Start off by saying, 'I tend to. . . .'"

Fallon told her partner, "I tend to do a lot of wonderings. But the thing is, I'm realizing that sometimes when I write 'I wonder,' it's really going to be a prediction, and other times when I write 'I wonder,' I'm asking a question." She covered her hand with her mouth. "Uh oh! Maybe I should put 'I predict' for when I'm making a prediction, and 'I wonder' for when I have a question. Wait, what do you do a lot, Josh?"

Josh ignored Fallon's efforts to deflect the focus from her reading to his own and observed, "Well, I'm thinking that really, you do two kinds of thinking as a reader."

"Yeah, I predict *and* question. I envision, too, but I don't write it. I don't know if I gotta push myself to write more notes about what I see in, like, my mind movie."

Josh said, "You should. Definitely. Then you'll have three sides."

"My envisionment would get fuller. So I'll try to read more with my eyes."

Meanwhile, Sam said to Aly, "I'm looking at my Post-it notes now, and I'm seeing that they are all predictions and questions. I'm not sure, but I think there are more questions. I gotta see if I ask questions when it's a really easy book, or it's that the book is confusing."

Aly then set a goal for herself. "Well, I mostly make ideas about characters. Now I want to try something else. I've decided that today I'm going to push myself to pay attention to the author's writing, the author's craft. I never ever *dreamt* of doing that before now, but I already see a bunch of Post-its I could write."

You may feel that asking readers to think like this, to be metacognitive about their own reading work, is a bit advanced. I tend to think differently. I think having readers actively researching and naming their own reading strengths helps them take this invisible thing called reading and make it more visible. I'm asking readers to think every day, and here, I'm pushing them to think about their thinking. Still, if you aren't comfortable with this minilesson, revise it to match your own ideas on how children grow as readers.

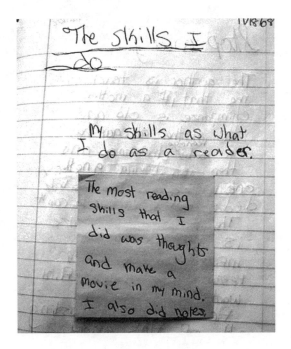

LINK

Rally your children to live as researchers of their reading lives and to realize that analyzing oneself sets the stage for generating goals.

"Readers, I hope you are realizing that to be authors of your reading lives, you also need to be researchers, studying what works and what doesn't work for you as a reader. Today I hope you have learned that readers can spy on our own thinking and say to ourselves, 'So far, I'm the sort of reader who does a lot of this (or that) kind of thinking.' And I'm hoping you've learned you can set goals for yourselves. When you get to your reading spot, please take a minute to jot down your goals in your reading notebook and read with these in mind today. Off you go!"

You may decide to be more or less definitive. You can, for example, ask readers to set goals for the thinking work they will do in the upcoming reading workshop while remaining on the carpet, perhaps recording those goals in a goal box or a self-assignment box within their notebooks. Or you may just mention that goal-setting is wise and leave this up to them. You'll gauge how explicit you need to be in all your teaching as you note whether invitations alone actually affect your readers' behaviors or whether you need to be more controlling. Always use the lightest touch possible, and remember, the goal is not for every child to do the same thing in the same way! Your hope is that a minilesson gets some new work into the classroom and generates some energy around that new work. You'll then be able to celebrate what children do, to make a fuss about it, and that, too, will build momentum.

CONFERRING AND SMALL-GROUP WORK
Lift the Level of Children's Work with Text

A large part of conferring and small-group work during this unit is watching and listening carefully to what your children are doing and then thinking of ways to lift the level of their work so that it's more effortlessly independent as well as more infused with thought and intention. Often the most meaningful and lasting support comes when we are engaged in a task and someone gives us a tip or a strategy to help us do that task even better. When a young child is learning to ride a two-wheeler, for example, and struggles to get the pedals going, we can either continue to run along behind her, holding the seat until she's propelled by her own pedaling, or we can provide a valuable tip that will allow her to take off on her own. We can say, as she straddles the two-wheeler, "Start with your foot on the higher pedal and your other foot on the ground next to the pedal. Push the higher pedal and that will help you go." She may wobble at first and have a few false starts, but she'll be much more likely to ride on her own sooner than if you had continued to hold the seat to keep her steady. Reading is no different. As we watch and listen to children read and talk

about their ideas, we always try to think of a tip or strategy that will help their work, for this book and beyond. Therefore, you will want to think about some things that readers in your room tend to do as they think and talk about books and then imagine ways to push their work forward, so they can take off as readers, independently and thoughtfully.

Teach Children to Extend the Connections They Make with Texts so that They Understand Their Characters and Their Stories Better

One particular trend that often emerges when studying characters is that children make connections to their own lives. They are quick to make connections like Isaac, who said, "Rob reminds me of me when I had to ride the bus and there were some bullies who bothered kids," and then he launched into a story about his experience, relating how the bullies got in trouble with the bus driver. Making connections with characters and texts is an important part of reading, and we want to foster this. However, there is an important dis-

---

> ### MID-WORKSHOP TEACHING POINT
> #### Readers Put Their Goals into Action
>
> In a voiceover, as children continued to read, I said, "Readers, I see that most of you have already jotted a few Post-it notes as you've been reading. I just wanted to remind you to keep your reading goals in your minds as you read today. Sometimes when we set new goals, we have to push ourselves to meet them. Grace is already working on her goal of reminding herself to stop and jot her thoughts so that she can think more deeply. I noticed just now that she has three new Post-its already!" I gave Grace a thumbs up.
>
> "And when I was talking with Kadija just now, she realized that she had been forgetting to go back to look at older jottings to see how they connect and to discover how her thinking—and her character—is changing over time, so she did it right there as we were talking, and discovered something new about her character. To meet our reading goals we have to read with those goals in our minds, and sometimes we need to stop and practice right then whatever it is we want to get better at. Before we go back to reading, I want you to turn to your partners and take a minute to remind each other what your goals are, and then say what you've done so far today to meet those goals. If you realize you haven't done anything yet to meet your goals, don't worry. You still have some reading time left today, and I bet you can figure out a way to put one of your goals into action. Go ahead and talk for a minute, and then we'll get back to reading."
>
> *continued on next page*

tinction to consider: We do not make connections just to see parallels in our lives and the lives of our characters, but to learn more about our lives and the characters' lives and to go deeper with our thinking. That is, connections help us to crawl inside of our characters, walking through life as our characters would so that we gain a deeper understanding of who they are and, quite possibly, who we are.

To help direct children toward this powerful reading work, you will want to help them see that their connections give them great insight into their character and their story, but the connection itself is only the first step in gaining insight. When they say, "This reminds me of one time in my life when . . . ," you might push them to deepen the connection by teaching them to say, "This reminds me of my life because . . . and so it makes me think . . . will happen next." Or "This character reminds me of myself when . . . and so it makes sense that he/she is feeling/thinking/going to . . . because. . . ."

So when Isaac said, "Rob reminds me of me when I had to ride the bus and there were some bullies who bothered kids . . ." and began to regale me with the story of the time the bus driver stopped the bus because of the bullies, I gently interrupted him and said, "So the part about the bullies on your bus reminds you of your life. Hmm. Using this connection, what do you think might happen?" At this point, Isaac can imagine possible scenarios, using his own connection alongside what he knows about the story to make predictions that are based both in the text and in his life experiences.

I could have also said, "So, you, like Rob, know what it's like to ride a bus with bullies. Really think about that connection, how you were feeling and what you were thinking, and use it to understand Rob better. How might he be feeling? What might he be thinking?" In showing readers how they can take their connections a few steps further and deeper, they will learn to use them not simply as a list of similarities with their

characters, but they will use their connections to get inside their characters' heads and hearts.

Teach Children to Not Just Ask Questions, But to Consider the Realm of Possible Answers

Children are naturally curious and ask dozens of questions across the day. They wonder why red lights mean stop, and who decided red would be the color for stop, anyway. "Why can't it be purple?" they ask, almost annoyed at the conformity. They notice a caterpillar making its way across a busy sidewalk, and they stop to move it to one side, wondering where the rest of its family is and what kind of butterfly it will be. This wondering and questioning stance will follow them into their reading, and you are apt to notice that many of your children will ask questions as they read, wondering why a character behaved a certain way, how the Magic Tree House really works, and whether or not Opal's dad will let her keep the scruffy, dirty dog.

Sometimes your students' questions will be more literal, and it is quite possible that they will be answered as the child reads on. For example, when a new character is first introduced, a reader might wonder who the character is in relation to the others or why the character said a certain thing. So, you might want to coach children to read with their questions in mind, entertaining them as they go. You might say, "The most thoughtful readers don't just ask a question and then leave it behind. No, we read on, staying alert for the answer. What you can do with your questions is jot them on a Post-it and stick the Post-it to the edge of the page with a little question mark symbol in the corner, so when you discover the answer, you can go back to the question and either jot the answer on the Post-it or pull it out altogether."

Then, too, children will ask questions that have no one answer. The beauty of these kinds of questions is that they often lead to theories and

---

MID-WORKSHOP TEACHING POINT

continued from previous page

The class buzzed with conversation. I moved around the room, briefly listening in on a few partnerships. Isaac was telling his partner that he realized he was paying more attention to his characters' relationships with each other over time, and Tyrell was saying that he wanted to go back and check his Post-its to see if he could use more specific words to describe them.

"Let me stop you, readers," I said after just a moment. "As you get back into your books, keep your new reading goals in mind, and if you haven't yet put any of them into action, make sure you start doing that before it's time to stop for math."

ideas that can be explored and revised as a reader continues reading. These questions might often start, "Why would . . ." or "Why does . . ." or "How can. . . ." For example, when we began *The Tiger Rising*, many students were asking, "Why does Sistine talk so harshly to Rob?" When students ask questions that may not have an answer or that won't be answered in the text itself, we can teach them to read with these questions in mind as well. "Any of our questions are worth carrying with us as we read. Some of them might be answered in the text itself, but other questions are the kind of questions that have no one absolute and obvious answer. These questions call on us to think deeply and to probe the nooks and crannies of the story to find hints of the answer. So when students ask, "Why does Sistine talk so harshly to Rob," you might respond, "Wow. That is a huge question! We can try to answer that now, and then as we read on and learn more, you can revisit this answer and ask yourself, 'Do I still think the same thing I did before? Has my thinking changed?'"

When I walked up to Brianna who was reading *The Miraculous Journey of Edward Tulane*, she was awash in questions and was, in fact, a bit overwhelmed. I asked her what her questions were, and she began to rattle them off. "I wonder what it must have been like for Brice to watch his sister die. And, I want to know: What did Edward wish on the shooting star? What did Sarah wish? How come Sarah's dad left?" I nodded my head emphatically and responded, "I know exactly how it is to have a pile of questions as you read. As you're asking these important questions, come up with possible responses, based on what has already happened in the book. Then, as you read on, sometimes the question will be answered and sometimes not. For example, your question about how it was for Brice to watch his sister die is an important one. Questions about how a character was feeling in a scene usually don't get answered later. You have to rely on what you know about the character to come up with some possibilities. Either way, come up with possible answers and then read on. When you find out the answer—or find more information that helps you answer the question—you can think about whether your first ideas were correct." My teaching point in this conference was a simple one: carry your questions along as you journey through a book. Some might be answered easily and quickly, while to answer other questions, you'll need to combine your own ideas with what the text offers.

I jotted down a note to myself to check in with Brianna the next day, which I did. I briefly interrupted her reading to make this suggestion: "Think back to the possibilities you came up with yesterday in answer to your questions. Now, compare that with what you are thinking today. I bet some of your ideas changed as you read on and got more information. For example, yesterday you said, 'I think Edward wished that he could be with Abilene again.' Do you still think that? When you find yourself revising your thinking about a question, it's helpful to frame your idea by saying something like, 'At first I thought . . . but now I think . . . because. . . .'" This little tip suggests to Brianna, and readers like her, that we're constantly thinking and rethinking as we read.

TEACHING SHARE

Readers Share Their Reading Talents

Remind children that as they've been studying themselves, they'll have discovered they have particular reading talents. Ask the children to present a bit about their reading talents to the group.

"For weeks now as you've been reading and thinking and talking and working together, I've been spying on you and finding out all of the things that you've gotten really good at. I could go around the room and say something that each of you is great at now. I'm not going to now, though, because I'm guessing you've done a little spying on yourselves as well and have noticed yourselves gradually becoming experts at various things we've worked on together. So when you notice that you're really good at something, it's important—almost like it's your job—to teach it to others. We all need each other to bring the things we're good at—our talents—to the whole community, so we can learn from each other and all get better at those things. So before we wrap up, we're going to have a little talent show, where a few kids are going to talk about their talents. It's not going to be like a real talent show where you perform your talent, because some of these talents we're developing are quiet and invisible and happen in your mind as you're reading and writing, so the kids presenting are going to talk about their talents to let us in on them."

Taking on the role of an emcee momentarily, I said, "First up, please make your way to the front of the classroom, Fallon and Josh! Let's hear it for Fallon and Josh, everyone!"

Loving an excuse to applaud and whoop, the class did just that as Fallon and Josh grinned hugely in front of them.

"Fallon and Josh," I said, continuing in my emcee role, "what talent are you presenting us with this morning?"

"Well, we got really good at having grand conversations about our characters," said Josh, "and pushing each other to say more about them."

"Yeah, for example, Josh helped me realize that I could be stronger at envisionment and that I could be writing more notes about the movie in my mind as I read. And whenever we thought we were out of ideas, we just kept talking and pushing each other to say

You could angle this kind of impromptu series of presentations in a few different ways, depending on your own preference and on the personalities in your class. You may choose to arrange kids' sharing of what they're good at as little seminars, where they simply stand in front of the class and discuss what they've learned. You may want to ham it up a little bit and bring a festive vaudeville sort of feeling to the event, especially if you have a lot of performers in your class! You will, of course, want to prepare the children you'll ask to speak in front of the class so that they know what's coming.

more. So we ended up learning lots more about our characters than we would have otherwise."

"Yeah, sometimes Fallon was kind of annoying." He gave her a sideways grin "because she always makes me clarify what I mean, and to do that I have to think more carefully and clearly myself. So. That's our talent."

"Fallon and Josh, everyone!" I said. "Grand-conversation havers! A round of applause, please, as they make their way back to their seats! And now, our next act will be the talented Tyrell. Come on up, Tyrell."

Tyrell stomped his way up to the front of the room with his hands in the air, to the great delight of his classmates. Stepping outside of my emcee persona for a moment, I quieted them before encouraging Tyrell to begin.

"Tyrell, tell us about your talent."

"Well, a long time ago when we first started this talking about characters stuff, I used to kind of read without paying attention. So my goal was to read more carefully and not on autopilot, so I wouldn't miss so much stuff about my characters. And I did, like with Andrew in *Freckle Juice*, I really got to know him well because I wasn't just reading without paying attention."

Nearby students reached up to give popular Tyrell high fives. Tyrell, savoring the moment, walked slowly back to his seat, arms in the air again.

I find that children really want other children to succeed, and I knew that Tyrell's classmates were genuinely happy that he'd made such leaps as a reader recently.

You may choose to have as many children share their talents as you have time for. If you have lots of children who want to "perform," you may even steal moments from other times during the day so that more voices are heard. This activity builds energy in the class for the imminent end of the unit and class celebration, so taking a bit of extra time to make students' hard work known is useful and fun.

Celebration: Creating a Self-Portrait in Books

As any unit in the workshop draws to a close, it is worthwhile to be especially deliberate. A unit can end with the abruptness and harsh finality of a shrill school bell, or it can come to a conclusion. Like storytellers, speechwriters, or writers of any genre at all, curriculum writers, too, must conclude with care, fine-tuning that final note with which we leave our kids. And, of course, our *conclusion* may very well be that we aren't ending this work at all, that the strategies kids picked up in this unit will be revisited in later units, in later grades, in later years. "Today is the start of the rest of your reading life," we could decide to say. "You'll be carrying a suitcase in your head like Rob, but instead of emotional baggage, yours will be a bag of strategies, close at hand for you to call upon whenever you pick up fiction literature."

Even though this solemn rhetoric may sound grand to our ears, and—if we state it with enough conviction—to the kids' ears, we need to remember that our words alone won't make the difference in kids' lives. To have lasting influence, our teaching needs to not only tell kids how to live; our teaching also needs to get them started on that living, nudg-ing them into real action in hopes that at the very least, Newton's first law will take effect, and kids will stay in motion for the rest of their lives.

Such longevity isn't easy to initiate. Sending kids off with balloons or certificates doesn't do the trick. Balloons pop and certificates are soon forgotten. We want to hand kids a gift that has greater lasting power—greater soaring power. Of course, like all grand aims, this is easier said than done. The kids that filed fresh-faced into our care in September will soon be filing out again, faces fuller and more mature. The ending of a unit heralds the ending of the year, remind-ing us that our goal must always be to make a lasting dif-ference. And so, in the final moments of this important unit of study, we might think of celebrating our children's grow-ing identities, their growing independence, and their grow-ing sense of self. After all, helping youngsters build lives and identities as readers was our goal at the start of the school year. A goal like that requires sustained attention over time. It merits becoming a motif. We hope that when this goal reoccurs, like the motifs we've taught kids to recognize, it will have greater effect and stronger staying power.

GETTING READY

- Ask kids to have a paper and pencil at hand, ready for quick jotting.
- Make copies of the self-portraits of van Gogh and Cézanne.
- Prepare blank bookmarks with the caption: My Self-Portrait in Books—enough for each student to have one.

"Who are you now?" we might ask our students. Specifically, "Who are you now as a *reader*?" If allowed to hang unthreateningly in the air, such questions themselves have enormous power. Our teaching thus far has been all about urging kids to carve a reading identity by choosing and investing themselves in books. We've urged our children to spy on themselves as readers; to set self-initiated goals; to read long, strong, and above all, with growing independence. More than just showing our kids that we take them very seriously, the question "Who are you now as a reader?" invites the sort of serious introspection necessary for true ownership. As kids ponder their emerging reading identities, as they pour over their logs to self-assess, as they list the books and authors that will forever be part of them, and as they aspire to next steps in their lives as fiction readers, they're enacting the same concept of self-creation and self-discovery that determines their decision to wear their hair a certain way or sign their name as a specific doodle. Kids are deliberately, thoughtfully, carving out identities for themselves. Our contribution is significant if we ensure that this identity is a consciously literate one.

In the final moments of this important unit of study, we might think of celebrating our children's growing identities, their growing independence, and their growing sense of self.

MINILESSON

Celebration: Creating a Self-Portrait in Books

CELEBRATION

Suggest that people are recognizable by their choices in clothes or music, possibly using examples from your own classroom and life to prove your point.

"Readers, you know how we can recognize someone by their choices in clothes or by their iPod playlist? Like if I were to walk into this room and see a baseball cap and red sunglasses lying at a certain desk, I'd know Kobe sits there. And if I were to see a pencil box or file cover with Kanye West's face staring back at me, I'd know it probably belongs to Brianna. Our choices in what we wear and what we carry sort of determine who we are. Like if I did something uncharacteristic such as dye my hair pink or wear a halter top to school, or if you heard me suddenly humming rock music, you'd be surprised. You'd think, 'What's up with her?' because pink hair and halter tops and rock music probably aren't characteristics that you associate with me. Or you might think, 'Maybe I didn't know her as well as I thought I did!'

"All the things that you associate with me—with any person—are part of who that person is. I want to suggest to you that what we wear and what we like doesn't simply occur by accident. We can *choose* who we want to be. And reading is a big, big part of this. If you want to know what makes me *me*, I have a list of books and authors I can rattle off for you: Enid Blyton, Annie Dillard, Thomas Hardy, Don Murray.

"For instance, I can tell you that Enid Blyton made me fall in love with reading, that Annie Dillard made me long to build a cabin in the woods and to lose myself in words and the cry of the loon, that Thomas Hardy's books bring me back to a year when I found my footing on the windswept moors of England. Every book that I pick up to read and, especially, every book that I decide to *reread* makes me the person I am today. Have you ever heard the saying, "You are what you eat?" Well the real truth is, you are what you *read*. In other words, you don't just recognize a person by his or her choices in clothes or iPod playlist. You can just as easily recognize people you know well by glancing at the contents of their bookshelves.

Teachers, think about it. Have you ever been in a presentation and lo and behold, the speaker mentioned you personally, by name? You probably find yourself sitting a little taller, listening more acutely. Your children, too, long to be seen and heard. I once passed a sign outside a church that said, "Give what you can. To someone it will mean more than you can imagine." Simply referring to a child by name, showing your attentiveness to the details of that child's life, will mean more than you can imagine.

It's a powerful thing to suggest we are what we read. And that's true for children as individuals and also true for your class as a whole. The community in your class will be shaped by the books you share together.

"Today, readers, as we end this unit on following characters into meaning, I want you to think about the characters you've come to know through books, characters that will stay with you long after this unit ends. I'm going to give you a minute to name a few characters that you've loved and will remember from the books you've read—and to jot these.

"I'm going to give you another minute to think of the book titles and the writers you've read this past month or in the past two months that you want to carry with you as part of who you are and who you want to be."

Suggest to kids that contemplating characters and books that we want to hold onto is the start of constructing an active self-identity as a reader. Do this by referencing the self-portraits of famous artists as a way to drive home your point.

"Readers, eyes up here. What you've just begun doing with those names you've jotted is thoughtful, serious work. Consider this picture." I showed kids a copy of one of van Gogh's self-portraits. "Or this picture." I showed Cézanne's self-portrait.

"These are paintings by the grand masters of art in which they've painted themselves. In fact *this* artist, van Gogh," I said, revisiting the first picture, "painted as many as *thirty-five* self-portraits in his lifetime. Artists make self-portraits to present themselves to the world but also to answer the question, 'Who am I?' And as they paint their own features, artists can literally construct who they *are* and also who they *want to be*." As I spoke, I touched my own face and features.

Of course, there are countless choices in the portraits you might show your students. You could decide to show self-portraits by Andy Warhol, Frida Kahlo, and Norman Rockwell instead, not only because of their powerful visual message but also to drive home the point that an artist deliberately constructs the self on canvas, choosing a specific face he or she wants to put on public display. You might even decide to showcase Facebook profile pictures—or dig from New York artist Matt Held's painting archives of powerful Facebook profiles to demonstrate the deliberate construction and projection of identity. You might even choose to use portraits of some of your students' favorite authors: Shel Silverstein, Gary Paulsen, or Patricia MacLachlan, for example. You might ask, "Why did Patricia MacLachlan choose to show herself hugging her dog in her portrait? What does this tell us about her?" Whatever portraits you choose to use for this lesson, they should resonate for you so that you can make them resonate for your students.

Note that I contrast the two concepts of who I am versus who I want to be. Though I've tucked this reference to the real self versus the ideal self casually into the discussion, in fact this touched on humanist psychologist Carl Rogers' perspective on personality. True self-actualization occurs, in Rogers's opinion, when we bridge the gap between how we perceive ourselves and how we would ideally like to be perceived. How consequential our teaching could be if ours was the classroom in which kids realized that they have active control in bridging this gap between who they are and who they want to become, and if they saw the vehicle for bridging that gap as involving active control of their own literacy.

Make the point that conscious choices in reading allow us to create a self-portrait in books—a powerful literate identity.

"Readers are the same way. When we read, what we're doing is creating a *self-portrait in books*, and in a way this is as powerful as a van Gogh painting in determining who we are. What I read, the books I choose to identify with, are as much a part of my identity as my hair color or the shape of my nose. These are the books that will shape my *brain*.

"So I want you to look again at the names and titles you've jotted on the paper in front of you and realize this: Rob and Sistine will be part of you forever. Stone Fox will be part of you forever. Whenever you see a boy being bullied, or a faithful dog that looks at its owner as if it might lay down its life in loyalty, you'll remember their stories. More than being memories, these stories, the struggles that these characters have been through, will guide your actions in life.

"There will be other books that shape you as well. How exciting to discover what those books will be, and how they will become part of your identity!

"Just like van Gogh chose the colors and the outfit in which to paint himself, you can decide to let a certain story shape you by reading it like it's gold, stepping into the skin of the character, and by rereading it, talking about it, letting that one book lead you to other related books.

Pass blank bookmarks around the room, inviting readers to use these as blank canvases on which to create their self-portraits as readers.

"Right now, I'm going to pass around some bookmarks. You could say that these bookmarks are *blank,* but I have a different way of looking at them." I held up a bare, unmarked bookmark and displayed it. These bookmarks are clean slates. Fresh beginnings. Ready to be filled with a million possible things and full of potential and possibility. Like you all.

"Just as van Gogh literally created himself thirty-five different times, you are going to use these bookmarks to create a self-portrait of yourselves—a self-portrait in books.

"In this unit we've learned about characters and about stories. Specifically, we've learned how to step inside a character's shoes and to literally climb the story mountain, struggling with our character as he or she faces a problem and grows toward its solution. Now that we've begun this work, let's use these bookmarks to continue it. You'll be picking up book after book from the library in the coming days and the com-

Of course you will want to add in or substitute those characters who have been most meaningful and resonant to your own class.

I wonder what it's like in your family, when it's time to end a long summer vacation together and to head home. Do you find that the last days brim with nostalgia as you prepare yourself for saying, 'the end,' 'Amen,' 'Goodbye'? I find that endings are always a time to look back. You'll see that this final session and all the final sessions throughout the series are filled with references to earlier work. I'm hoping that is a way to hold tight to all we've experienced and learned.

Notice the phrase "in the coming days and the coming months." This is a new way to say, "Today and every day . . ." Both phrases are important in a workshop because we're not teaching into today only but also tomorrow.

ing months. As you read, tuck your bookmark between the pages of the book and think, 'Should *this* character and *this* story contribute to my self-portrait in books? Am I learning and changing because of having met this character and having gone on a journey with him or her?' If so, you may choose to write the name of the character or a quote that captures his spirit or personality. Or instead, you may want to draw a picture of her, or a motif or symbol, that represents the character or the book, or you might even want to draw the object that the character kept close on your bookmark.

"The bookmarks, then, will become reading self-portraits of yourselves, portraits you'll continue to add to across the year. To get ourselves started, why don't we spend some time looking through our reading logs and remember all of the books we've read this year. Once you've got some books in mind, books that you'll carry in your head and heart always, you can collect them from the library and skim through them. You'll be looking for inspiration for the way you'll represent what the book or character means to you on your bookmark. As you are rereading, find the one quote or excerpt that resonates the most for you. In a while, we are going to get together and read those parts to each other like they are gold and to talk about why we've picked that particular excerpt as the one that has moved us or stuck with us the most."

I wasn't surprised at all to see Sam rereading *Wringer*. He had been so invested in that book when he read it. I recalled that he had done a book buzz on it. Sam had drawn a pigeon on his bookmark. I asked Sam, "Are you going to read aloud from this book or another one?"

"This one. I'm trying to find the perfect part. I think I'll read aloud the part where Palmer tells Dorothy that he wished he'd never joined up with Beans and the gang and how he didn't want to be a wringer. She tells him not to be one. But he feels pressure to be one."

"That's interesting. That's such an important part of the book, isn't it? What I'm wondering is why *that* part in particular? How does that section of the book fit into your reading self-portrait? I guess that also means, what does your choice say about you?"

Sam was quiet for a moment, looking off across the classroom. Then he said, "Well, I want to be like Dorothy, who isn't afraid to be herself and tell the truth. I think Palmer learned that, too. If he had told the gang about Nipper and that he didn't want to be a wringer, Nipper would be alive. It kind of reminds me of how last summer there was this new kid in my cabin at camp, and he was kind of weird, and we all kind of teased him. I felt bad after, because he was actually pretty nice. It's like Palmer, I know how it feels to wish you'd done something different when you had a chance."

As your students study their logs, reread books, and make their bookmarks, you'll want to watch and learn about them as readers. You might be surprised by what they pick or by what they say about the characters or books. Your students might reveal things about themselves that you didn't know.

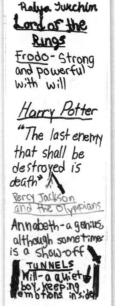

Impressed with the depth of Sam's response, but not totally surprised, knowing Sam the way I was coming to know him, I said, "Sam, that is such an important thing you've recognized. I can see why you've chosen this book as part of your portrait. Speaking up in the face of peer pressure and standing up for what you know is right is one of the most important (and sometimes one of the hardest) things ever. I can tell you're on your way just by how you're thinking and talking about it now."

I left a smiling Sam at his table and stood up to scan the room. I saw Fallon putting Post-its in *When You Reach Me* and then furiously scribbling in her notebook. I remembered that she had read this book in practically one day because she couldn't put it down. When I walked over and looked at her bookmark, I saw that she had written "lifting my veil" next to the title of the book. I asked her if she'd mind reading to me what she'd written in her notebook. Without looking up, Fallon nodded and read,

> I couldn't bear to put *When You Reach Me* down. When I get involved and really care about a book, it does that to me. The biggest thing I thought about is Miranda's veil and my veil. Veils are keeping both Miranda and me from doing things we want to do. We also both have times where it is hard to stay on our feet, where our pride sort of disappears."

"Wow. What a connection you've made with Miranda! I'm so interested in what you mean by the veils. I know about Miranda's from the book, but how does the idea of a veil fit into your life?"

Fallon looked up, frowning slightly, and began, "Well, I think I'm a lot like Miranda because we don't really show people how we really feel or what we really think. I mean, sometimes I do. But sometimes I don't. It's like how Miranda was scared. Sometimes I guess I feel like that, too. But Miranda lifted her veil, and when she did, good things happened—and she was ok. She is like, maybe, a role model to me."

"How so?" I asked, surprised by bold and outspoken Fallon's candor and insight.

"Well, sometimes it's hard for me because I come on kinda strong, and sometimes people see me one way, but really I'm not that way. Like I don't always say what I'm really thinking, or sometimes I argue because I don't want to say how I really feel. Miranda got more confident in the book, though."

Because you'll be reminding children of how much they've grown, you may want to carry your conferring notes with you. It's helpful to show children that these are tools that remind you of the progress a child has made, because children tend to think of them as "grade sheet" and to worry. You can turn them into sources of compliments.

This activity can inspire some really thoughtful and unexpected introspection in students. Not all children will make connections to such deeply personal ideas as Sam and Fallon did, but being asked to define themselves by books or characters that resonate for them is an activity that helps children not only think back over the books they've read and loved but also unfold themselves a little as they make connections between themselves and the things these books taught them.

Fallon's voice trailed off and she looked back at her paper. "Well it takes a lot of confidence to realize those things about yourself, Fallon, and to say them," I said quietly. "That's some really deep thinking. Thanks for sharing this with me."

"Readers, as I am walking around, I see *The Tiger Rising* and Kate DiCamillo in a lot of self-portraits as well as *Stone Fox* and little Willy. That's interesting. Like the portraits of a family reveal some common physical feature that they all share, the portraits of this reading community also reveal a common feature. It's like you're all related to each other now because you've all been shaped by the same book or books. I can't wait to hear why you've chosen these books. So right now, I want you to get into groups of four and read those excerpts of the books you've chosen to each other like they are gold, like they are treasured—because they are—and then explain why this book or character matters to you."

With a minimum of negotiation and discussion, the children were able to get themselves into groups of four, eager to share. I listened in to Jasmine talk about how she wants to be more like Willie May and really tell people what she is thinking and feeling, but maybe not so rudely, like the time Willie May called Sistine an angry liar. Jasmine said, "But when I talk I want to say things that make people think, like Willie May does. She doesn't just go blah, blah, blah. She only says things that are really important somehow. She's wise." Then she read from *The Tiger Rising*.

> "Ain't that just like God," she said, "throwing the two of you together?" She shook her head. "This boy full of sorrow, keeping it down low in his legs. And you,"—she pointed her cigarette at Sistine—"you all full of anger, got it snapping out of you like lightning. You some pair, that's the truth."

I leaned in and asked, "Jasmine, how does this connect to you as a reader?"

"As a reader? Hmm . . . . Well, I want to say wise things about the books I read—wise just like Willie May says wise things to people. She studies people really closely. I like to do that, too."

Moving to another conversation, I heard Tyrell finish reading his excerpt from *Freckle Juice* and then say, "I love this guy, Andrew. He's so weird. He's funny, too, which I am sometimes." Tyrell grinned and continued, "And he likes to try experiments, like me."

I smiled to myself, remembering how Tyrell had really gotten into that book—how he'd worked so hard to be able to read that level fluently and how he'd sat on the rug chuckling to himself during reading time.

Emma had in front of her *The Great Gilly Hopkins* by Katherine Patterson and *Journey* by Patricia MacLachlan. I was curious to see which she'd chosen to reference. She began, "I had a hard time choosing between Journey's grandmother and Ms. Trotter. I hope both of these characters will stay with me forever. But I hope that I will find more characters in books like Ms. Trotter because of her compassion. At first I saw her as Gilly did, kinda dumb and unaware. But she wasn't. She saw through Gilly's tough outside, and no matter how much Gilly pushed her away, she responded to her with kindness. When Miss Ellis, the caseworker, said to Gilly that her mother wasn't going to come and get her," Emma read,

> It's been over eight years, Gilly. Even when she lived close by, she never came to see you.

Emma looked up and said, "Trotter could've agreed with Miss Ellis, but instead, even after all the unkind things Gilly had done, she said,

> If she knowed you—if she just knowed what a girl she has—she'd be here in a minute.

"I wrote that quote on my bookmark so I won't forget Trotter and what she taught me as a reader and as a person. As a reader she taught me that the next time I am thinking that a character may be just as the main character sees him or her I'm going to look at her through the other characters' eyes and my eyes. And as a person she's taught me to be more compassionate."

It felt like the children could go on forever and ever. Huge conversations were erupting as children added their thoughts to each other's. I hesitated to intervene, but I knew the last part of this celebration was important, so I stopped them. "Readers, it seems fitting that we begin the journey to fill up this bookmark today. So now I'm going to ask you to keep in mind what you know about the characters and books that matter to you as you grab a new book baggie and begin to fill it up with three or four books that you will take home with you to read in the next month alongside the nonfiction reading we'll be starting to read, too. Even though parts of our minds will be busy absorbing nonfiction, we still want to do the kind of reading where we fall in love with characters, like you've obviously been doing already this year!"

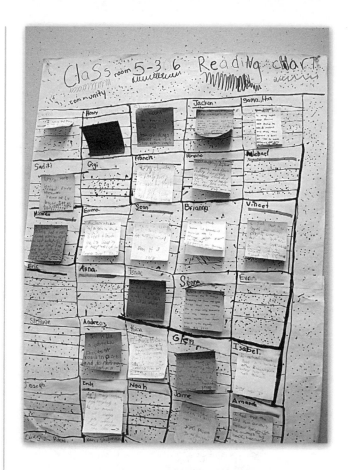

Taking Stock of All We've Learned

ou'll have come to the end of the character unit, and also to the end of a stretch of time in which fiction reading was front and center in the reading workshop. It will be time, soon, to shift the spotlight onto nonfiction reading. Before doing this, you will certainly want to take a little bit of time to help children take stock of all they have learned.

At this stage, it will be helpful to you to conduct some kind of ending assessment. Give children another story to read with the same questions and prompts inserted into the story as we described in the informal assessment tool based on "Abby Takes a Shot." (The magazine *Cobblestones* is a great source of these stories, as is *Chicken Soup for Kids*). Then ask children to compare and contrast their efforts previously with their efforts now to envision, predict, and grow theories about characters. Or you might ask children to spend one reading workshop making Post-its that contain their very best predicting, envisioning, and growing theories about characters, and then set them up to make posters of "I used to predict (envision, theorize) like this: . . . , but now I predict (envision, theorize) like this. . . ."

Ask children to study their logs, too, noting whether they are reading more pages and more minutes a day, or a week, than they were at the start of the year. Above all, give children chances to tell the stories of how they have changed as readers. Peter Johnston, in *Choice Words*, stresses the importance of helping children notice what they are doing well, particularly the leading edge of what is going well. "This leading edge is where the student has reached beyond herself, stretching what she knows just beyond its limit, producing something that is partially correct. This is the launching pad for new learning." He adds, "Showing children that they have changed as community members, learners, readers, and writers reveals that they are in the process of becoming. . . . The

advantage of drawing attention to change in learning and behavior is that children can then project learning futures" (p. 12).

For kids, this is a time to pat themselves on the back, to name the progress that they've made. But you, meanwhile, will continue the long-term journey toward coming to understand your children in deep enough ways that you'll be in a position to help them. In this section, I'll describe yet one more informal assessment tool that my colleagues and I have used, and again, you'll see that the decision to jump off the treadmill of teaching, teaching, teaching and to take some time to observe, to piece together what kids show us when we listen and look, proves worthwhile.

A Second Informal Assessment Tool: Study Readers' Responses to Questions, Inserted into Novels that Represent Particular Bands of Text Difficulty

The comprehension assessments I've described prior to now have all aimed to understand the meaning readers make as they read short stories or short passages. Recently, my colleagues and I decided we needed to bring our lens to the responses kids give to full-length novels, to try to understand their understandings.

Choose Benchmark Texts to Use

We began by trying to select texts that represented the start of each of the three predominate bands of text difficulty in grade 3–5 classrooms (N–Q, R–T, U–W). We wanted texts that are relatively well known so that many teachers would have a leg up understanding kids' responses to the texts, and we wanted books that are fairly brief so that this assessment would require a day or two, not a week of required reading. Above all, we wanted texts that felt to us as if they embody the band of text difficulty in which they're located. We finally settled upon:

Amber Brown Is not a Crayon (N)

Skylark (S)

The BFG (U)

Insert Prompts and Questions into the Text, Based on the Reading Work Needed

Then we worked with these texts as I described us working with the short stories into which we inserted prompts. We read the books and spied on the reading work we found the text practically requiring us to do. Then we looked at the new work we anticipated children would need to be doing as they moved into that band of text difficulty and framed questions that we hoped would reveal the reader's abilities to do the work required of that band of text difficulty.

For example:

- Because readers of level N often need to deal with plays on language, we asked a question or two about places where the reader needed to understand puns in order to get the joke—including, for example, a question about the title of the book, *Amber Brown Is not a Crayon*.

- Because readers of level N are expected to understand that sometimes there are a couple of layers to the central problem in the text and in this story, we asked questions such as "What is really going on between Amber Brown and Justin?" and "Why do you think Justin is acting the way he is?" (Amber Brown is upset with her best friend Justin first because he is moving away and then second, because he doesn't seem as devastated as she is over the thought that he is going.)

- Because we were interested in readers' abilities to grasp the main drift of the story and to use that to predict an outcome, we asked, "How does this connect with what happened earlier in the story?" and "What do you think will happen at the end of the story?" (*Skylark* is historical fiction, and our work with that text informed

that unit of study, so I write about this research in the assessment section of Unit 4 *Tackling Complex Texts*. The full set of questions is available on the CD-ROM.)

Ask Readers to Read the Text and Respond to the Questions and Prompts

We then asked approximately 100 readers to read each of the three texts and to pause to respond to questions that we inserted into the text on Post-its. We began by only doing this research with children who had been assessed in such a way that these texts would be just right (that is, those reading *Amber Brown Is not a Crayon* were reading N books, for example). We asked teachers to be extra cautious that children were, in fact, reading at these levels—that is, that when reading a 200-word passage at this level of text difficulty, they'd been able to read with 96% accuracy, fluency, and enough comprehension to be able to retell or to answer a few literal and inferential questions.

We later studied what readers for whom these levels were "supposed to be" hard or easy did with the texts, but that will be another story for another day!

Collect Answers from Children; Sort Responses into Categories and Study Them

It was as if we hit the jackpot! What amazing data. First, and above all, it was absolutely mind-blowing to glimpse the wildly divergent understandings that readers constructed as they read *Amber Brown Is not a Crayon*. Although all of these readers had been assessed as children for whom N texts are "just right," their work with the book-length text highlighted how different these readers are, one from the next. I was struck by the fact that we tend to document and to pore over and find patterns in children's miscues (their mistakes) when they read a text aloud, but we are far less apt to pore over and study and find patterns in their comprehension miscues. If we study children's comprehension, our attention is usually local—we notice what one reader makes of one part of the text—and it is rare that we look at multiple readers, making sense of many parts of a text. When one does look in these ways, patterns emerge that are fascinating.

Some Children Don't Understand the Whole Text

First, it is important to note that children's understandings of the book were often weak in spots. This could, of course, fan the feelings of anxiety that all teachers feel when a child reads books silently, gleaning from those books whatever meaning that child constructs. We can all drive ourselves crazy worrying over the reader who reads *Stone Fox* on her own and entirely misses the fact that at the end of the book, Searchlight dies. Although this can drive us crazy, the truth is that there is absolutely no getting away from the fact that when we teach readers to read, we must set them loose. We must at some point say, "Go to it!" And readers will then construct the stories as they read, bringing together the pieces they notice, the meanings they infer, and the associations they bring, and just as each of us will not construct the same thing from looking at a painting, we will not construct the same thing from reading a text. Even you, reading this text, will pull from it what you will. Certainly I hope that you are reading this in the company of others and that other readers will say, "Wait—where did you see that?" and "Whoa! I definitely didn't get that from her book!" But ultimately, the important thing is for teachers to realize that because readers inevitably do co-construct the texts we read, it is important for teachers to draw up a chair, to witness that happening, and to teach in response.

Certainly this highlights the value of reading in book clubs, where readers co-construct a sense of the text, and the value also of rereading, expecting to see whole layers and chunks that one missed during a first read.

Some Children Understand the Text and Character Relations Very Well

When we do watch kids construct meaning from a full-length text that we know well, patterns of meaning-making emerge that distinguish some kinds of readers from others. Let's take a single question: What's really going on with Justin and Amber? Remember, the entire book is about the fact that Justin is moving away and his best friend, Amber, is devastated at the prospect of him leaving and angry at him for not seeming to be as upset as she is. Here are the answers that a few readers for whom this text is just right gave to that question:

Jorge provided an answer that is not all that different than the one many proficient adult readers would probably have provided. He wrote,

> "They are being mean to each other because Justin is moving to Alabama because of his dad's new job. If they are mean to each other, then it will not hurt as much when they move apart and are separated—but it will. Deep down Amber just wants Justin to be sad too."

The answer links early and later parts of the story, explains surface-level and deeper meanings, shows cause and effect, and includes details that are specific to the story. Good answer.

Some Children Respond in True and Revealing Ways

But let's look at Lisa's response to the same question. She wrote,

> "Amber is getting annoyed by his kangaroo jumping, being like a monkey and also he wanted to eat a leaf. Amber stopped him because if you eat a leaf you'll get infected and she keeps saying what if a bird drops something and what if you get a poison leaf."

The interesting thing about that response is that all these things that Lisa mentions actually did happen. These are true details from the story. But it is as if Lisa has missed the forest for the trees. She is holding so tightly to details she recalls (and in this answer and others it often seemed she recalled details that were especially odd or gross or bizarre) that she cannot seem to grasp the bigger generalizations that are applicable. And Lisa was not alone in doing this.

For contrast, listen to Roy's answer to 'What's really going on with Justin and Amber?' He responds,

> "Amber Brown is not taking Justin's parents' divorce seriously."

In the book, Justin's parents are not getting divorced. The father is moving for a new job.

> "She is having a good time, she's just having fun at the party."

In the book, Amber is unhappy, not having fun, and there is no party.

> "Their relationship is breaking up."

There is truth to that in the book.

"His father said he was going to start treating him as a grown boy because he wants him to start helping. Since his father toughened him up Justin is acting a little uncaring about Amber."

Justin's father did not toughen him up, though we could say Justin is acting a little uncaring about Amber.

Roy, unlike Lisa, has a whole story-drama in mind. He has constructed a text that perhaps bears some connection to the actual text at hand. That is, Amber's parents, not Justin's, are divorced, and although this is not a big part of this particular story, Roy could have recalled the divorce and brought it to this story to explain why one child is moving from another. Then, too, Justin's dad did leave his son behind—for two days—not for the purpose of toughening him up, but so the father could shop for a new house. It *is* the case that Justin has at times shown Amber a tough exterior, not showing that he is sad over the move, though there is no link between this tough exterior and the father's weekend of house-shopping. Again, the interesting thing is that Roy's reading was not entirely idiosyncratic.

Finding Patterns within the Strugglers

As always, it is especially interesting and revealing to study the work of children who are struggling. I've always said that proficient readers essentially pull things together, so in the end, one proficient reader is not all that different from another. But struggling readers draw on a limited set of strategies, and this means that one struggler can be entirely distinct from another. When assessing a child's ability to read with accuracy, for example, skilled readers draw on meaning, syntax, and phonics, while strugglers tend to draw on one or more of these cueing systems to the exclusion of the others. There was a parallel situation when studying children's comprehension. Readers like Jorge seemed to pull things together—and one successful reader was not remarkably different than another.

There were two extremely different patterns to the children who struggle with comprehension.

- **Top-Down, Meaning-Based Misreading**

  Some readers make meaning in a top-down, meaning-based way. These readers generally create a text that has drama and tension, cause and effect relationships. It just is not rooted in the actual text. For example, Roy read *Amber Brown* as a story about Justin's parents getting divorced, deciding to ask more of Justin, requiring him to toughen up, and then Justin in turn being tougher on Amber. Roy seems to have a sense for how stories go, and he can spin whatever scraps of the actual text he notices into a full-fledged story that has its own logic and drama—but that is only tangentially related to the actual facts of the story.

- **Bottom-Up, Detail-Based Misreading**

  Meanwhile Lisa's responses to the questions time and again showed that she has practically memorized the precise details of the story. But she does not seem to have any sense for how stories hang together, for the larger meaning of this story or the larger patterns of any story, and her tenacious hold on what seemed to be fairly inconsequential details (although perhaps to her they were the juicy ones) functions like a decoy, preventing her from seeing the main drift of the story.

The notion that some readers who struggle with comprehension are far too glued to the specifics of the text in hand and that others are exactly opposite seems to me to be important, and I suspect that these differences might be reflected also in what these readers do when they encounter difficult words—with the one thinking about meaning, the other about the details of the letters on the page, and both having trouble integrating both top-down and bottom-up sources of information.

There are far more conclusions to be drawn from the data. For instance, children who struggle to comprehend regularly are overly reliant on their personal experience. Also, a surprising number of readers can read three or four chapters while still having no idea who the narrator is, and figuring that out does not seem to be a high priority for them, even when the text isn't making sense. But the most interesting thing of all was learning that we need to take time to understand children's understandings, in their entirety, and to look across responses to questions to try to understand children's ways of making sense as they read entire texts.

Adler, David A. 2004. *Cam Jansen Series*. Madison, WI: Perfection Learning.

Allington, Richard L. 2006. *What Really Matters for Struggling Readers: Designing Research-Based Programs* (2nd ed.). Boston: Pearson Education.

Allen, Debbie. 2000. *Dancing in the Wings*. New York: Puffin Books.

Armstrong, Lance. 2001. *It's Not About the Bike*. Berkeley, CA: Berkeley Trade.

Barth, Roland S. 2004. *Learning by Heart*. Somerset, NJ: Jossey Bass.

Bradbury, Ray. 1980. "All Summer in a Day" from *The Stories of Ray Bradbury*. New York: Alfred A. Knopf.

Bear, Donald, Marcia Invernizzi, Shane Templeton, and Francine Johnston. 2010. *Words Their Way*. Boston: Pearson.

Blume, Judy. 1971. *Freckle Juice*. New York: Yearling.

——- 1977. *Starring Sally J. Freedman as Herself*. New York: Bantam Doubleday Dell Books for Young Readers.

——-1990. *Fudge-a-Mania*. New York: Puffin Books.

Boelts, Maribeth. 2007. *Those Shoes*. Somerville, MA: Candlewick.

Bulla, Clyde Robert. 1998. *The Paint Brush Kid*. New York: Random House Books for Young Readers.

——— 1987. *The Chalk Box Kid*. New York: Random House Books for Young Readers.

Bunting, Eve. 2006. *One Green Apple*. Boston: Clarion Books.

Calkins, Lucy, and Cory Gillette. 2006. "Breathing Life into Essays." *Units of Study for Teaching Writing, Grades 3–5*. Portsmouth, NH: Heinemann.

Catling, Patrick S. 2006. *The Chocolate Touch*. New York: HarperCollins.

Cisneros, Sandra. 1984. *The House on Mango Street*. New York: Vintage Books.

Cleary, Beverly. 2001. *Ramona and Her Father*. New York: HarperCollins.

Clements, Andrew. 2007. *Jake Drake, Know-It-All*. New York: Atheneum.

————2001. *The School Story*. New York: Aladdin.

Creech, Sharon. 1996. *Walk Two Moons*. New York: HarperCollins.

Curtis, Christopher Paul. 2004. *Bud, Not Buddy*. New York: Laurel Leaf.

Dahl, Roald. 2007. *The BFG*. New York: Puffin Books.

Danziger, Paula. *Amber Brown* series. New York: Scholastic.

DiCamillo, Kate. 2009. *The Miraculous Journey of Edward Tulane*. Somerville, MA: Candlewick.

Didion, Joan. 2006. *The Year of Magical Thinking*. New York: Vintage Books.

Drucker, Peter. 1993. *The Effective Executive*. New York: HarperCollins.

Fox, Mem. "Ten Read-Aloud Commandments." www.memfox.com/ten-read-aloud-commandments.html

Fullan, Michael. 1993. *Change Forces: Probing the Depths of Educational Reform*. Levittown, PA: The Falmer Press.

Gannett, Ruth Stiles. 2009. *My Father's Dragon*. New York: Random House.

George, Jean Craighead. 2003. *Julie of the Wolves*. NewYork: HarperTeen.

Gipson, Fred. 2001. *Old Yeller.* New York: Harper Perennial Modern Classics.

Gladwell, Malcom. 2005. *Blink: The Power of Thinking Without Thinking.* New York: Little, Brown and Company.

Going, K. L. 2007. *Liberation of Gabriel King.* New York: Puffin.

Goldberg, Natalie. 1993. *Long Quiet Highway: Waking Up in America.* New York: Bantam Books.

Goodlad, John I. 2004. *A Place Called School.* Boston: McGraw-Hill.

Graham, Steve. April 12, 2010. "Writing to Read: Evidence for How Writing Can Improve Reading." Panel discussion. Washington DC.

Harris, A.J., and E.R. Sipay. 1990. *How to Increase Reading Ability: A Guide to Developmental and Remedial Methods* (9th ed.). White Plains, NY: Longman.

Johnston, Peter. 2004. *Choice Words.* Portland, ME: Stenhouse.

Keene, Caroline. *Nancy Drew* series. New York: Grosset & Dunlap.

Lewis, C. S. 2005. *The Chronicles of Narnia: The Lion, the Witch and the Wardrobe.* New York: HarperCollins.

Lowry, Lois. 1984. *Anastasia Krupnik.* New York: Yearling.

Luckette, Dave. 2004. *The Girl, the Queen, and the Castle.* New York: Scholastic.

———— 1998. *What You Know First.* New York: HarperCollins.

———— 1995. *Baby.* New York: Yearling.

———— 1994. *Cassie Binegar.* New York: HarperCollins.

———— 1993. *Journey.* New York: Yearling.

Mathis, Sharon Bell. 2006. *The Hundred Penny Box.* New York: Puffin.

Myers, Walter Dean. 1999. *Monster.* New York: HarperCollins.

Naylor, Phyllis Reynolds. 1995. *Boys Against Girls.* New York: Yearling.

Nye, Naomi Shihab. 2008. *Honeybee.* New York: Greenwillow.

Paterson, Katherine. 1995. *Bridge to Terabithia.* New York: Harper Trophy.

———— 1987. *The Great Gilly Hopkins.* New York: HarperCollins.

Paulsen, Gary. *Dunc and Amos* (Culpepper Adventures) series. New York: Yearling.

———— 2006. *Hatchet.* London: Aladdin.

———— 1993. *The Monument.* New York: Yearling.

———— 1993. *The River.* New York: Yearling.

Peterson, John. *The Littles* series. New York: Scholastic.

Rogers, Carl. 1995. *On Becoming a Person.* Boston: Mariner Books.

Roy, Ron. 1997. *The Bald Bandit.* New York: Random House.

Ryan, Pam Muñoz. 2002. *Esperanza Rising.* New York: Scholastic.

Rylant, Cynthia. 1993. *The Relatives Came.* London: Aladdin.

Sharmat, Marjorie W. 2002. *Nate the Great.* New York: Delacorte Books for Young Readers.

Spinelli, Jerry. 2004. *Crash.* New York: Laurel Leaf.

———— 2004. *Wringer.* New York: HarperTeen.

———— 2003. Loser. New York: HarperCollins.

———— 1999. *Maniac Magee.* New York: Little, Brown Books for Young Readers.

Stead, Rebecca. 2009. *When You Reach Me.* New York: Wendy Lamb Books.

Thomas, Jane Resh. 1981. *The Comeback Dog.* New York: Clarion Books.